Praise for ECOMMERCE

"What Traian has written here is very needed in the online marketing space. Not only does he walk you through the technical SEO process, he also gives you very practical and step-by-step tactics to use to increase your organic traffic. A recommended read for intermediate to advanced SEO specialists."

John Doherty – Online Marketing Manager at Zillow and Global Associate at MOZ

"I was impressed with the breadth, depth, accuracy and nuances (which only come from years of direct, hands-on experience) displayed in Traian Neacsu's eCommerce SEO book. His recommendations on handling everything from pagination to faceted navigation are the same ones I'd give. I was also impressed that Traian mentioned other business considerations in the book, rather than sacrificing conversion rates and usability for a moderately effective "SEO Tactic". The fact that he discusses the use of "map elements" inside hero images speaks to the deep level of experience Traian has with eCommerce. It just isn't something most SEOs even think about, but anyone who works with enough retail brands - especially in apparel - has to balance "optimal SEO" with equally important factors like the brand's image (they often want a catalog-style look), merchandising strategies and conversion-rate optimization. Traian knows all of the eCommerce SEO best practices - and when to break them. Long story short: Get this book. It's the real deal."

Everrett Sizemore, Director of SEO Strategy – inflow.com

"If you're looking for a soup-to-nuts handbook on search optimization, Ecommerce On-Page SEO covers not just marketing but the IT aspects of the trade. Whether you're just starting up or need to take audit of your SEO practices, this guide will give you insightful strategies and tactics for higher rankings."

Linda Bustos, director of ecommerce research, Elastic Path Software, author GetElastic.com

"A well written and highly informative guide that's up-to-date with proven SEO techniques and strategies. This is an SEO resource done right.

Antonino Ciappina, Ecommerce Marketing Director, Kenneth Cole Productions, Inc."

"If you are looking to take your SEO from intermediate to the advanced skill level, this is the book to help you get there.

Micah Fisher-Kirshner, Senior SEO Manager at Zazzle Inc"

ECOMMERCE SEO

AN ADVANCED GUIDE TO ON-PAGE SEARCH ENGINE OPTIMIZATION FOR ECOMMERCE

Traian Neacsu

Traian Neacsu
neacsutraian@gmail.com
www.ecommercemarketingbooks.com

Ordering Information:
Special discounts are available on quantity purchases by corporations, associations, and others.

Engaging the author:
If you would like to invite the author to speak at an event or to your organization, or if you need help with your ecommerce strategy, please contact the author.

Editor: Laura Woods
Stylistic editor: Dr. Dania Sheldon
Cover Designer: Bogdan Rusu

ECOMMERCE SEO, Traian Neacsu —1st edition
ISBN 978-0-9939372-0-0

Contents

To my daughter Anna, with regrets for all the precious time that writing this book took away from us. I love you!

To my parents, who miss their son. I miss you too!

To my investors Amar, Nav and Sukhi: thanks for your trust.

To my business partner and friend, Siva: I appreciate your support.

To all my past, current and future clients: see you at the top!

And last, but not least, I dedicate this book to all hard-working SEOs out there, and to all ecommerce websites that aim for top rankings. It's not easy, but it's achievable.

A man should never neglect his family for business.

—WALT DISNEY

CHAPTER ONE

Introduction

Ecommerce appeared in its basic form (electronic business transactions) in the late 1970s.[1] At that time such transactions happened at the B2B level, mostly for invoices and purchase orders. B2C ecommerce as we now know it started around 1994, after the launch of the Netscape browser. By 2013 ecommerce had boomed to $261 billion in the US alone.[2] In 2014 China's ecommerce is expected to grow 64%, with sales around $1.5 trillion.

You can therefore expect to see new ecommerce websites showing up every day, catering to an audience that is increasingly comfortable shopping online. Most shoppers will initiate their research on a commercial search engine like Google, Yahoo, Bing, Baidu (China) or Yandex (Russia). For ecommerce businesses, this means that the competition is getting tougher all the time.

So how do you get ahead of competitors or maintain your existing edge in terms of search visibility? *Optimize the website for search engines and their users.*

We'll start with the foundation, the architecture of the website, and then we'll continue with keyword research, which is essential for determining your content strategy. Next we'll learn how to guide crawlers to avoid traps, and then we'll explore using internal linking to improve relevance and create strong topical themes.

We'll continue by deconstructing the most important pages for ecommerce websites—the home, subcategory and product detail pages—each in a separate chapter.

About this book

This book evolved from the desire to offer those involved in ecommerce access to on-page search engine optimization (SEO) advice in a single place. The Internet contains a large amount of SEO information, and the online SEO community is amazing; in fact, I'm not aware of any other online community that shares information at the level SEOs do. However, the SEO resources that ecommerce professionals need are widely scattered.

So I decided to put everything I have researched, learned and practiced about SEO since 2002 into a single resource. For now, that resource is a book, but this medium may change. SEO is too dynamic, and keeping a book up to date simply takes too much time.

The current edition addresses *on-page SEO issues only*. Link development is a big part of the rankings equation and requires a book of its own. But while links have been the main target of SEOs for a very long time, I believe that you should optimize your website by putting people and content first. Then you can think of search engines, and finally of backlinks.

What level of SEO expertise is required?

This book contains *intermediate* to *advanced* SEO advice and tactics. You may find that the book gives particular advice or an opinion about a topic without getting into details—that may be because that topic is basic SEO knowledge. In many such cases, I reference others' work, so please check out those resources. In other cases, I don't reference because I don't consider it necessary. I also skip rudimentary topics such as how search engines work.

Who should read this book?

If you're a *small or medium business (SMB) owner* who runs an ecommerce website, then this book is for you. You've probably realized that running an ecommerce business requires a lot of skills. Depending on your background, you're either putting a lot of time and work into learning various other disciplines—like programming, design, usability and copywriting—or you're contracting qualified help.

This book will help you realize how complex SEO really is, and it should help you set realistic expectations. That means: don't expect to get qualified personnel if you pay peanuts. More importantly, don't expect organic traffic to be the silver bullet of your marketing campaigns. It's a good idea to diversify your acquisition channels to email, social, referral and more while working your way up in organic results.

If you're an *ecommerce executive* in an SMB or large organization, read this book to understand how complex on-page SEO is, and how almost any decision you make regarding the website might affect its search visibility. The book will show you what needs to be done to have an SEO-friendly ecommerce website, but it's up to you to prioritize based on your current situation and objectives.

Even if you work in a medium-sized business, you may realize that you don't have all the expertise or resources in-house, so you will have to contract/hire outside talent. If you don't feel like reading technical stuff, at least pass a copy of this book onto the IT, marketing and production departments.

If you're a *search engine optimizer (SEO)*, I hope you will find this book helpful not only because it presents most of the SEO issues encountered by ecommerce websites in a single resource, but also because it provides advice and options for addressing those issues. You can show the book to your employer or your clients to help them understand that ecommerce SEO cannot be addressed overnight, nor does it have strict rules. SEO is an art, and it involves risks.

This book will also be valuable to *IT professionals* involved with ecommerce. The book discusses on-page SEO issues and proposes solutions; however, it doesn't go into the technicalities of fixing them. While working with your colleagues to address a particular issue, you should decide which approach is best given your particular technical setup.

For example, sometimes a 301 redirect is not possible, whereas a *rel="canonical"* is. While I may recommend one approach over another, you will have to decide whether it's possible to implement the recommended method.

What websites is this book for?

Ecommerce extends across a multitude of segments, such as travel (air tickets, railway tickets, hotel bookings, tour packages, etc.), retail, financial services and many others. While the vast majority of the examples presented in the book are for retail, the SEO principles discussed here also apply to all other ecommerce segments.

This book is for websites that face complex issues associated with faceted navigation, sorting, pagination or crawl traps, to name a few. However, a website's complexity is not directly tied to how big a business is in terms of revenue. Start-ups, SMBs and enterprises can be complex no matter what their revenues. This book is therefore just as useful for *large websites* (e.g., with tens of thousands of items)—which are many levels deep, are made up of numerous subsections and cater to many audiences—as it is for *small and medium websites* (e.g., with tens to thousands of items).

Throughout this book I will, for simplicity, use the terms *item* or *product* to refer to a tangible good. But *item* or *product* will have a different meaning depending on your business. For an online hotel reservation business the *item* will be the hotel, and it will be presented on the hotel description page; for a paid content publisher the *item* may be a journal excerpt page; for a real estate listings website the *item* will be a property-details page, and so on. Also, I will refer to *items* and *products* interchangeably.

Companion website

The book has a companion website, where you can download several sample files mentioned in this book. The website URL is *www.ecommercemarketingbooks.com*

CHAPTER TWO

Website Architecture

This chapter will explore the concepts behind building optimized ecommerce website architectures. Having a great website architecture means making products and categories findable on your website so that users and search engines can reach them as easily as possible.

There are two concepts search engine optimizers (SEOs) should be aware of in relationship to information architecture (IA):

- Efficient crawling and indexing (let's call this *technical architecture*, or ***TA***).

- Classifying, labeling and organizing content (let's call this *information architecture*, or ***IA***).

An understanding of the above concepts will help SEOs build search engine optimized websites that are both search engine and user friendly.

To avoid confusion, it's important to differentiate between IA and TA:

- *Information architecture* is the process of classifying and organizing content on a website and providing user-friendly access to that content via navigation. This is done (or should be done) by ***information architects***.

- *Technical architecture* is the process of designing the technical and functional aspects of a site. This is done by ***IT professionals***.

Together, the two form the ***site architecture (SA)***. Keep in mind that SEOs should be involved in both IA and TA.

Information architecture

The Information Architecture Institute's definition of information architecture is:[1]

- The structural design of shared information environments.

- The art and science of organizing and labeling web sites, intranets, online communities and software to support usability and findability.

- An emerging community of practice focused on bringing principles of design and architecture to the digital landscape.

This definition shows that information architecture goes beyond websites, and it hints at IA's complexity. It also reveals how flexible and theoretical IA is.

From an ecommerce standpoint, let's oversimplify the definition of IA to:

The classification and organization of content and online inventory.

SEOs should be familiar with two other IA concepts.

The first is **taxonomy**, which is the *classification* of topics into a hierarchical structure. For ecommerce, this translates into assigning items to one or more categories. Ecommerce taxonomies are usually vertical, *tree-like*. A website's taxonomy is often referred to as its hierarchy.

To visualize a taxonomy, think of *breadcrumbs*:

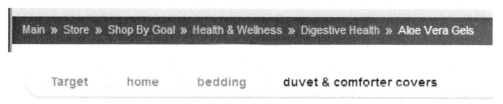

Figure 1 Breadcrumbs can mimic the website taxonomy.

The structures above, ordered hierarchically using a parent-child relationship from broader to narrower topics, are called *taxonomies*. One way to create ecommerce taxonomies is to use a *controlled vocabulary* (a restricted list of terms, names, labels and categories). Information architects develop these.

In terms of SEO, you should use semantic markup to help search engines understand *breadcrumb* taxonomies.

Microdata or RDFa[2] markup are used by search engines to generate breadcrumb-rich snippets similar to the one on the next page:

Cheap **car rentals in New Orleans** from $15/day - Find a rental car i…

www.kayak.com › Cars › United States › Louisiana ▾ | Kayak ▾

Compare prices from Advantage, Avis, Budget, Dollar, Enterprise and Hertz. Save 35% or more. Find **New Orleans car rental** deals and discounts on KAYAK.

Figure 2 Sometimes, search engines display the website taxonomy directly in the search engine results pages (SERPs).

We will discuss breadcrumbs in detail later in this book, but briefly, this is how the source code for the above rich snippet looks:

```
</div>
<div class="clear"></div>
<div class="citiescolumns cityCarsBreadcrumbs">
    <div>
<div class="seoWidget innerWidget seoHotelBreadCrumbs">
                    <span itemscope itemtype="http://data-vocabulary.org/Breadcrumb"><a href="/cars" itemprop="url"><span
itemprop="title">Cars</span></a></span>
        <span class="divider"> /</span>            <span itemscope itemtype="http://data-
vocabulary.org/Breadcrumb"><a href="/United-States-Car-Rentals.253.crc.html" itemprop="url"><span itemprop="title">United
States</span></a></span>
        <span class="divider"> /</span>            <span itemscope itemtype="http://data-
vocabulary.org/Breadcrumb"><a href="/Louisiana-United-States-Car-Rentals.136.crr.html" itemprop="url"><span
itemprop="title">Louisiana</span></a></span>
        <span class="divider"> /</span>            <span itemscope itemtype="http://data-
vocabulary.org/Breadcrumb"><a href="/Cheap-New-Orleans-Car-Rentals.22085.cars.ksp" itemprop="url"><span itemprop="title">New
Orleans</span></a></span>
```

Figure 3 The highlighted text shows the breadcrumb vocabulary markup.

The second term you need to be aware of is ***ontology***. It means the relationships between taxonomies.

If an ecommerce hierarchy can be visualized as an inverted tree (home page at the top), then an ontology is the forest showing relationships between trees. An ontology might encompass various taxonomies, with each taxonomy organizing a topic in a particular hierarchy.

Simply put, an ontology is a more complex type of taxonomy, containing richer information about the content and items on a website. We are just at the beginning of building ontology-driven websites. One common ontology vocabulary for ecommerce is GoodRelations.[3]

The Semantic Web is aimed at helping artificial intelligence agents such as search engine robots crawl through and categorize information more effectively, as well as at helping identify relationships between items and categories (e.g., manufacturers, dealers, prices and so on).

Was this product information helpful? ○ Yes ○ No

Related Categories
- Fashion Women's Watches
- Luxury Women's Watches
- Diamond Women's Watches
- Michael Kors Women's Watches
- Geneva Women's Watches
- Bangle Women's Watches
- Stainless Steel Women's Watches
- Timex Women's Watches

Figure 4 Related categories or related products can be considered a form of ontology.

As an SEO, you probably won't be too involved in identifying related categories and products (sometimes they are identified automatically by the ecommerce platform), but it's important to know these terms in your discussions with information architects.

Why IA is important for SEO

A correctly designed IA will result in a tiered website architecture with an internal linking structure that will allow *child pages* (pages that link up in the hierarchy, such as product detail pages or blog posts) to support the more important parent pages (upper-level pages that link down in the vertical hierarchy, such as category and subcategory pages).

Parent - Child   Sibling - Sibling

Figure 5 Pages that link to each other at the same level of hierarchy are called siblings. They share the same parent.

With correct internal linking, the blog article "Top 5 New Features of Canon Rebel T5i DSLR" will support the product details page *Canon Rebel T5i DSLR; Canon Rebel T5i DSLR* will support the category *Digital Cameras,* and will further support the top-level category *Electronics.*

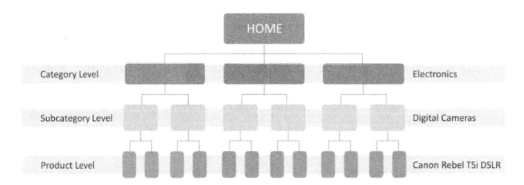

Figure 6 This pyramid-like structure is a very common architecture for ecommerce.

Note: One of the questions that often comes up when deciding on hierarchy is "What is the best number of levels to reach a product detail page?" The famous "three-click rule" (every page on a website should take no more than three clicks to access)[4] is good to follow, but don't get stuck on it. If you need a fourth level, that's fine.[5]

IA will help identify relationships between categories, subcatego
Based on these findings, you will decide on rules for an internal link
rules can in include:

- Only highly related categories will interlink.

- Categories will link only to their parents.

- Subcategories will link to related subcategories and categories.

- Product pages will only link to related products in the same category, and to parent categories.

A proper website architecture will help your website rank for the so-called *head terms*. For ecommerce these are usually the category and subcategory pages. However, internal linking is not enough for a subcategory page to reach the top of the search engine results pages (SERPs) for category-related search queries. That page should also have:

- Relevant and useful content (more than just listings, in the case of a listing page, and more than just a picture and pricing for product detail pages).

- Links from external websites.

Additionally, good IA means good usability. Great usability creates a good user experience, which then leads to less SERP bounce[6] (aka *pogo sticking*[7]). A lower SERP bounce rate is good for SEO, since it hints to search engines that a document is relevant for a particular search query.

Navigation (primary, secondary, breadcrumbs, contextual and so on) is also one of the key components of an ecommerce website architecture. Navigation is jointly crafted by many members of the web team, led by the information architect. Given that the primary navigation will be present on almost every page of the website, it will influence how link signals (PageRank, anchor text) are passed to other pages.

Fortunately for everyone involved with ecommerce marketing, there are ways to give users what *they* want (findability and usability), and at the same time guide search engine robots towards what *you* want them to discover, crawl and index.

How SEO can add value to IA

Remember, IA is not about technical issues but about organizing digital inventory. So while SEO has an important role to play with IA, SEO should not dictate how information is labeled and organized. IA is about making content easy to find and helpful for users. However, because most SEOs are biased towards marketing and technology

.ather than user experience and usability, it's advisable to involve both an information architect and an SEO consultant.

Try to involve the SEO consultant from the early stages of the IA process, to provide suggestions and feedback from a search engine standpoint and to contribute to the website architecture discussion. Once the information architect designing the draft IA listens to what the SEO has to say, he or she can brainstorm with the other teams involved about how to implement the SEO recommendations with minimal changes to the initial IA format.

Many times, technology and marketing teams will dismiss a certain proposed information architecture simply because it doesn't have traffic potential. Don't make this mistake. As an SEO, you should listen to what the other teams have to say and only then suggest solutions to the technology team.

As mentioned, the SEO's role is to provide consultancy from the perspective of search engines. Let's take a look at how to prepare the feedback.

The concept of flat architecture

In good, flat architecture, deep pages (pages at the lower levels of the website hierarchy—usually the product detail pages) are accessible to users and search engine bots with a balanced number of clicks (not too many, but also not too few).

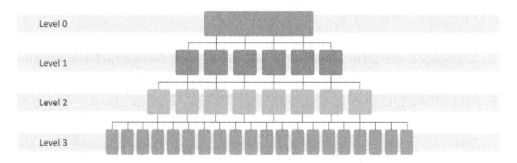

Figure 7 This is what flat website architecture looks like.

The opposite of flat architecture is the so-called *deep architecture*[8], which looks like the example on the next page:

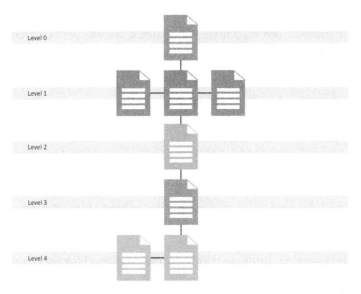

Figure 8 In a deep-architecture model, pages are mostly linked in a vertical structure.

We'll use math to illustrate the concept behind flat architecture:

- At level 0 (home page), you link to 100 category pages; 100^1 = 100 pages linked.

- At each page in level 1 (category), you link to 100 subcategory pages; 100^2 = 10,000 subcategory URLs.

- At each page in level 2 (subcategory), you link to 100 product pages; 100^3 = one million product page URLs.

So in three "clicks", search engines can index a million pages.

Note: The 100 links-per-page limit was used as an example only. In real life it can be more or less than that, depending on your website authority.

Let's look at the scenario of a direct visit to your home page. To reach a product— e.g., *MyChelle Minerals Eye Shimmer Champagne*—a user will perform:

- First click on *Cosmetics* category page.

- Second click on *Eye* subcategory page.

- Third click on *MyChelle Minerals Eye Shimmer Champagne* product details page.

If no external links point directly to this product page, search engines will find the product URL in a similar way to users, crawling from an entry page (search engines enter your website through multiple URLs, not only the home page) to the product details page. In our scenario it took only three clicks, but if the website is structured on a deep IA it will take users and search engines more clicks.

How and why did SEOs adopt flat architecture?

The concept of flat website architecture seems to have its roots in web design. The three-click rule started becoming a "best practice" circa 2000.

But when usability experts tested this rule, they found it was not necessarily good. As a matter of fact:

> *"Users' ability to find products on an ecommerce website increased by 600 percent after the design was changed so that products were four clicks from the homepage instead of three" (p. 322).*[9]

Then SEOs jumped in, thinking that if the rule was good for users, then it should be good for SEO as well. SEOs found a way to funnel more PageRank to deeper levels and optimize crawling by providing better paths for search engines. Initially the goal was to avoid pages ending up in the supplemental index because of their very low PageRank.[10]

Here are a few important pointers about flat architecture:

- Unless you sell a limited number of products (e.g., just 10 diet supplement pills) or have a very limited number of pages on the site, do not flatten to the extreme. This means don't link from the home page to hundreds of product detail pages, just to build a flat architecture.

- Flat architecture is about the **distance between pages in terms of clicks**, not about the number of directories in the URL. For example, you can link from the home page directly to a subcategory URL at the fourth level of the hierarchy (e.g. *mysite.com/Home-Garden/Furniture/Living-Room-Furniture/Recliners/*) to promote a subcategory that generates high profits. In this case the *Recliners* page is only one click away from the home page (flat) but is four levels down in the directory hierarchy (deep).

- If you have already organized your hierarchy using directories in URLs, do not remove them just for the sake of flattening.

As long as the directories don't generate super-long URLs, they have advantages, such as:

- Easier "theming" (see the next section in this chapter, *Siloing*).

- Presenting users with a clear delineation of the categories on your website.

- Easier SEO, IA and web analytics analysis (e.g., you can use *site:domain.com/directory1/* to troubleshoot indexation problems).

- Google may use your directory structure to create rich-snippet breadcrumbs.[11]

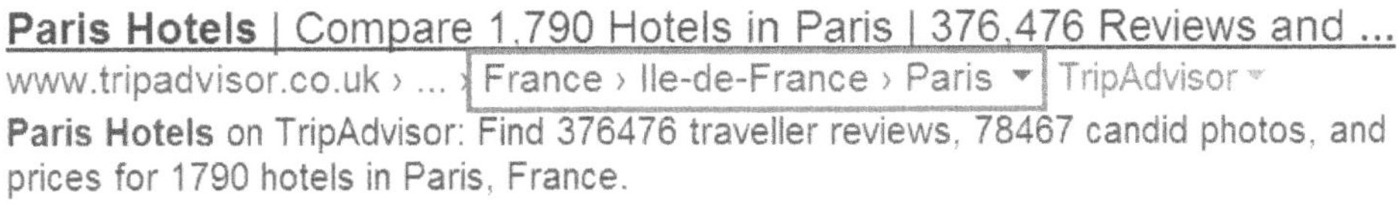

Paris Hotels | Compare 1,790 Hotels in Paris | 376,476 Reviews and ...
www.tripadvisor.co.uk › ... ⟩ France › Ile-de-France › Paris ▾ | TripAdvisor ▾
Paris Hotels on TripAdvisor: Find 376476 traveller reviews, 78467 candid photos, and prices for 1790 hotels in Paris, France.

Figure 9 These SERP breadcrumbs show up only if the directory hierarchy is clear.

It is not mandatory for a URL to replicate an exact website taxonomy. If you want, you can keep the URL's structure below two directories. Here's an example.

On hotel reservation websites, it is common to have a taxonomy based on hotel geo-locations:

Taxonomy: *Home > Europe > France > Ile-de-France > Paris*

URL: *domain.com/europe/france/ile-de-france/paris/*

Even though this URL clearly reflects a hierarchical taxonomy, the URL is too long and too difficult to type or remember. An alternative URL for users/searchers might be:

domain.com/france/paris/ — in case the website does only hotel bookings.

domain.com/car-rentals/france/paris/ — in case the website offers other travel services (air tickets, car rentals, etc).

Regarding the directory structure above, it's worth noting that hotels are a special ecommerce case, because you can't move the products (hotels) from one geo-location (city page) to another. But for online retailers, product re-categorization happens a lot.

To avoid issues associated with moving products from one category to another, or issues with poly-hierarchies (items in multiple categories), keep the item URLs free of categories whenever you can. Setting product names in stone is also a good idea. For example, to reach the *3 Level Carrousel Media Center* product page a user will navigate through:

mysite.com/

mysite.com/office-furniture/

mysite.com/office-furniture/storage-shelving/

mysite.com/office-furniture/storage-shelving/media-storage/

But once he or she reaches the product details page, the URL is free of categories and subcategories: *mysite.com/3-level-carrousel-media-center.html*

Notice a couple of things about the above URLs:

- The product page URL is free of categories and subcategories.

- The category and subcategory URLs have the trailing forward slash (/) at the very end. This hints to search engines that the URLs are directories and there is more content to be found on those pages.[12]

- The product page has an .html file extension (it could be .php or .aspx—the file extension doesn't matter at all to search engines), but it hints to the search engines that this is an item page and not a directory.

Removing categories and subcategories from a URL is a trade-off with your data analysis, as it will make the web analysis harder (grouping products by directories), but this difficulty is surmountable.

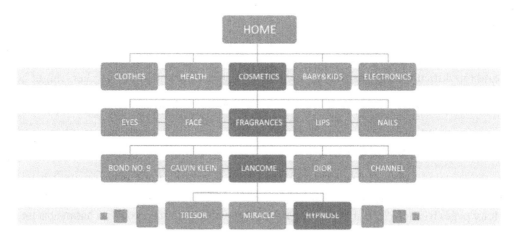

Figure 10 The flat architecture concept on an ecommerce site.

Flat website architecture is closely tied to another important SEO topic, *siloing*.

Siloing (theming)

In the simplest terms, siloing means creating an architecture that allows users to find information in a structured manner (a vertical taxonomy), while linking pages in a specific manner to guide how search engines crawl the website.

Siloing sounds like a fancy term, but in reality it is just good information architecture, because siloing is one part website hierarchy and the other part navigation (internal linking).

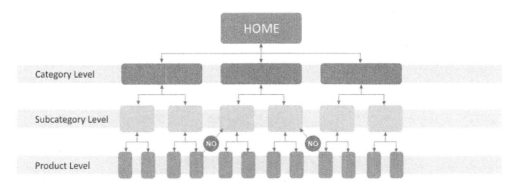

Figure 11 Product pages don't link to subcategory pages from other silos.

In practice, a *strict hierarchy pattern* like the one in Figure 11, where child pages are only linked to and from their respective parent pages, is not possible without strictly controlled internal linking. That is mainly because (i) primary navigation is present on all pages, (ii) there is a poly-hierarchy (multiple categorizations, e.g., *Office Furniture* in *Office Products* and *Furniture*), and (iii) there are subcategory cross-links and crossover products (*Home Theater* in *TVs* and in *Audio*).

Because ecommerce websites are complex, they are most likely to have a hierarchy with frequent interlinking between silos:

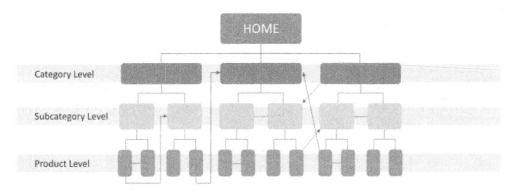

Figure 12 In practice, it's very difficult to prevent interlinking between silos.

In practice, the internal linking architecture can be very complex and difficult to control, even for ecommerce websites with just a few hundred products, as you can see on the next page:

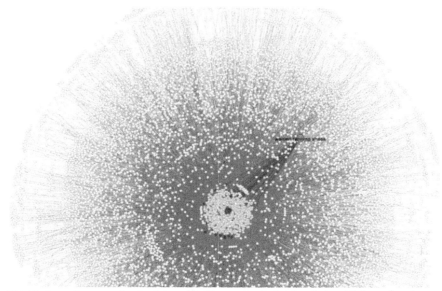

Figure 13 This shows how complex the internal linking can really be. A website with just a few thousands pages generated more than 250,000 internal links.

The siloing method

Conceptually, siloing is done by identifying the main themes of the website (for ecommerce, those will be departments, categories and subcategories) and then interlinking only pages belonging to the same theme (category). The good part is that ecommerce websites are usually developed using a similar architecture, with separate hierarchies (themes) for each department or broad product category.

The idea is that by siloing the website into themes, you will be able to rank for semantically unrelated keywords—e.g., "hard drives" and "red wines" within the same website—even though the themes are totally different.

You can achieve silos with directories or with internal linking:

- Directories

  You create the hierarchy using user research and testing (done by information architects), keyword analysis and research, and web traffic analysis. Your silos will be the *directories* in the URLs. Whenever possible, have a directory hierarchy.

- Internal links

  With internal linking you can create *virtual silos*, as pages in the same silo don't need to be placed under the same directory. You achieve virtual silos by controlling internal links in such a way that search engine robots only find links to the pages in the same silo. This is a very similar concept to *bot herding*[13]or *PageRank sculpting*[14](with subtle differences in meaning and application).

Siloing with directories

This is the easiest to implement on new websites during the IA process. From a user experience perspective, creating the website's hierarchy with directories is the best way to go. In the end, siloing with directories is actually creating good vertical hierarchies, which the URLs reflect. Many online retailers create them naturally by branching out all categories, without thinking too much about SEO and without being obsessed with either keywords in the anchor text or internal linking patterns.

A sample silo with directories would look like:

Mysite.com/category1/subcategory1/

Mysite.com/category1/subcategory2/

Mysite.com/category1/subcategory3/

....

Mysite.com/category1/subcategoryN/

Does this "siloing" look familiar now? It should if you use directories in your URLs, because it's actually nothing more than a good hierarchy. So if you design your website hierarchy properly, you don't even need to worry about siloing.

Note: You need to have fewer than three directory levels.

Siloing with internal linking

Siloing with directories may not always be possible (for example, if you wish to change an existing hierarchy on an established website). In this case, you can create virtual silos using carefully controlled internal linking. Generally, pages in a silo need to pass search engine authority (PageRank) and relevance (anchor text) **only with respect to other pages within the same silo**. This is to prevent the dilution of a silo's theme and to send the maximum power to the main silo pages.

There are rules about linking within and between silos. A page within a silo:

1. Should link to *parents*.

2. Can link to *siblings* (pages at the same level in the hierarchy) if appropriate.

3. Should not link to *cousins*.

4. Could eventually link to *uncles/aunties* (siblings of that node's parent).

Linking to uncles/aunties means that if you have to link two related supporting pages found in separate silos (*cousins*), you should link only to the silo's main page (*uncles*).

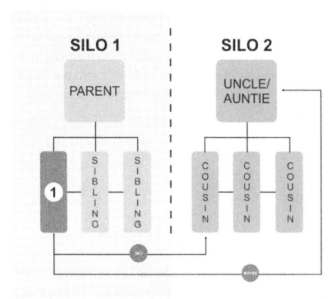

Figure 14 Sibling number one could eventually link to uncles (siblings of that node's parent). This means that if you have to link two related supporting pages found in separate silos (cousins), you should link only to the silo's main page (uncles).

There are rules about linking within and between silos. A page within a silo:

5. Should link to *parents*.

6. Can link to *siblings* (pages at the same level in the hierarchy) if appropriate.

7. Should not link to *cousins*.

8. Could eventually link to *uncles* (*siblings* of that node's *parent*). This means that if you have to link two related supporting pages found in separate silos (*cousins*), you should link only to the silo's main page (*uncles*).

If you need to link to pages outside the silo, hide those links from search engines (e.g., with Flash, Asynchronous JavaScript and XML [aka AJAX], iframes or JavaScript). Note, however, that there is a fine line between white hat and gray SEO, and such siloing may cross that line at some point in time. This is because Google's definition of manipulative techniques is generated in answer to the question: "Would you do it if search engines didn't exist?" For now, though, it seems that some big brands deploy siloing, and they are not being penalized.

But don't take siloing to the extreme. If a page is more relevant and you want to link to it, then do so, regardless of whether it's in a different silo/theme.

Siloing with internal links is a powerful advanced SEO technique, especially for large websites with multiple departments (themes, categories) that are not semantically related (grocery with mobile phones, for example). But it's important to know that siloing is not easily achieved, and it pays to be aware of the existing dangers.

If you want to silo with internal linking, know that:

- PageRank sculpting with *rel="nofollow"* is not recommended.

- Virtual siloing means you somehow have to hide internal links from search engines, and doing so can fall outside a search engine's guidelines.

- Hiding internal links from search engines using iframes, AJAX, JavaScript or other similar techniques can qualify as cloaking, since you show different content to users than to search engines; this could result in penalties.

- If you hide links with AJAX and/or JavaScript, make sure your website works properly with JavaScript turned off (i.e., users can finish ALL macro conversions).

- Trading away too much for SEO in terms of usability and accessibility is not the right way to go.

- Siloing may require hiding entire navigation elements, such as facets and filters, from search engines. There are risks associated with such bold tactics.

Figure 15 Only the top-level categories (women, men, baby, etc.) and the immediate next hierarchy level of subcategories (clothing, shoes, accessories, etc.) pass indexing signals. All the categories marked with a border are nofollowed.

Proper internal cross-linking is helpful and necessary for good rankings (we will discuss this in detail in the *Internal Linking* chapter), but remember that internal linking has to be built for users first, and only then for search engines. You have to link consistently, thematically and wisely (using synonyms, stems, plurals and singulars, and so on) to support rankings for categories and subcategories.

As an SEO, you should not ask information architects or developers to remove navigation elements just for SEO purposes. Keep links that are useful for users, and if you want to remove links for SEO reasons (i.e., to hide them from search engines), then do it with an SEO-unfriendly technique like AJAX or JavaScript.

Another method for theming online stores is to evolve taxonomies into ontologies. Instead of linking based strictly on a vertical taxonomy, interlink items that are conceptually related, not hierarchically (e.g., interlink a particular fragrance with some sunglasses from the same manufacturer). This requires defining semantic and conceptual relationships between categories and items and deciding on the internal linking based on predefined business rules.

One business rule example is crowd-sourced recommendations (aka *Customers Who Bought This Item Also Bought ...*). Do users often buy certain products together? If yes, then cross-link those product detail pages, even if they are in different silos.

And if this type of linkage generates too many internal links on those pages, you can always AJAX the ones that are less important (you'll have to define how many is too many in your particular case). But for the sake of users, interlink whenever is necessary, without being too concerned about siloing.

If the business rules are based on data, then you won't be linking from adult toys to lawn mowers. You won't link to hundreds of related products, but just to a few that are highly related.

Here's what Google has to say about the subject of theming an internal architecture, in a post on its official blog:[15]

> Q: *Let's say my website is about my favorite hobbies: biking and camping. Should I keep my internal linking architecture "themed" and not cross-link between the two?*
>
> A: *We haven't found a case where a webmaster would benefit by intentionally "theming" their link architecture for search engines. And, keep-in-mind, if a visitor to one part of your website can't easily reach other parts of your site, that may be a problem for search engines as well.*

This is a reminder not to take soloing to extreme. But siloing with directories is natural, and the resulting internal linking is also good.

This is why I lean towards a "hybrid" siloing concept combining the following:

- Good website hierarchy, reinforced by directory structure (directory structure is a patented Google signal for classifying pages[16]).

- Rule-based internal linking.

- A reduced number of links available to search engines (with or without AJAX/JavaScript, depending on the case).

Generate content/information ideas

Keyword research enables you to expand from a relatively narrow set of keywords (category and subcategory keywords) to a large number of long tail keywords. These long tail keywords can then be used to generate content ideas or to identify products' attributes, features and descriptions.

Based on the initial taxonomy that the information architect creates, SEOs can identify keyword patterns, tag user intent, group keywords according to buying stages, and find search volumes (we'll cover this in the *Keyword Research* chapter). This type of research provides great insights that are usually overlooked by the other teams in an ecommerce business.

If you want to consistently publish content that your target market will find relevant, you'll have to know not just the exact words they're using in searches, but more importantly, what it is they're searching for. Are they looking for information about your products? If so, you'd do well to put more emphasis on review-type content and how-to articles. Are they searching for products? If so, you could improve the content on a particular product detail page. You can address your target market's needs better once you gain an understanding of what they really want, by discovering the user intent behind the search query. When you do so, you'll be better able to address their needs on your landing pages. And when your landing pages address people's needs, they'll be more likely to convert their visit into a product purchase.

Here are some interesting facts about search queries:

80% of web queries are informational in nature, while about 10% are navigational and another 10% transactional.[17]

You can't afford to ignore the long tail of organic search traffic—it can amount to 70-80% of the total traffic.

The earlier in the buying stage you can reach the customer, the higher the chances of closing the sale later on (this is true for both B2B and B2C).

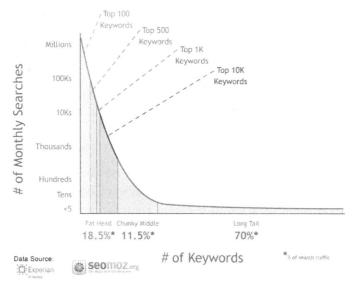

Figure 16 The search demand curve, by MOZ.com.[18] Notice the long tail and chunky middle.

Why do I mention the above facts?

Because the correct way to start keyword research and to build website architecture is by recognizing that only a small fraction of your target market is ready to buy at any given moment. A lot of ecommerce websites mistakenly focus on targeting keywords such as department, category or subcategory names while completely ignoring the large amount of informational (and even navigational) search queries.

Let's look again at a common ecommerce website architecture:

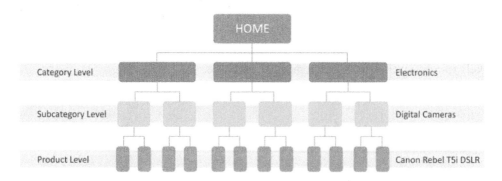

Figure 17 With this architecture, product detail pages are not supported by any other pages.

There are four levels in this architecture: The first level is the home page, which is supported by category keywords (second level) and subcategory keywords (third level). The subcategory pages are then supported by product keywords (fourth level).

When an ecommerce website doesn't support the product detail pages with an additional level in the hierarchy (a content-heavy level, such as a blog) it can miss a huge amount of organic traffic coming from informational search queries. It also misses out on creating contextual links to product, subcategory and category pages.

For example, on the Victoria's Secret website, I was not able to find a single reference to their blog, as of March 2014. This is bad for them but good news for the small guys competing in their niche, lingerie.

Figure 18 Only five pages on victoriassecret.com contain the word "blog", and none of them are part of a real blog.

Here's what you have to do:

1. Add a new layer of support for all pages (especially for product and subcategory pages) on the website. This layer can be a blog, forum, expert Q&A, how-to guides, buying guides, white papers, workshops and so on. This will help achieve additional organic traffic and provide support for contextual internal linking. Plus, it may help in building a community around your brand.

2. Conduct keyword research with this new level in mind, which means you won't dismiss informational keywords. Categorize such keywords into the "informational" bucket in your spreadsheets, and plan content based on them.

Let's say you sell woodworking tools, and you want more people to come to your website to buy them. Why not create a series of DIY woodworking projects and publish them on your blog, or on a dedicated *Projects* page?

Take a look at this inspiring piece of content on Home Depot's blog, on the next page.[19] Home Depot is not at all into selling instructional DIY DVDs, but they are attracting the target market with related content. As a matter of fact, Home Depot has an entire DIY section on their blog.[20]

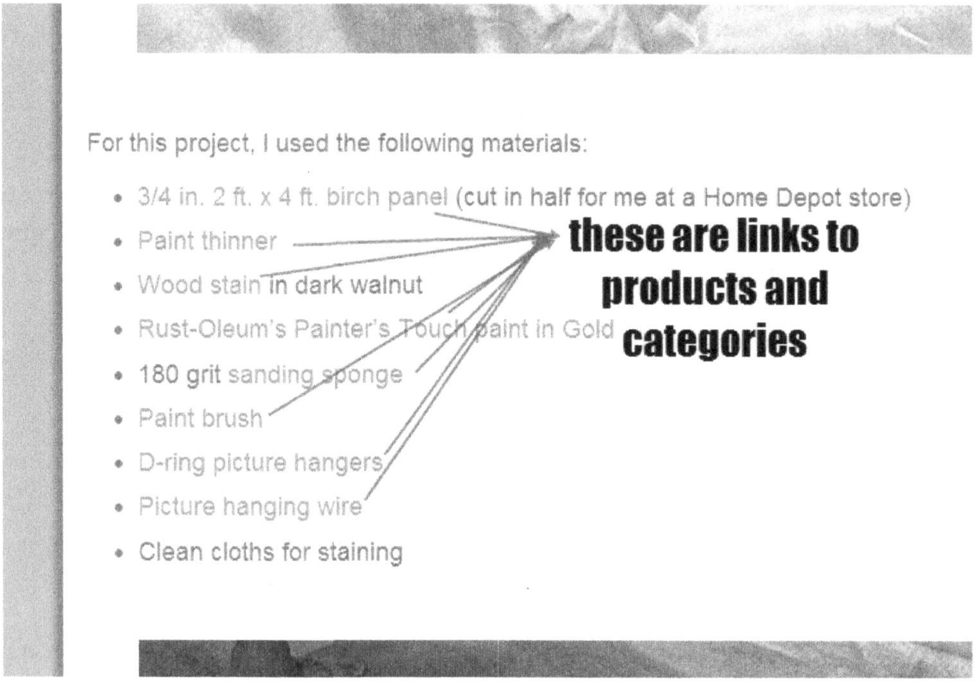

For this project, I used the following materials:

- 3/4 in. 2 ft. x 4 ft. birch panel (cut in half for me at a Home Depot store)
- Paint thinner
- Wood stain in dark walnut
- Rust-Oleum's Painter's Touch paint in Gold
- 180 grit sanding sponge
- Paint brush
- D-ring picture hangers
- Picture hanging wire
- Clean cloths for staining

these are links to products and categories

Figure 19 Notice how this DIY project page supports category and product pages by linking to them.

When you add a new, content-rich layer in the hierarchy, you:

- Come up with a new way to generate more traffic.

- Give visitors more reasons to buy from you.

- Reinforce product and category pages with better internal linking.

Let's see how SEOs can help with IA.

Evaluate information architect's input

Planning an ecommerce architecture starts with information architects identifying the navigation labels (e.g., the departments, categories and subcategories).

In many cases, IAs don't associate this process with keyword research (which is good, because navigation has to serve the users, not the robots). However, you should evaluate their input from a search engine perspective.

Here's an example of how to evaluate IA input with Google Trends. If the information architect wants to label one of the categories in the primary navigation as "mp3 players", the search trend comparison below might change his or her mind.

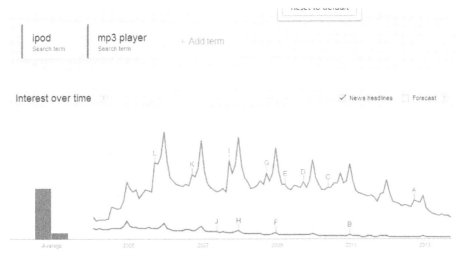

Figure 20 The trend for "iPod" is downwards, but it's still a few times more than the one for "mp3 player".

Indeed, "iPod" can be a child of the "mp3 player" parent, but you should brainstorm with the others in the team to decide whether making the "iPod" category easier to find would be more beneficial for most users, which may mean having it directly in the primary navigation.

Usually, the search volume for a parent category should be higher than the search volume for the child category, but as you see in the example above, this is not a definitive rule.

Note: Google Trends displays data on a scale of 1 to 100 (100 being the highest search volume recorded). Google Trends doesn't display absolute search volumes.

Website navigation

All ecommerce websites will have *primary navigation* (aka global navigation or main navigation), *secondary navigation* (aka local navigation) and *contextual navigation*. Another form of navigation specific to complex websites is faceted navigation.

Primary and secondary

Primary navigation is the easiest type for most users to identify. It allows direct access to the website's hierarchy and is present on almost all pages. Primary navigation represents all of the top-level categories.

Figure 21 Sample primary navigation on Kohl's website.

It will be difficult for Kohl's to rank for top-level category keywords (e.g., *Home, Bed & Bath, Furniture, Outerwear*, etc.), since they will have to compete with niche-specific websites that are laser-focused on one particular segment—for example, a company that sells only furniture.

However, it's not impossible for Kohl's to achieve good rankings, but it will require significant work, including onsite SEO and quality back link development.

Regarding secondary navigation, even IA experts like Steve Krug, Jesse James Garret and Jacob Nielsen can't agree on a definitive definition. For many ecommerce websites, primary navigation consists of category links, while subcategories links can be found in secondary navigation.

Strongly connected with navigation links is an SEO best practice that recommends keeping the number of links on a page below 100. Don't be stuck on this number, as you can have more than 100 links, depending on the authority of your website. You will see high PageRank websites like Walmart having 600 links:

```
627  http://www.walmart.com/c/kp/bluetooth-headphones?povid=P1171-C1093.2766-L105

628  http://www.walmart.com/c/kp/baby-shower-party-favors?povid=P1171-C1093.2766-L106

629  http://www.walmartstores.com/PrivacySecurity/9243.aspx?povid=P1171-C1093.2766-L107
630  https://www.facebook.com/walmart?povid=P1171-C1093.2766-L108
631  http://pinterest.com/walmart/?povid=P1171-C1093.2766-L109
632
633  http://www.walmart.com/cp/Walmart-App-for-iPhone/1087865?povid=P1171-C1093.2766-L111
```

Figure 22; 600 links is a lot, unless you have a very good authority.

The large number of links results from the use of the fly-out *mega menu* in primary navigation, for usability reasons (it makes deeper sections easily accessible to users).

Mega menus allow direct linking to subcategories and even to products, but you have to be careful to keep that number to a reasonable limit. Since the primary navigation is present on the majority of the pages on a website, it can have a pretty big influence.

Let's take another example, Walmart. Notice the *See All Departments* link at the bottom of the primary navigation?

Consolidating a long list of departments into a single resource probably has to do with design considerations (limited screen real estate) and user experience (too many options to skim at once), but it also has an effect on the PageRank passed to the other pages.

Figure 23 Design considerations made Walmart reduce the links in their navigation.

However, Walmart has a separate page for the complete list of their departments and categories:

All Departments

Halloween	Books	Health	Movies	Photo Center
Game Time	New Releases	Diet & Nutrition	Blu-ray Discs	Available in 1 Hour
College Living	Our 200 Top Sellers	Home Health Care	Moviecenter	Available same day
Back to School	Preorders	Medicine Cabinet	Movies (DVD)	Blankets
Made in the USA	Clearance	Oral Care	New Releases (Blu-ray & DVD)	Calendars
Empowering Women Together	Electronics	Personal Care	Preorders (Blu-ray & DVD)	Canvas Wall Art
Man Cave	Accessories	Vision Center	TV Shows (DVD)	Cards & Invitations
Character Corner	Auto Electronics	Vitamins	Video on Demand by VUDU	Mugs
Super Heroes Store	Cameras & Camcorders	Wellness Shops	Music	Photo Books
Apparel, Shoes & Accessories	Cell Phones & Services	Home	CD Store	Posters
Accessories	Computers	Appliances	Musical Instruments	Prints
Baby	GPS & Navigation	Bath	New Releases	Wedding Stationery
	Theater	Bedding		See all Products
	Infant & C...			
Bath & Body	Meal Solutions, Grains & Pasta	Bill Pay & Money Order		Nintendo DS
Fragrances	Snacks, Cookies & Chips	Check Printing		Nintendo Wii
Hair Care				Nintendo Wii U
Makeup	Grocery Delivery - Beta			PlayStation 3
Massagers & Spa				PlayStation 4
Men's Grooming				PlayStation Vita
Shaving				Xbox One
Skin Care				Xbox 360
				PC Gaming

Figure 24 This may be a good idea, since this page will act as a site map for both people and search engines.

You can help the information architects decide which categories are the most important for users and should be listed on the primary navigation. Use the web analysis tool to identify the most searched terms on the website, the most viewed pages, the highest pay-per-click (PPC) traffic keywords or other similar metrics.

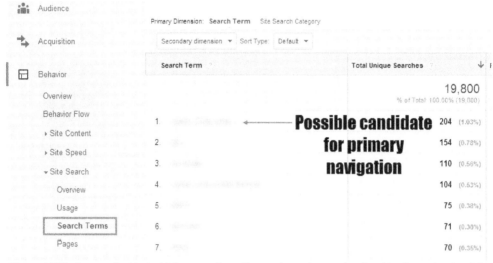

Figure 25 The keyword with the highest number of internal searches can be placed in the navigation (if it makes sense), or it can be placed near the search field.

Contextual navigation

Contextual navigation refers to the navigation present within the main section of web pages. It excludes boilerplate navigation items such as those found in the header, sidebar and footers.

Examples of contextual navigation on ecommerce websites include:

Figure 26 Customers who ...

Figure 27 Best sellers

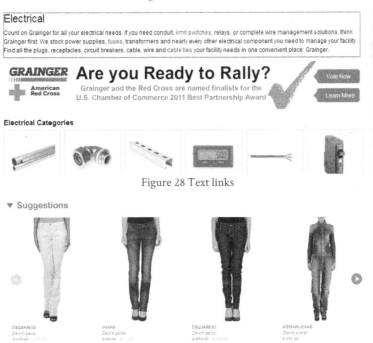

Figure 28 Text links

Figure 29 Recommended products

You will need to discuss contextual navigation with the information architect to identify relevant relationships between categories, subcategories and products, and to plan the internal linking accordingly.

Prioritization

You need to know how many pages will be linked from the primary, secondary and footer navigation on each page template. This is important to estimate, because you need to determine how many links you can display in the contextual navigation.

If you have a new website, it's a good idea to keep the number of links on each page to a maximum 200. This is because you will have only a small authority (PageRank) to pass along to lower levels in the beginning.

Some prioritization guidelines:

- Keep the number of top-level categories/departments in the primary navigation low to avoid the paradox of choice.[21] Research has established that having too many choices is bad for decision making.[22] The short-term memory rule of seven items doesn't apply to primary navigation, as users don't need to remember the menus.

- You can list more in a *view-all departments* or *view-all categories* section.

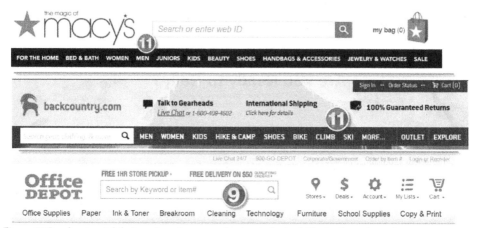

Figure 30 In a horizontal design, the primary navigation is limited. Notice how short the category names must be.

- Vertical primary navigation placement allows room for more categories:

Figure 31 Specialty retailers will probably have no more than two or three departments. General department stores can have up to 20.

- You can break each category level into 20 to 40 subcategories, depending on how large your inventory is.

- If a parent category needs more than 40 subcategories, you may want to consider adding a new parent category and/or implementing faceted subcategories.

- The hierarchy to reach a product details page should be fewer than four (maximum five) levels deep:

  o Three levels deep means *home, category, product details page* (this is for a niche retailer).

  o Four levels is *home, category, subcategory, product details page* (this is the most common setup).

  o Five levels means *home, department, category, subcategory, product details page* (this setup is for large department stores).

- If the hierarchy has more than four or five levels, consider using faceted navigation and filtering by product attributes.

- To improve the authority (PageRank) and the relevance (anchor text) of product detail pages, add a layer in the hierarchy just below the product details page level and link to relevant items from there (e.g., blog, community forums, user reviews and so on).

- Ordering the categories (or items) alphabetically is not always the best option. You should prioritize based on popularity and logic whenever possible, and eventually complement with an alpha navigation (if user testing proves that such navigation type is useful).

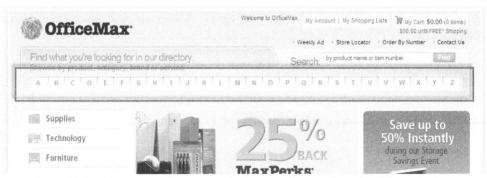

Figure 32 An older version of primary navigation on OfficeMax, featuring alpha navigation.

Figure 33 OfficeMax tested an alpha navigation before reverting back to category name navigation.

- If a category has too few items, consider moving them to an existing category with more items. Only do this if the new categorization makes sense for users.

- If a category has too many items (thousands), it may generate information overload. In this case, you can break the category into smaller subcategories.

Keyword variations

Planning a categorized product hierarchy is not easy. At the top category level, the labels in the primary navigation must be intuitive, have the appropriate search volume and be concise enough to support menu-based navigation. It's worth repeating that determining the hierarchy of an ecommerce website based solely on keyword research is neither ideal nor recommended. However, keyword research should complement and support IA.

One common question regarding keywords is how to handle misspellings, synonyms, stemming or keyword variations for a category. Where do you place them in the website's IA?

For your own internal site search this should be easy to handle: you have to associate each keyword variation, misspelling, etc. to a product/category and redirect users to the respective canonical product or category page. For example, when someone searches for *tees*, *tee shirts* or *tshirts*, you return results for *t-shirts* (or redirect them to the t-shirt category listing page).

Your search for "t-shirt" has returned 515 results
"t-shirt"
Sort by Best Match
View Sears.ca products only
COMPARE SELECTED
$13.99
$29.99
$68.99
$38.00

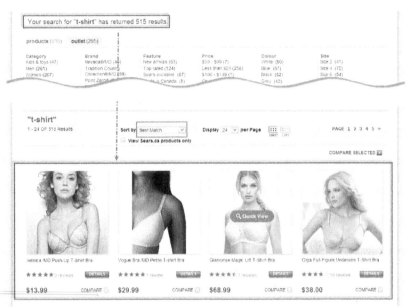

Figure 34 Make sure that your internal site search works properly and doesn't return wrong products (i.e. returning bras when someone searches for t-shirts).

It's a bit more complicated for *commercial search engines* like Google and Yahoo! to understand and connect keyword variations with the right content on your website. But here are some ideas:

Create new categories/pages

You can create individual pages to target keyword variations (or a group of keywords), but this requires a decent content creation budget. On the other hand, if you create pages that target keyword variations using just boilerplate text, you generate significantly similar content across multiple URLs, which is Panda's favorite target.

Budgetary constraints almost always rule out creating new pages. However, some ecommerce websites are implementing this strategy.

Target the most common variations in the title and/or description

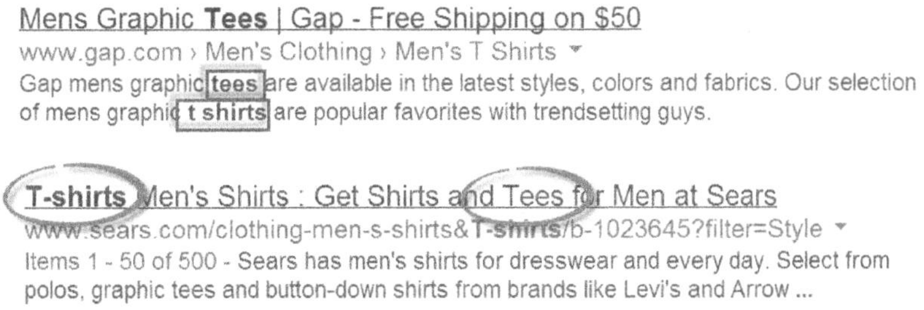

Mens Graphic Tees | Gap - Free Shipping on $50
www.gap.com › Men's Clothing › Men's T Shirts
Gap mens graphic tees are available in the latest styles, colors and fabrics. Our selection of mens graphic t shirts are popular favorites with trendsetting guys.
T-shirts Men's Shirts : Get Shirts and Tees for Men at Sears
www.sears.com/clothing-men-s-shirts&T-shirts/b-1023645?filter=Style
Items 1 - 50 of 500 - Sears has men's shirts for dresswear and every day. Select from polos, graphic tees and button-down shirts from brands like Levi's and Arrow ...

Figure 35 Gap targets keyword variations in the description, while Sears uses the title.

Use product and category descriptions

One option is to use category or product description sections to add several keyword variations in the copy. The bottom of the image below highlights how this website uses two keyword variations of t-shirts:

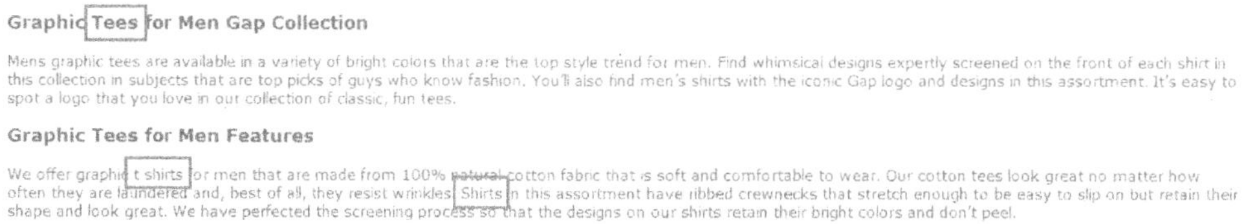

Graphic Tees for Men Gap Collection

Mens graphic tees are available in a variety of bright colors that are the top style trend for men. Find whimsical designs expertly screened on the front of each shirt in this collection in subjects that are top picks of guys who know fashion. You'll also find men's shirts with the iconic Gap logo and designs in this assortment. It's easy to spot a logo that you love in our collection of classic, fun tees.

Graphic Tees for Men Features

We offer graphic t shirts for men that are made from 100% natural cotton fabric that is soft and comfortable to wear. Our cotton tees look great no matter how often they are laundered and, best of all, they resist wrinkles. Shirts in this assortment have ribbed crewnecks that stretch enough to be easy to slip on but retain their shape and look great. We have perfected the screening process so that the designs on our shirts retain their bright colors and don't peel.

Figure 36 This retailer uses "tees" and "t shirts" in the category description copy.

Take advantage of related searches

This approach requires displaying a *related searches* section that contains several of the most used keyword variations:

Related Searches: card products, eco products, eco products promotional, eco friendly products, eco-friendly products, View all related searches zombies slayer undead

Figure 37 Related searches can be useful for users, too.

Identify possible IA problems

Perform "category_name site:mysite.com" (without quotes) searches to see whether search engines list the right page at the top. You can also use products and subcategories in the search. For example, you can query:

- *site:www.costco.ca/ gourmet products*
- *site:www.costco.ca/ "gourmet products"*

If what you deem to be the most relevant page doesn't show up at the top of the results, various reasons are possible, such as:

- Improper internal linking (the internal linking architecture doesn't support the correct page).

- Thin content, no content or inaccessible content (e.g., JavaScript reviews) on the right page.

- External links point to the wrong page(s), diluting and reducing the relevance of the correct pages. If people are linking to the wrong pages, you have to ask yourself why. (Maybe those other pages are more relevant!)

- Page-specific penalties.

Of course, a more in-depth analysis may be required to identify the root cause of these issues. However, it is important to understand how the page you want at the top of SERPs is linked from other pages on the website when attempting to identify the cause.

One of the tools for analyzing this is Google Webmaster Tools:

Figure 38 The Internal Links report will display the most important internal links, but only for the most important pages on the website.

This report is basic, but it can provide some immediate insights. Look for signals such as:

- Are there more internal links to the wrong page(s) than to the desired page?

- Is the desired page linked from parent pages (pages higher in the hierarchy)?

- Is the desired page linked from pages with high authority in terms of PR (PageRank) and DA (Domain Authority)?

- Is the desired page linked with the proper anchor text?

If there are issues with the above-mentioned items, it's time to restructure some internal linking. Keep in mind that Google won't allow you to download the complete list of links, just the top ones.

Another good method to assess the internal linking is to run a crawl on your website using tools like *Xenu Link Sleuth* or *Screaming Frog*, and export the results in Excel to play with.

It is also a good idea to run the most important terms on your internal site to check whether there is a match between the URL returned by your internal site search and the URL returned by search engines. For instance, say Google returns the category listing URL first when you search for "*site:www.costco.ca/ gourmet products*". If you click on it, the *Gourmet Products* page opens up:

Figure 39 Costco's organic search landing page, pointing visitors to the right category page.

However, Costco's internal site search returns a different page, which is actually a search results page. This is not the best approach from a usability point of view or even for search engines (Google doesn't want to list results pages).

Figure 40 This may happen because of the setup of the internal site search rules.

If there's an exact match between a user's query and a category name, then redirect the user to the category listing page instead of to a search results page.

Labeling

Labeling (in reference to choosing the names of the links in the navigation) is an area where information architecture and search engine optimization overlap. SEOs and IAs have to understand the user's mental model to properly label the navigation. This is not easy, and presents a real challenge for very large ecommerce websites. Research from eBay[23] shows how complex it can get.

While most ecommerce taxonomies can be architected based on a predefined vocabulary, SEO can assist in the labeling process.

Let's say you sell toys. Start by searching for the category name ("toys") on the AdWords *Keyword Planner*:

Figure 41 Don't forget to set up the targeting option based on your target market.

Download this keywords list and open it with Excel then tag each keyword with its category/attribute:

A Keyword	B Avg. monthly searches	C Category
toys	90500	top level category
fisher price	165000	brand
toy story	165000	theme
kids games	165000	age
toys for tots	74000	age
hasbro	74000	brand
toy story 3	74000	theme
car toys	60500	vehicles
melissa and doug	60500	brand
toy	49500	top level category
educational games	40500	activities
toy story 2	40500	brand
baby furniture	33100	age
wwe toys	33100	brand
stuffed animals	27100	stuffed
kites	27100	type
toy story characters	27100	brand
baby stores	22200	age
mcfarlane toys	22200	brand
baby walker	22200	age
toy box	22200	type
baby gifts	18100	age
baby stuff	18100	age
fat brain toys	18100	brand
mastermind toys	18100	brand

Figure 42 Categorize keywords into "buckets".

Insert a pivot table that counts the occurrences of categories:

Row Labels	Count of Category
brand	9
age	6
theme	2
top level category	2
type	2
age	1
vehicles	1
activities	1
stuffed	1
(blank)	
Grand Total	**25**

Figure 43 Visitors should be able to find the "brand" label in the main navigation.

Some navigation labels will be easy to identity after tagging fewer than a hundred keywords. For instance, in our example, it is clear that *brand* should be a primary/secondary navigation label and users should be able to navigate and to filter items by brands. Other possible candidates are *age, theme* and *character*. Take the findings from this type of research and discuss them with the information architect.

Another thing you should do with the keyword list generated by *Keyword Planner* is to get the individual word frequency, using Wordle.net:

Word Counts		
Word	**Frequency**	
toys	487	
toy	241	
for	54	
kids	43	
story	34	
baby	31	
stuffed	18	
games	18	
doug	16	
melissa	15	
and	14	
educational	14	
wooden	12	
animals	12	
us	12	
box	11	
online	11	
best	11	
storage	11	
learning	10	
toddlers	9	
guns	8	
r	8	
truck	7	
toddler	7	

Done

Figure 44 This will provide some interesting insights into which words your target market uses the most when searching for toys.

Visually, this is how it looks:

Figure 45 This is the word cloud, excluding "toys" and "toy".

Note: The frequency of the word *kids* is particularly interesting in this example. If you sell only toys for kids (no other target market segments like adult toys), then you probably should exclude the word *kids* from your analysis.

However, a few important segmentations/labels are missing from this keyword list, one being the *gender* label (girls' toys versus boys' toys). Is your target market price sensitive? Then pricing might be another segmentation/label (shop by *price*). These are insights that can't be discovered using keyword tools.

So how do you identify these "hidden" segments/labels? By conducting user research and testing, gathering data about users, and creating consumer personas and scenarios, user flows, website maps and wireframes.

Keep in mind that from an IA perspective, labeling doesn't stop with the text used for links and navigation. There are different types of labels as well:

Document labels

- *URLs* (whenever possible, URLs should contain keywords that make sense to searchers and to search engines).

- *File names* (having relevant keywords in filenames is important for SEO and for users).

Content labels

- *Page titles* should make sense to searchers and search engines. When there's a partial match between the keywords in the HTML title element and the search query, search engines will emphasize (bold) the matched keyword(s), which may help with the click-through rate (CTR).

- *Headings and sub-headings.* Headings use large fonts and attract the eyes almost immediately. Putting keywords in headings assures users they are in the right place.

Other types of navigation labels

Breadcrumbs. Since search engines are so popular, home pages are not the only entry points to websites. Use breadcrumbs to easily and quickly communicate the hierarchy of your site to users.

Contextual text links. Using keyword-rich anchor text placed in a sentence or paragraph is one of the best ways to interlink pages, either vertically or horizontally.

Footers. This is probably the place people spam the most, by creating tens of keyword-rich internal links.

Figure 46 The above looks like a good candidate for an over-optimization penalty.

This footer is just *boilerplate* text, meaning that search engines most likely ignore it when assessing this page's content and anchor text. And it doesn't help to repeat "men's jeans" across a million pages, since search engines can handle boilerplate text pretty well.[24, 25]

Minimize boilerplate repetition: For instance, instead of including lengthy copyright text on the bottom of every page, include a very brief summary and then link to a page with more details. In addition, you can use the Parameter Handling tool to specify how you would like Google to treat URL parameters.

Figure 47 An excerpt from Google's webmaster guidelines.[26]

It's funny how SEOs refer to the labels mentioned above as *on-page SEO factors*, while information architects refer to the same as *labels.* It seems to me that SEOs and IAs work with similar and related concepts, but they still can't get on the same wavelength when it comes to optimizing websites for both searchers and search engines.

Poly-hierarchies

Very often, multiple suitable hierarchies could be appropriate for a given item. It's important to help the information architect choose the best fit as the canonical hierarchy and to stick to it. From the primary/secondary navigation you should link only to the canonical hierarchies. Ideally, all links on the website should point to only one canonical hierarchy.

You can keep as many logical hierarchies as are helpful to users, but to avoid confusing search engines, link only to the canonical hierarchy.

For example, an Elmo toys category can be found under:

Toys > Stuffed Animals > Elmo (URL: mysite.com/toys/stuffed-animals/elmo/)

Gifts > Holidays > Christmas > Elmo (URL: mysite.com/gifts/Christmas/elmo/)

If you decide that the first hierarchy is the canonical one (usually canonical hierarchies are the shortest), then whenever you link internally to the Elmo category, ***always*** use the URL *mysite.com/toys/stuffed-animals/elmo/*

You can use your web analytics tool to see how most users reached a particular page. For example, take a look at the *Navigation Summary* report (under *Behavior* → *All Pages*) generated using Google Analytics, and see how most people reached the *Elmo* page:

Figure 48 For a more detailed analysis, use the *Visitors Flow* report under the *Audience* tab.

Additionally, you should take a look at the *Refined Keywords* dimension in the *Behavior* → *Search Terms* section to understand what keyword refinements were made after a search for "elmo".

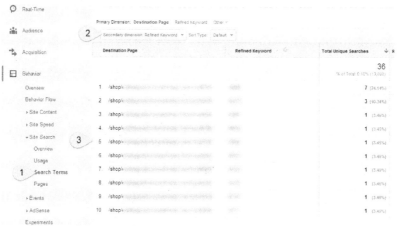

Figure 49 The *Refined Keyword* report can be a source of keyword variation.

Remember that there's no wrong or right way to classify a product into certain taxonomies, as long as you refine them over time, if need be. However, once you decide on a canonical hierarchy, it's a good idea to set that in stone.

Other SEO tips for ecommerce IA

- If you use Google Analytics (or any other web analysis tool), activate the *Site Search Tracking* option. Take a look at what users search for, and use that information to decide on the website's hierarchy. Don't rely solely on your web analytics data, though, because you will miss a lot of data that is sourced outside your website.

- Use keyword research tools to identify keyword variations and suggestions for the terms you have in mind or for those generated with user research and card sorting.

- Analyze your competitors' website architecture and navigation, but don't copy blindly. Use this information for inspiration, but create your own in the end.

- Use a crawler on your competitors' websites and sort their URLs alphabetically. You may need to crawl a large number of URLs, or even complete websites (100k+ pages), for this to work.

- Find your competitors' site maps (both the HTML site map and the XML Sitemap) and analyze them in Excel.

www.brooksrunning.com/Men/
www.brooksrunning.com/mens-and-womens/
www.brooksrunning.com/Mens-Be-Cool/
www.brooksrunning.com/Mens-Be-Dry/
www.brooksrunning.com/Mens-Be-Ready/
www.brooksrunning.com/Mens-Be-Warm/
www.brooksrunning.com/Mens-Be-WarmX/
www.brooksrunning.com/mens-closeouts/
www.brooksrunning.com/mens-cross-country-track-spikes/
www.brooksrunning.com/mens-guidance-shoes/
www.brooksrunning.com/mens-motion-control/
www.brooksrunning.com/mens-neutral-running-shoes/
www.brooksrunning.com/mens-pureproject-shoes/
www.brooksrunning.com/mens-racing-shoes/
www.brooksrunning.com/mens-running-accessories/
www.brooksrunning.com/mens-running-apparel/
www.brooksrunning.com/mens-running-pants/
www.brooksrunning.com/Mens-Running-Shorts/
www.brooksrunning.com/mens-running-socks/
www.brooksrunning.com/Mens-Shirts/
www.brooksrunning.com/mens-support-shoes/

Figure 50 Sorting URLs alphabetically can reveal the website structure.

- Download DMOZ's taxonomy[27] and look at the shopping categorization.

- When choosing the category names, use Google Trends to check whether there's a steep drop in what people search online over time.

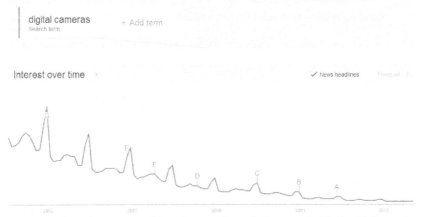

Figure 51 Notice how the interest in "digital cameras" trends downwards. Maybe this has to do with mobile phones that yield increasingly better pictures.

- Don't create the website hierarchy solely on keyword research data; validate with card sorting and user interviews. Nowadays, you can easily do that online, so you have no excuses not to.

- Perform simple navigational queries, like "contact {your_brand}", and make sure the contact URLs (and all other important URLs) are user friendly.

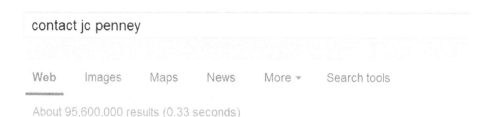

Figure 52 A not-so-friendly "contact us" URL.

Remember, labeling applies to URLs, too, not only to links. In our example, the URL is not optimized for users (nor for search engines). This may be limited by the CMS, but maybe it's time to ditch the old for new. A friendly URL will read like: *www.jcpenney.com/contact-us*

- If you need to categorize large volumes of items, you can use the power of *folksonomy,*[28] an academic term for *crowdsourcing*. Services such as Mturk, from Amazon, will allow you to quickly categorize products, or even relationships between products, using real people. However, you need to be careful in how you select participants and what instructions you give them.

- When card sorting tests are in progress, it's more important to listen and observe than to try to put words in your users' mouths.

- When you remove/update categories and subcategories from your website, make sure that the URLs belonging to the updated/removed categories redirect to the most appropriate working category or subcategory.

- When you develop/update the website, create a checklist of SEO requirements for the information architect (e.g., directory and file name conventions, canonicalization rules, lower casing all URLs, data quality rules for data input teams, seasonality and expired content handling, parameters handling, and so on). I won't provide an extensive checklist here because people tend to use such lists and believe they've done all that's necessary. After reading this book, you should be able to come up with your own list.

- Send email alerts to the search engine optimizer when someone removes or updates categories, subcategories and/or products, so that he or she can check the header responses for the new and old URLs. This task is easily automated.

Technical architecture

At the beginning of this chapter, I mentioned that website architecture is made of *information architecture (IA)* and *technical architecture (TA)*. We then looked at several IA topics. Now it's time to discuss TA.

While duplicate content and crawlability issues are well-known SEO headaches, many search engine optimizers categorize them under the IA umbrella. But they are in fact technical issues. Most of the SEO tips you will learn during the next chapters are technical architecture issues.

But before jumping into pure SEO stuff, let's continue with another pillar of search engine optimization: *Keyword Research.*

CHAPTER THREE

Keyword Research

While SEO is the abbreviation for "search engine optimization", SEO experts don't improve how search engines work; they optimize *for* search engines. And because the main purpose of search engines is to be helpful to the people who use them, SEO would be better thought of as ***optimizing a website for users and for search engines***.

The *search trifecta* includes three entities:

- The user
- The search engine
- The website

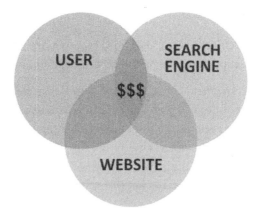

Figure 53 SEOs should pay attentions to users, search engines and websites.

When performing keyword research, SEOs very often skip the user and jump straight to the search engine. This chapter describes what I believe is a better approach to keyword research: start with the user, then move to the website, and finally consider the search engine.

In this book I refer to *keywords* and *queries* interchangeably, but there's a subtle difference between them.[1] A *search query* is a series of words users type into a search engine. A *keyword* is the abstract concept within a search query. A short query can be one and the same as the keyword.

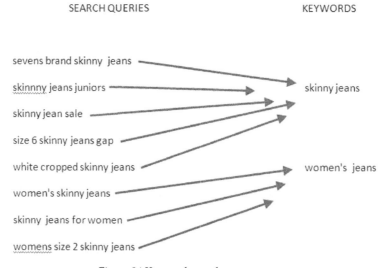

SEARCH QUERIES   KEYWORDS

sevens brand skinny jeans

skinnny jeans juniors

skinny jean sale   skinny jeans

size 6 skinny jeans gap

white cropped skinny jeans   women's jeans

women's skinny jeans

skinny jeans for women

womens size 2 skinny jeans

Figure 54 Keywords are abstract concepts.

For example, on ecommerce websites, keywords are represented by department, category or subcategory names. A search term that contains several words, including the keyword, is a search query.

Good information architecture and keyword research are at the foundation of great ecommerce websites that perform the best in search engines and convert at high rates.

In the *Information Architecture* chapter we found that deciding on primary and secondary navigation labels (or category and subcategory labels) solely based on keyword research is not optimal—it should be done based on user testing and research, using controlled and custom vocabularies. This is because the user's intent is not always reflected in what he or she types in the search engine. That is also why it is so difficult to estimate user intent purely by analyzing keywords or search queries.

Keyword/query research is a core concept of ecommerce SEO because it's important for both users and search engines to map keywords with the right type of content. Discussing search engines and keywords outside the context of users is not the correct SEO approach.

In terms of marketing, *research* means collecting all the raw data that you will later use to perform an *analysis*. In reference to keywords, research means collecting data including but not limited to:

- The keywords (or search queries) used by searchers on search engines.

- Their associated search volumes.

- Existing rankings for those keywords (if applicable). These rankings are difficult to measure accurately due to personalization and geo-location.

- Competition (average *DomainAuthority* and *PageRank* authority of the top 10 websites).

You will collect this data directly from search engines and/or third parties, or by using your own tools.

Gathering keywords

Gathering the initial set of keywords is straightforward, but the number of potential sources is overwhelming:

- The Google's Keyword Planner (good for discovery but unreliable for exact search volumes).

- Google's Display Planner.

- Google's autosuggest feature (crank it up with *Ubersuggest* or *Keyword Snatcher*).

- Google and Bing related searches.

- Bing's Keyword Research with Bing Webmaster.

- Brainstorming with various internal departments.

- Existing Google AdWords.

- Google Analytics data (this source has become less useful because Google now hides more and more keywords, bucketing them under the "not provided" label).

- Google Webmaster Tools.

- Social media sources (Twitter, Facebook, LinkedIn, etc.).

- Internal website search data.

- Voice-of-the-customer surveys and research.

- User testing.

- The anchor text of the natural links to your pages.

- Competitor analysis.

Even though there is a plethora of great keyword tools, arguably the largest set of keywords (and search queries)—and the most accurate search volumes—can be extracted from pay-per-click (PPC) advertising platforms such as AdWords. I recommend collecting keyword data using an actual AdWords campaign, rather than just the data AdWords provides without running a campaign. This is because when you run a live campaign, the AdWords data goes beyond the keyword suggestions within the Keywords Planner. A live campaign will help generate a list of long-tail keywords (use the *Search Terms Report* in AdWords) that are impossible to capture with any other tool.

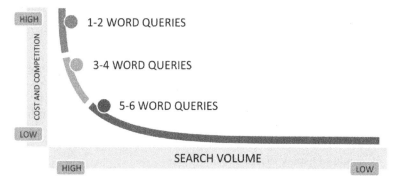

Figure 55 It is easier to rank for a search query that has more words in it, because the search query is usually less competitive.

Besides *Text Ads,* you should run *Product Listing Ads* in Google's AdWords, via the Merchant Center and *Dynamic Search Ads,* and then use the *Search Query Reports* to get an amazing number of relevant keywords.

Unfortunately, many people stop their keyword research after collecting just the quantitative data. This is a pretty common scenario:

"We identified that these keywords have the highest search volumes and so we should target them. We'll change page titles, go with a 3% keyword density and build hundreds of backlinks to pages targeting them."

Or, if the SEOs are more knowledgeable, it may sound like this:

"These keywords have a decent amount of traffic and have good conversion rates, as per your own analytics data. They are competitive, and that's why we should optimize the internal linking and build backlinks to the most appropriate SEO'd pages."

I call this the *traditional* keyword research approach.

Yes, search volume data research is necessary, but you need to go much deeper than this if you want to succeed (make revenue) with SEO. Volumes are just the starting point. You have to think of your users and the problems that may affect their purchasing decisions, and then create content to address such factors.

Seasoned marketers call this concept *Intent to Content.*

Creating personas

One of the best ways to map intent to content is by creating *personas*. Ecommerce websites (especially B2B) need to go above and beyond and develop well-researched *buyer personas* to address buyers in the early stages of the buying funnel, as well as to develop and market content for every stage of the buying funnel.

Let's say you sell promotional products to businesses. Here's what an oversimplified persona creation could be like.

Start by identifying the segments you need to market to and giving them names:

- Vera, the *Marketer.*

- Chris, the *IT Geek.*

- Brad, the *Economical Buyer.*

If you sell promotional products, your focus will be on *Vera, the Marketer.*

Creating Vera's buyer profile should be exhaustive. Everyone involved with marketing and sales needs to answer something called the "Persona Questionnaire", based on their experience, knowledge and online research. This questionnaire should be created by the marketing team and include questions such as:

- Where are they going to read online?

- Where do they go to ask for help?

- What kind of wording do they use?

- What challenges do they face right now?

- What are their goals?

- What does their career path look like?

- What motivates them to select a particular competitor brand?

- How do they take decisions?

Additionally, you can collect and analyze public résumés to identify career paths for people involved in marketing decisions. Here's what the word cloud for marketing managers' accountabilities looks like:

Figure 56 Responsibilities for marketing managers.

Some of the most important facts you have to uncover about Vera are her *pain points* and how she makes decisions. You will uncover such data by engaging on websites where she goes to read, be educated or ask for help.

Once you've identified Vera's pain points and top challenges in relationship to your vertical (promotional products), bucket them in different content types and rank them based on the most stringent challenges. Then prepare content to address each challenge (e.g., case studies, how-to, extensive guides, etc.).

One type of content can be targeted to *raise awareness* about a particular challenge. Another can be a *guide* on how to address the same challenge, with examples of how other businesses dealt with the problem. The third one can be a *case study*. But none of these should be salesy, just good and useful.

Simply put, you will identify Vera's most important problems, educate her and then prove that you have the products she needs.

The *Intent to Content* concept became more relevant and obvious after the Hummingbird algorithm update. Its focus was on processing conversational queries (longer, question-like queries—*how to..., where is..., where can...*), which is different from the traditional word-parsing approach. Another objective of Hummingbird was to match the user intent, to provide answers rather than just search results.

To map keywords to intent and then intent to content, we need to discuss two concepts, the buying funnel and the user intent.

The buying funnel

In U.S. ecommerce, conversion rates are still at about 3%[2] because online retailers focus on converting branded traffic and on marketing to consumers in the late stages of the funnel. Also, ecommerce websites usually will focus their link-building campaigns on category and subcategory anchor text.

Keyword research and web analytics tools, PPC data and other similar sources provide insights on *which* keywords the target audience members search for, *when* they search, and *where* they search from. But savvy online retailers must understand searcher context and create a content plan accordingly. User testing is one great way to gauge that, but it has limits.

Users don't just turn their computers on, navigate to your website and buy your products. First, they realize they have a *need*; next, they *research* online,[3] *decide* what's good for them and—only then—*purchase*.

This journey is called ***the buying funnel***.

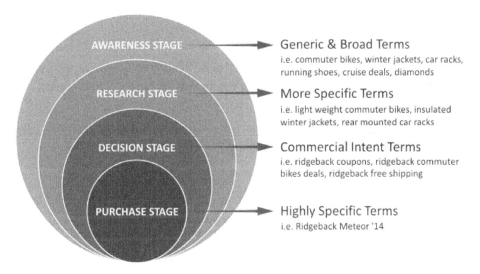

Figure 57 The stages of the buying funnel.

Although the keyword categorization above may seem easy and logical, in practice the keywords consumers use may belong to multiple categories. That's why you can't (and don't need to) be too particular about where to bucket a keyword.

Here are some great insights from one study that mapped 40,000 PPC keywords to the buying funnel:[4]

- Targeting only keywords in the *Purchase* and *Decision* stages of the buying funnel for ecommerce websites can, theoretically, lead to **79% *less organic traffic***.

- The buying funnel is representative of actual online consumer behavior, at least at the individual query level (*6. Discussion and Implications, p. 11*).

- Advertisers can use the model to organize separate campaigns targeting various consumer touch points (*6.3. Practical Implications, p. 14*).

- The implication is clear: do not ignore *Awareness* key phrases (*6.3. Practical Implications, p. 14*).

The research analyzed data from about seven million keywords from a large retail chain having both a brick-and-mortar and an online presence:

Stage of the Buying Funnel	Occurrences	%
Awareness	1,892,620	28%
Research	3,537,930	51%
Decision	1,174,251	17%
Purchase	266,660	4%
	6,871,461	100%

Figure 58 Stages of the buying funnel.[5]

The same research indicates high advertising (PPC) costs for the Awareness (25%) and Research (57%) stages. A staggering $4.6 million (57% of $8 million) could have been saved with a proper keyword to content strategy.

When you map keywords to buying stages and user intent and develop content accordingly, you will:

- Generate content that attracts organic traffic.

- Create content that can be linked to more easily.

- Support pages in the vertical silos up to top-level categories.

- Reduce advertising costs.

The awareness stage

This is the first stage in the buying funnel. Your potential customers realize they have *a need* or *a problem*, and they start researching general information about what would help them fill that need or fix that problem. They want to know what types of products or services are available on the market.

For an ecommerce website, the queries that can be associated with the awareness stage are the broadest, most generic terms, such as department, category or subcategory names (e.g., *commuter bikes, winter jackets, car racks, running shoes, cruise deals, diamonds,* and so on).

However, longer queries and natural language queries are also found in the awareness stage. For example, someone wants to know how to save on his daily commute; he starts by typing "best ways to save on commuting", then reads an article about *commuter bikes.*

At this stage, consumers don't yet know what will address their needs and are still seeking information, so awareness queries usually contain neither brand names nor specific full product names. They can contain an action or a problem that needs to be solved—e.g., *removing wine stains.*

According to the same study cited earlier,[6] an awareness search query:

- Does not contain a brand name.

- Could contain the partial product name/type.

- Could contain the problem to be solved.

At this stage, the *user intent* is mostly *informational.*

Tactics for this stage

The search queries associated with the awareness stage (departments, categories and subcategories) are what most of the ecommerce websites go after. These search terms are super-competitive, and realistically, ranking for such keywords won't happen unless your website has a significant amount of authority in the industry (backlinks), and a lot of content that clearly establishes your website subject matter.

Some tactics associated with attracting traffic for these keywords are:

- Creating content at the lower levels of the website hierarchy (community pages, articles, guides, how-to pieces) and linking vertically from these pages. You will need a significant amount of content and consistent linking to support category pages.

- Siloing the website with directories and internal linking.

- Building themed backlinks to the content-rich pages and articles.

- Blogging, then blogging, then blogging again.

- Shooting instructional videos and featuring them on your website and through social media.

The research stage

At this point, the consumer has identified the type of product/service he or she believes can help, and can recognize brands in your industry, but has not yet decided on a definitive brand to choose from. The consumer still needs to refine his or her knowledge before making a purchasing decision.

While the search queries are still broad, instead of generic searches the consumer now uses more specific terms, including keyword modifiers such as brand names or geo-locations.

The queries may look like "light weight commuter bikes", "insulated winter jackets", "rear mounted car racks", "cross training running shoes", "European cruise deals", or "4 carat wedding ring". The queries can be subcategories, sub-subcategories or product attributes.

Again, long-tail queries can be found at this stage as well. In our biking example, the consumer may type *what are the best brands for commuter bikes, which brand is more reliable, compare {brand1} with {brand2}, what bike size do I need, what is the cost of an electric bike, how much will it cost to maintain a bike,* and so on.

At this stage, the user intent is still mostly informational, but transactional intent may be there too.

Tactics for this stage

- Write product reviews and product comparisons, as well as plenty of articles to answer your target market's questions.

- Write extensive user guides (e.g., *How to Select {category_name}, How to Choose a Commuter Bike in 10 Easy Steps*). This type of content is an organic traffic driver and has the potential to become a real link magnet. The backlink developers will promote this content and generate backlinks as well.

- Create buyer personas to identify where the target market goes to read information and what questions they have (identify those questions with AdWords; group them into topics, and write articles to respond to those questions). Because the authoritative businesses you compete with on SERPs have a lot of inventory and themes to create content for, this is where you can have an edge. It's a well-known fact that BestBuy creates buyer personas.[7]

- Keyword-rich internal linking is also important at this stage. Internal linking is actually important at all stages of the buying funnel, so make sure you correctly cross-link from informational pages to subcategory and category pages.

The decision stage

Now your prospective customer has an idea of what solution is good for him. He will research the best store to buy from and how to get the most value. His logic and emotion will incline him towards a particular brand, and he will be much closer to making a purchase decision. At this stage, the consumer has chosen a product and brand but not the exact model number or version of that product. In our bicycle example, the searcher knows he wants the *Ridgeback* (brand), and he knows he needs a *commuter bike* (category).

The *Decision* stage is where comparison shopping occurs, so it often includes brand names and technical specifications. At this point, his queries will be more focused than in the previous two stages and can include very strong commercial intent keyword modifiers like *sale, discount, coupon, buy* or *buy online*.

His keywords can be *ridgeback coupons, ridgeback commuter bikes deals, ridgeback free shipping, ridgeback bike size guide, ridgeback commuter bikes comparison* and so on. At this stage, the user intent is mostly transactional, with some commercial intent. Some navigational queries may occur when consumers check the manufacturers' websites directly.

Tactics for this stage

1. Make sure that your website (or the websites complementary to your brand) shows up for branded searches, *{brandname} reviews*.

   Your website can take the first positions if you have pages that target those keywords and you build just a couple of good backlinks from external websites.

   Having a dedicated template page for *{brandname} reviews* will allow you to publish all the reviews for that particular product/brand.

Figure 59 This website has a "reviews and news" template for each brand.

Here's how the above website ranks for "ridgeback reviews":

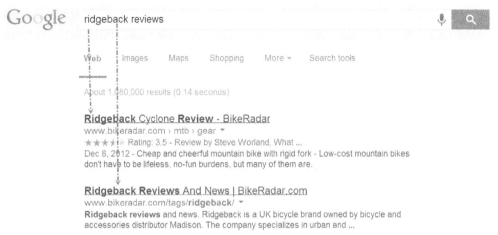

Figure 60 It ranks #1 and #2 for "ridgeback reviews". If you are the owner of the brand, your website should come at the top for your brand's name, even without backlinks.

2. Distribute coupons to build links and brand awareness.

3. Write how-to content, user guides and product comparison pages.

4. Optimize your brand pages and product descriptions to include reassurances, shipping estimates, refund policies and so on—think about optimizing your content for conversions rather than SEO.

5. Have a *Promotions* page for your own brand.

Figure 61 Macy's is ranked #2 for its own brand name plus "coupons".

6. If you accept coupon codes at checkout, make no mistake; consumers will leave the checkout process to find the coupons. Instead of allowing them to leave the checkout to find current promotions outside your website, use a pop-up window (or open a page in a new tab) that lists all of your current promotions. Create interactive tools for finding, comparing or visualizing product (e.g., virtual eyewear, try before you buy, see the painting in your room, etc.).

The purchase stage

This is the stage at which consumers know either exactly what they want to buy or, at least, the brand. The queries contain specific product names and the exact model number or version of that product (e.g., *Ridgeback Meteor'14*). The keywords are the most focused at this stage.

These are probably the easier keywords to classify, because they often contain the product name or the brand name. For ecommerce websites, the landing pages most associated with these queries are the product detail pages.

At this stage, the user intent is mostly transactional, with some navigational intent as well (for example, typing *amazon* in a search engine to buy a book, or purchasing directly from the manufacturer's website).

Tactics for this stage

1. Engage appropriate influencers for product reviews and send qualified traffic.

2. Develop backlinks to product pages.

3. Optimize product detail pages to include detailed product specifications and descriptions, images, Q&As, technical specifications, and so on.

4. Offer coupons. Product and/or service coupons can attract traffic, but not as much as "*{brandname} coupons*".

More sophisticated marketers and sales professionals have gone into greater depth about the buying funnel and broken it down into even more detailed stages. But if you start with these four stages and develop content based on them, you will see traffic and sales increase nicely over time.

Keep in mind that a purchasing decision is never going to be linear. You will have prospective customers who start their journey in the middle, at the end, or at the beginning of the funnel. But you will be able to capture consumers at any stage if your content is well planned.

Knowing about the buying funnel stages is important for understanding another keyword research concept, the ***user intent***.

The relationship between these two concepts is pretty tight. Usually, a consumer who is in the *Awareness* buying stage is going to use informational search queries. When he is in the *Purchasing* stage, he will mainly use transactional intent keywords that have a strong commercial intent.

The user intent

When users go to search engines and type queries, they are trying to accomplish something. This can be finding a business (online or offline), getting more information about a product or service, or purchasing an item online or offline. Search engine users have a goal in mind, and this is called the *user intent*.

Users type phrases that represent their intents, and Google tries to match those intents with the most relevant results. If you understand this concept, then you understand the importance of mapping keywords to intents and developing content accordingly.

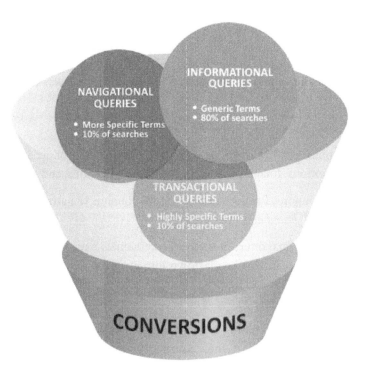

Figure 62 Three types of user intent keywords.

The specialty literature[8] breaks down the user intent into three categories:

- *Navigational*, when searchers use a search engine to navigate to a specific website.

- *Informational*, when searchers want to find content/info about a particular topic.

- *Transactional*, when searchers want to engage in an activity, such as buying a product online, downloading or playing a game, seeing pictures, viewing a video, and so on. Transactional intent doesn't necessarily involve a purchase.

Google's guidelines for quality raters[9] refer to the user intent categories above as *Navigation*, *Informational* and *Action* (instead of *Transactional*).

When discussing user intent types, it's worth mentioning *commercial intent*. This is a rather independent dimension that can apply to all three types of user intent, with transactional queries probably carrying a higher commercial intent than the other two. A Microsoft Research study found that 38% of queries have a commercial intent, and the rest are non-commercial.[10]

	COMMERCIAL	NON-COMMERCIAL
NAVIGATIONAL	Amazon	Yahoo! Mail
INFORMATIONAL	Digital camera	Vancouver, Canada
TRANSACTIONAL	Canon EOS Rebel T4i	U2 beautiful day lyrics

Figure 63 Navigational and informational keywords can have commercial intent, too.

For example, when a consumer wants to buy a car, he will perform the research online but seal the deal in the dealership. His queries, whether informational, transactional or navigational, will all have some commercial intent since his final goal is to purchase a car.

Mapping keywords to user intent is not an easy task. Even search engines are not able to accurately classify user intent in general, let alone commercial intent.

So map keywords to user intent as best you can. As long as you start categorizing based on intent, you will start generating ideas for content that matches that intent, which is the best SEO approach to stand the test of continuous algorithm updates.

Below are some guidelines for classifying user intent, but remember that many keywords can be placed into multiple intent buckets.

Navigational intent, the "go" queries

- Queries containing companies, brands, organizations and/or people's names.

- Queries containing parts of full domain names.

- Queries containing *website* or *web site*.

Navigational queries are the easiest to spot during keyword research.

For this type of query, make sure you show up for your own brand or your domain name. If not, you have a bigger problem than understanding user intent.

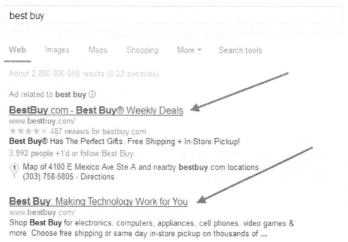

Figure 64 Best Buy pays for its own brand name to appear on AdWords.

Generally, it's not a good idea to put effort into ranking at the top of SERPs for the brand names you sell, because this means competing directly with the brand owners and their social media profiles. Overtaking them in rankings is not possible—unless the brand really sucks—and is going to require significant effort.

If you sell your own products, make sure your website shows up for variations of the product names. For example, if you manufacture and sell RAM, your website should rank with or without spaces between words (e.g., "Kingston 1GbRAM" and "Kingston 1 Gb RAM").

Informational intent, the "know" queries

- Queries containing question words (e.g., *ways to, how to, what is*, etc.).

- Queries containing informational terms (e.g., *list, top, playlist*, etc.).

- Queries containing anti-commercial queries (e.g., *DIY, do it yourself, plans, tutorial, guide*, etc.).

- Queries containing words like *instructions, information, specs.*

- Queries containing word like *help, resources, FAQ.*

- Queries that contain a category or subcategories (e.g., *digital cameras, rain coats,* etc.).

If you have difficulty classifying keywords based on intent, one trick is to find the navigational and transactional intent queries, then assume that the rest are informational. If you want to learn more about how Google teaches its own search quality raters to classify search queries, I recommend reading Google's "Search Quality Rating Guidelines", especially Chapter Two.

Informational intent is the type of intent ecommerce websites should start shifting their attention to, because keywords with informational intent provide the chance to get in front of the target market in the early stages of the buying funnel. The earlier your audience is exposed to your brand, the higher the chances of closing the sale later.

The content that addresses informational queries encompasses all types of media (text, video, audio, etc.), and all types of content (product descriptions, technical specs, expert reviews, infographics, instructographics, blog posts, how-to guides, etc.).

Your goal is not to sell your products with this content, but rather to position yourself as the authoritative source. You need to become a publisher of trustworthy, useful content. Informational queries are perfect for this because they represent a great opportunity to increase brand awareness and show expertise.

The fact that 80% of search queries are informational[11] represents a huge opportunity for those who plan for long-term gains. These queries can be very generic (head keywords like category and subcategory names, e.g., "cars" or "insurance brokers"), but long-tail keywords will be there as well. For example, keywords like "what is the most fuel efficient car on the market?" or "life insurance brokers in New Westminster, BC" are informational (note, though, that either of these could be a transactional query as well).

To cover as many informational queries as possible, you will need to create educational content for those consumers who are not yet ready to buy or don't even know what they need. Your goal is to give them content that will answer their questions, fill their need for information and help move them further in the buying funnel.

Informational intent queries appear at the Awareness, Research and Decision stages, and you have to guide consumers towards content that is more transactional, which will eventually lead to conversions. After all, a macro-conversion (e.g., a web sale) happens only at the end of several micro-conversions (reading an article about a problem, finding the right product, adding to the shopping cart, etc.).

One way to check whether there's a disconnect between user intent and the content on your website is by looking at the ecommerce transactions (and conversion rates) for your keywords:

Keyword	Acquisition			Behavior			Conversions eCommerce ▾		Ecommerce Conversion Rate
	Visits ↓	% New Visits	New Visits	Bounce Rate	Pages / Visit	Avg. Visit Duration	Transactions	Revenue	
	67,459	67.84%	45,765	46.16%	3.81	00:04:04	283	$42,959.26	0.42%
	% of Total 27.65% (244,012)	Site Avg 03.59% (0.69%)	% of Total 29.45% (155,103)	Site Avg 48.65% (-5.13%)	Site Avg 3.91 (5.62%)	Site Avg 00:03:58 (2.83%)	% of Total 30.43% (230)	% of Total 28.54% ($150,546.50)	Site Avg 0.38% (10.07%)
1. (not provided)	40,438	70.35%	28,449	45.41%	3.79	00:04:02	163	$28,315.46	0.40%
2.	3,392	75.12%	2,548	49.12%	3.54	00:03:43	1	$483.98	0.03%
3.	1,900	31.26%	594	24.89%	6.49	00:08:02	24	$4,146.57	1.26%
4.	1,093	67.25%	735	44.46%	4.43	00:04:03	15	$633.85	1.37%
5.	941	69.71%	656	45.80%	3.40	00:03:18	0	$0.00	0.00%
6.	597	82.08%	490	53.77%	2.37	00:02:43	0	$0.00	0.00%
7.	462	33.98%	157	25.97%	6.93	00:08:47	2	$406.59	0.43%

Figure 65 Using Google Analytics, you can look at which pages/keywords perform poorly. 3.3k organic visits and just a single conversion is a sign that needs to be taken seriously.

Another way of finding this disconnect is by analyzing the keywords' bounce rate:

Keyword	Acquisition			Behavior		
	Visits ↓	% New Visits	New Visits	Bounce Rate	Pages / Visit	Avg. Visit Duration
	3,392	89.92%	3,050	88.24%	1.25	00:00:54
	% of Total 76.80% (4,412)	Site Avg 87.94% (2.25%)	% of Total 78.61% (3,880)	Site Avg 87.32% (1.17%)	Site Avg 1.26 (-1.19%)	Site Avg 00:00:53 (1.73%)
	3,187	90.15%	2,873	88.30%	1.25	00:00:54
	5	0.00%	0	80.00%	1.20	00:00:20
	5	100.00%	5	60.00%	1.40	00:00:08
	3	66.67%	2	86.67%	1.33	00:08:55
	3	33.33%	1	66.67%	1.67	00:01:45
	2	100.00%	2	50.00%	1.50	00:00:48
	2	50.00%	1	50.00%	3.50	00:16:59

Figure 66 A high bounce rate is usually a bad thing, because it shows that the consumer landed on your website and didn't find what he expected.

As you start looking at keywords through the user intent prism (as opposed to just numbers) and try to solve high bounce rates, low conversion rates and low transaction numbers, you'll start to learn more about your visitors. This will help not only with SEO, but with everything marketing and sales.

When analyzing the performance of the informational queries, keep in mind that such keywords will most likely not convert at the first visit.

Transactional intent, the "do" queries

These are queries that contain:

- Calls to action (*subscribe, purchase, pay, play, send, download, buy, listen, view, watch, find, get, compare, shop, search, sell,* etc.).

- Entertainment terms (*pictures, movies, games,* and so on).

- Promotional terms (*coupon, deal, discounts, for sale, quotes*).

- Complete product names.

- Comparison terms (*where to buy, prices, pricing, compare prices for*).

- Terms related to shipping (*next day shipping, same day shipping,* and *free shipping*).

Note that:

- Not all transactional queries contain verbs. For example, "Dell Vostro 1700" can be both transactional and informational, because the user either wants to read more about this product or wants to buy it.

- Transactional queries don't necessarily have to involve money and/or a purchase. They reflect the desire to perform some action on the Internet.

Transactional queries with commercial intent occur more frequently in the decision and purchasing stages. Such keywords should land visitors on category and product detail pages, or on landing pages that have been built to funnel visitors to a page where a commercial transaction occurs (e.g., comparison tool, finder tool, etc.).

Transactional queries are most likely to generate the highest return on investment (ROI) for pay-per-click campaigns, and that is why their cost per click can be high. However, the ROI would be even greater if you had previously "touched" the PPC clicker with an organic result—your brand would ring a bell with them after they clicked on your ad.

A smart way to connect user intent and search queries is with user surveys sourced from your organic traffic. You can implement a modal window (pop-up) that tracks the search query used by visitors (whenever you can—nowadays, search engines no longer pass search queries) and ask a simple question, such as "What is the goal of your visit to our website today?" to which you provide two possible answers:

- I am shopping for something to buy, now or in the future.

- I am looking for more information about some products/services.

Mapping intent to content

Understanding (i) where in the buying funnel the user is when he types in a search query, (ii) his user intent and (iii) the persona he belongs to should guide your content strategy, rather than dictating where to stuff keywords into a specific page.

Let's take a look at the following scenario:

"Tired Jamie" (persona name) can't sleep at night and wants to improve her sleep. She found that an old mattress may be the cause of her poor sleep, and she decides it's time to buy a new mattress. She then hunts for info on how to choose a mattress that can provide the best night's sleep. She discovers a useful mattress finder tool that recommends foam mattresses, based on her input. Next, she starts researching which brands are out there and which product has the best reviews. Tempur-Pedic seems like a trusted brand, so she investigates their various types of mattresses. Finally, she knows what she wants and now is actively looking for that product.

First, map her keyword journey, which might look like this:

Keyword	Theme/Silo	Primary User Intent	Content Type
tossing all night	resources	informational	blog article/video
how to improve my sleep	resources	informational	how to guide/ blog article
how to choose a mattress	mattresses	informational	buyers guide/mattress finder tool or quiz
foam mattresses brands	mattresses	informational	guide/comparison tool
tempur pedic mattresses	mattresses	transactional	content-rich category page with tools for comparison, ask an expert, etc
tempur pedic cloud luxe breeze	mattresses	transactional	content rich product detail page with expert reviews, q&a, etc

Figure 67 Try to assign each keyword to the most suitable silo.

Next, map the keywords to the user intent (remember that there can be multiple intents behind a query).

Then, add the type of content that fits the intent and search query (e.g., for *how to choose a mattress* you can build a mattress finder tool).

Now you need some more details:

- The **URL** represents the page you want to rank in SERPs.

- The *Anchor Text(s)* is the internal anchor text used to link to the targeted URLs (this can be used as anchor text for your backlinks as well).

Keyword	Theme/Silo	Primary User Intent	Content Type	URL	Anchor Text(s)
tossing all night	resources	informational	blog article/video	mysite.com/blog/mattresses/tossing.html	poor sleep, tossing at night
how to improve my sleep	resources	informational	how to guide/ blog article	mysite.com/blog/mattresses/improve-sleep	improve your sleep
how to choose a mattress	mattresses	informational	buyers guide/mattress finder tool or quiz	mysite.com/educate/mattresses/mattress-finder-tool mysite.com/educate/mattresses/mattress-buyers-guide	how to choose a mattress mattress finder tool
foam mattresses brands	mattresses	informational	guide/comparison tool	mysite.com/educate/compare/foam-mattress-brands	foam mattresses brands
tempur pedic mattresses	mattresses	transactional	content-rich category page with tools for comparison, ask an expert, etc	mysite.com/bed/mattresses/tempur-pedic/	tempur pedic mattresses
tempur pedic cloud luxe breeze	mattresses	transactional	content rich product detail page with expert reviews, q&a, etc	mysite.com/tempur-pedic-cloud-luxe-breeze.html	tempur pedic cloud luxe breeze

Figure 68 The table above doesn't look like the volume-based keyword research you're used to.

Keep in mind that failing to establish contact and presence with consumers who perform informational queries is one cause of single-digit conversion rates. Too often, ecommerce websites try to sell too early.

If you have content for all buying stages and for all intents, you can land the consumer on your website at the research stage and then gradually advance him to the purchasing stage right on your website, without having him exit to find answers on competitors' websites. If one of your competitors becomes the trusted source of advice for him, you've lost the sale.

So make sure that you optimize the right pages for the right queries. If the query is informational, you want to rank a page that provides informational or educational content. Likewise, if the query is transactional, you need to optimize and rank with pages that have transactional intent.

Prioritization

Keyword prioritization is tough because:

- You need to take into account many and various metrics.

- The SERP ranking factors are not publicly available.

- Several metrics, such as competitiveness, come from third-party sources (not directly from search engines).

Therefore, any keyword evaluation model based on rankings factors and competitiveness metrics is subjective.

Prioritization methodologies are usually based on factors such as keyword difficulty, search volumes, business goals, margins and profits, or conversion rates, or a combination of these.

One lesser-known method for keyword prioritization is based on the *revenue opportunity of forecasted rankings*. This evaluation model determines a monetary value for top 10 rankings, using the average SERP CTRs.

Note that this model is meant only as a tool to help you identify the lowest-hanging opportunities, not to make a business case.

Keyword	[Search Volume]	Current Ranking	Organic Visits	Per Visit Value		Revenue	Rev. if ranked #1	Rev. if ranked #2	Rev. if ranked #3	Rev. if ranked #4	Rev. if ranked #5	Rev. if ranked #6	Rev. if ra #7
tossing all night	345	200	1	$ 2.00	$	2.00	248.40	86.25	65.55	54.51	42.09	28.29	
how to improve my sleep	480	134	2	$ 3.00	$	6.00	518.40	180.00	136.80	113.76	87.84	59.04	
how to choose a mattress	1900	45	20	$ 7.00	$	140.00	4,788.00	1,662.50	1,263.50	1,050.70	811.30	545.30	50
foam mattresses brands	30	30	2	$ 10.00	$	20.00	108.00	37.50	28.50	23.70	18.30	12.30	
tempur pedic mattresses	600	15	6	$ 15.00	$	90.00	3,240.00	1,125.00	855.00	711.00	549.00	369.00	34
tempur pedic cloud luxe breeze	50	12	5	$ 25.00	$	125.00	650.00	156.25	118.75	98.75	76.25	51.25	

Figure 69 Obtain *Per Visit Value* by dividing Revenue by Organic Visits.

In the table above, the section displaying the *search volume, current ranking, organic visits, per visit value* and *revenue* columns contains advertising and/or web analytics data.

Note that I purposely exclude metrics such as *conversion rate* or *number of conversions*. This is because ecommerce websites have multiple micro- and macro-conversions (e.g., a web sale, a newsletter subscription, reaching a key page, submitting a form, etc.), and the evaluation method is based solely on revenue, not conversion rates. If you want to dig into details and evaluate based on each type of conversion (for example, if you want to prioritize keywords that generate more email subscriptions), then use only the newsletter revenue data for each keyword, and prioritize accordingly.

The columns named "Rev. if ranked N" represent the revenue opportunity for various positions if they are ranked organically.

% clicks on #1 results	36.0%
% clicks on #2 results	12.5%
% clicks on #3 results	9.5%
% clicks on #4 results	7.9%
% clicks on #5 results	6.1%
% clicks on #6 results	4.1%
% clicks on #7 results	3.8%
% clicks on #8 results	3.5%
% clicks on #9 results	3.0%
% clicks on #10 results	2.0%

Figure 70 The organic SERP CTRs are based on research by Optify.[12]

Looking at the "Rev. if ranked 1" column, you can see that although the keyword "tempur pedic cloud luxe breeze" currently has the highest *Per Visit Value* ($25) and is a transactional keyword, it's not the keyword with the highest potential (increase in revenue). That keyword would be "how to choose a mattress".

The next step is adding keyword competitiveness data. There are a few different methods for assessing the competitiveness of a keyword. The easier ones are:

- The average PageRank, Domain Authority (DA) or Page Authority (PA) of the top 10 ranking pages and root (sub)domains.

- The keyword difficulty score computed by MOZ, or the CI index from serpIQ.

Keyword	Avg PR root domains	Avg PR URLs	Avg DA	Avg PA	MOZ KD
tossing all night	4.5	2.4	45	22	30
how to improve my sleep	3.7	2.1	65	31	64
how to choose a mattress	4.6	1.9	48	26	56
foam mattresses brands	2.9	1.4	74	17	50
tempur pedic mattresses	2.2	0.7	45	12	40
tempur pedic cloud luxe breeze	3.4	1.3	35	15	34

Figure 71 The keyword difficulty score computed by MOZ, or the CI index from serpIQ.

Now that you have some quantitative information, you can slice and dice the keyword data any way you like. However, I suggest analyzing data in sets/themes only. If you mix keywords related to mattresses with keywords related to dressers, your data will be skewed.

Also, it's important to find a balance between the forecasted revenue and the costs associated with obtaining the necessary rankings to achieve that revenue. Keep in mind that you will need to produce content, promote it through social media and develop backlinks to it. All these are costly.

Keyword	Avg PR root domains	Avg PR URLs	Avg DA	Avg PA	MOZ KD	Content Creation Cost	Cost per Link	Costs	ROI
tossing all night	4.5	2.4	45	22	30	$250	$200	$2,050	0.12
how to improve my sleep	3.7	2.1	65	31	64	$250	$200	$2,850	0.18
how to choose a mattress	4.6	1.9	48	26	56	$250	$200	$2,170	2.21
foam mattresses brands	2.9	1.4	74	17	50	$250	$200	$3,210	0.03
tempur pedic mattresses	2.2	0.7	45	12	40	$250	$200	$2,050	1.58
tempur pedic cloud luxe breeze	3.4	1.3	35	15	34	$250	$200	$1,650	0.27

Figure 72 Take content creation and promotion into consideration.

Content creation cost is an estimate of how much it will cost to create the content necessary to promote the keyword. (Note that each keyword might have a different cost, depending on the type of content you need to create; creating an article is less expensive than creating a video, which in turn is less expensive than creating an interactive tool or a mobile app.)

The *cost per link* is an estimate of how much it will cost you to build a link to that piece of content.

Costs = content creation cost + (cost per link * (average DA / 10)*2)

The 2 in the above formula is a cost coefficient tied to your own domain's authority. The lower the domain's authority, the higher the coefficient. You can use the following brackets as guidelines for adjusting the coefficient, based on your DA:

- DA 0–20, coefficient = 5.

- DA 21–40, coefficient = 4.

- DA 41–60, coefficient = 3.

- DA 61–80, coefficient = 2.

- DA 81–100, coefficient = 1.

Basically, the *Costs* formula says that the lower your DA, the more links you need to build to achieve first-page ranking.

For example, for the keyword "tempur pedic mattresses", if your website DA is 65, the coefficient is 2 and the *Costs* formula is:

*Costs = $250 + ($200 * (45/10)*2) = $250 + ($200 * 9)*, where 9 means you will need to build nine good-quality links.

The Excel file can be found on the book companion website at *http://www.ecommercemarketingbooks.com/companion-files/*.

Going back to user intent, remember that the ultimate goal of search engines is to provide straight answers for search queries and to provide the best possible results for keyword searches (remember the difference between search queries and keywords). If search engines fail at this, they'll lose users, market share and advertising revenue. It's therefore crucial for search engines to identify user intent as best as they can (Google's Hummingbird update focuses a lot on this).

So, whenever you are in doubt about how search engines map keywords to intent, use Google's help to assess what type of pages it returns for a specific keyword. First, log out of all your Google accounts. Then, clean out the browser cookies, open a private/incognito session and type in the keyword you want to research.

For example, let's take a look at the results for the keyword search "digital camera", on the next page.

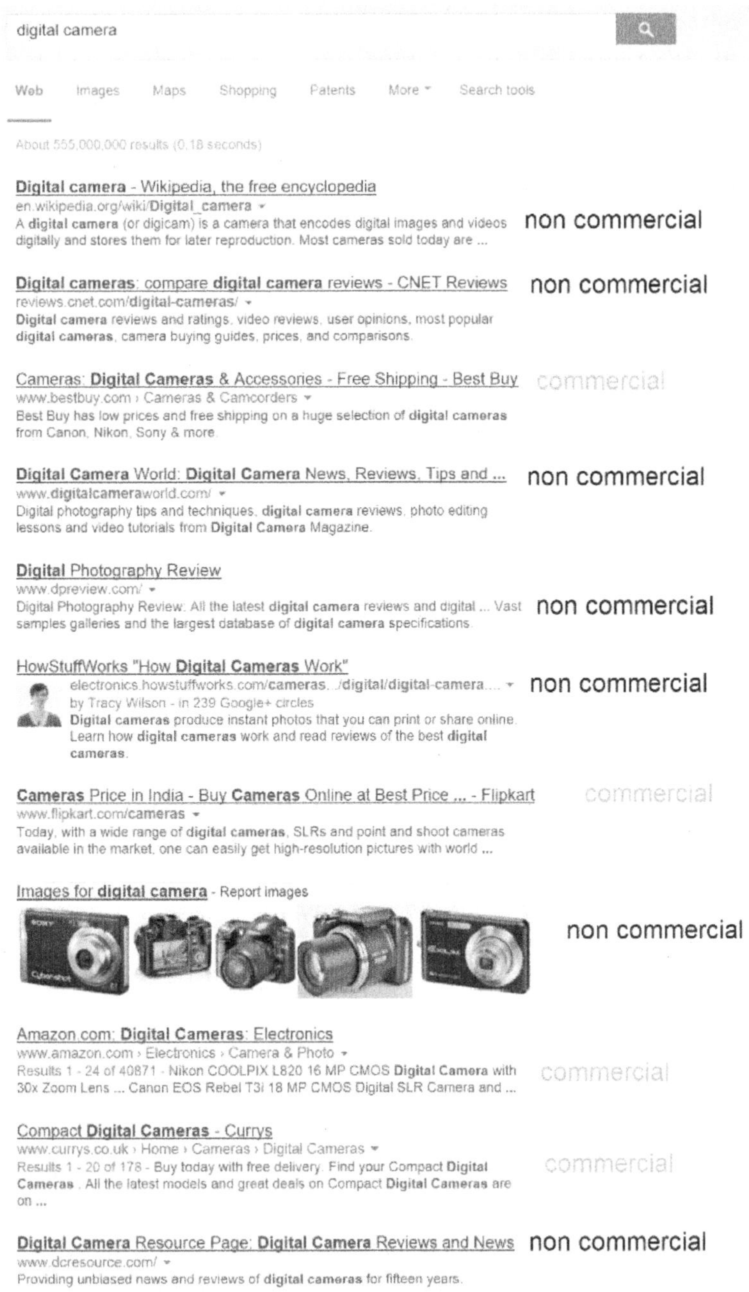

digital camera

Web   Images   Maps   Shopping   Patents   More ▾   Search tools

About 555,000,000 results (0.18 seconds)

Digital camera - Wikipedia, the free encyclopedia   **non commercial**
en.wikipedia.org/wiki/Digital_camera ▾
A **digital camera** (or digicam) is a camera that encodes digital images and videos
digitally and stores them for later reproduction. Most cameras sold today are ...

Digital cameras: compare **digital camera** reviews - CNET Reviews   **non commercial**
reviews.cnet.com/digital-cameras/ ▾
Digital camera reviews and ratings, video reviews, user opinions, most popular
digital cameras, camera buying guides, prices, and comparisons.

Cameras: **Digital Cameras** & Accessories - Free Shipping - Best Buy   commercial
www.bestbuy.com › Cameras & Camcorders ▾
Best Buy has low prices and free shipping on a huge selection of **digital cameras**
from Canon, Nikon, Sony & more.

Digital Camera World: **Digital Camera** News, Reviews, Tips and ...   **non commercial**
www.digitalcameraworld.com/ ▾
Digital photography tips and techniques, **digital camera** reviews, photo editing
lessons and video tutorials from **Digital Camera** Magazine.

Digital Photography Review
www.dpreview.com/ ▾
Digital Photography Review: All the latest **digital camera** reviews and digital ... Vast   **non commercial**
samples galleries and the largest database of **digital camera** specifications.

HowStuffWorks "How **Digital Cameras** Work"
electronics.howstuffworks.com/cameras.../digital/digital-camera.... ▾   **non commercial**
by Tracy Wilson - in 239 Google+ circles
Digital cameras produce instant photos that you can print or share online.
Learn how **digital cameras** work and read reviews of the best **digital cameras**.

Cameras Price in India - Buy **Cameras** Online at Best Price ... - Flipkart   commercial
www.flipkart.com/cameras ▾
Today, with a wide range of **digital cameras**, SLRs and point and shoot cameras
available in the market, one can easily get high-resolution pictures with world ...

Images for **digital camera** - Report images

non commercial

Amazon.com: **Digital Cameras**: Electronics
www.amazon.com › Electronics › Camera & Photo ▾
Results 1 - 24 of 40871 - Nikon COOLPIX L820 16 MP CMOS **Digital Camera** with   commercial
30x Zoom Lens ... Canon EOS Rebel T3i 18 MP CMOS Digital SLR Camera and ...

Compact **Digital Cameras** - Currys
www.currys.co.uk › Home › Cameras › Digital Cameras ▾
Results 1 - 20 of 178 - Buy today with free delivery. Find your Compact Digital   commercial
Cameras. All the latest models and great deals on Compact **Digital Cameras** are
on ...

Digital Camera Resource Page: **Digital Camera** Reviews and News   **non commercial**
www.dcresource.com/ ▾
Providing unbiased news and reviews of **digital cameras** for fifteen years.

Figure 73 Microsoft used to have a commercial intent detector tool, but unfortunately, it's been
discontinued. So, you will have to classify the results manually.

Seven out of the eleven listings are educational resources (non-commercial intent
such as reviews, news, images, tips, wiki, etc.) and four are online retailers (commercial

intent). If you sell digital cameras and want to rank for this keyword, you now know that you have to create great educational resources on your website and promote them heavily, on both your website and others' sites.

Given the number of informational results for "digital camera", it seems Google doesn't assign a strong commercial intent to this keyword.

Then why do ecommerce websites try to rank their *Digital Cameras* category URL rather than a *Digital Camera University* page dedicated to educational content and tools? Wouldn't the category page create a disconnect between the user intent and the content on that page?

Imagine you walk into a store to gather information about which digital camera best suits your needs, only to encounter a pushy sales person who tries to sell you items **he** thinks you need, rather than what **you** think you need. You'll probably thank him nicely and leave without buying. The same applies for online experiences. If consumers land on a page that doesn't fit their intent, they will bounce.

Creating content based on keyword research has to address not only the possible buyers of your products, but also those who will link to your content. That is because most of the people who buy from you won't link to a product or category page. It is possible that customers will share the purchase socially, but linking is going to happen only from people who believe the content they link to is valuable. The buyers think in terms of the value they get by buying the product from you, but those who link to you think in terms of the value they offer to their own website visitors.

Product attributes and keyword variations

Online retailers often find themselves selling products with a multitude of similar attributes and therefore would like to rank for a large number of keyword and product variations. For example, you sell a sweater that comes in red, blue and green and in three different sizes. This 3x3 matrix will generate nine SKUs (small red sweater, large red sweater, extra-large blue sweater, etc.).

In the chapter dedicated to product detail pages, we will discuss how you should approach product variations, but for now let's say that creating separate URLs and content (product descriptions) for each product variation may not be the best idea. Rather, you should handle product variations in the interface (AJAX).

If you already have unique URLs for product variations, then choose a canonical URL and point all product variation URLs to it. However, if the URLs are clean (i.e., they don't have too many URL parameters), don't change the URL structure without properly consulting your SEO expert.

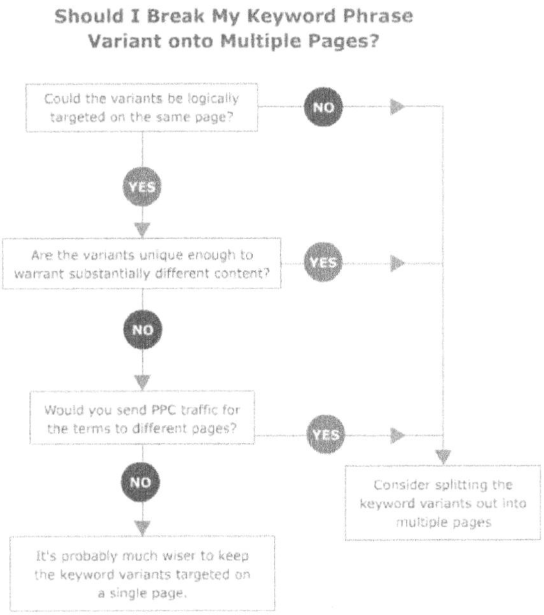

Figure 74 A simple keyword variation process inspired by MOZ.[13]

Keyword strategies

In this section I'll discuss a couple of less talked about keyword strategies for ecommerce websites.

Target the lowest-hanging keywords

When you run an ecommerce website, the number of keywords you want to rank for is huge, so it's not economically feasible to target all of them with link-building campaigns. You can rank some keywords (the long-tail ones in particular) naturally just by supporting them with content. Others, usually more competitive terms (head and body terms, aka category and subcategory keywords), will rank only if you support with links from external websites.

An often overlooked keyword strategy is to focus on a large number of keywords ranking on page 2, especially those between #11 and #15. Moving a keyword from the second page to the first page is usually less competitive than moving from position #5 to #1 (four positions up). In the same way, moving from #21 to #17 (also four positions up) is not going to generate a substantial increase in visits.

Let's illustrate with a keyword that has 1.22 million searches a month, "wedding dresses". Moving this keyword from position #11, where it gets less than 2.6% of the clicks (around 3,100 visits), to position #6, where it gets 4.1% of the clicks (around 4,900 visits), represents a 158% improvement in traffic. Yet moving the same keyword from #21 to #16 will generate a minimal rise in visits.

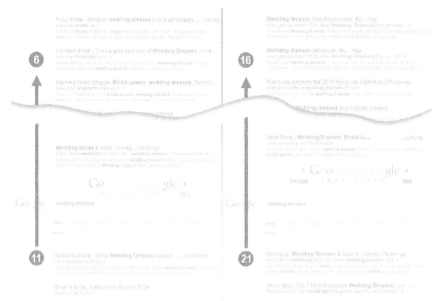

Figure 75 Keyword ranking at the top of page 2 can be a good target for link development.

The idea is that by building links to keywords ranking on the second page, you gradually increase your website's authority and, at the same time, organic traffic. And in time, these links will support the link-building campaign for more competitive terms.

Of course, you should not focus solely on keywords ranking on the second page. A thorough analysis will identify keywords that rank on the first page and don't have much competition—it makes sense to target those ones as well.

Target holidays and retail days search queries

Holidays such as Christmas, Hanukkah, Thanksgiving and Easter, and major retail events (Back to School, Halloween, Cyber Monday, Black Friday, Boxing Day, etc.) represent major traffic and revenue opportunities for all ecommerce websites, and for online retailers in particular. Shoppers are more open to spending on themselves and on others. But their search patterns change around these special shopping days.

The 2013 ecommerce shopping days calendar created by Shopify [14] shows there's not a single month without a major shopping event. Promotions change very rapidly, and shoppers will shift their search queries very quickly. Smart ecommerce websites have to adapt to and capitalize upon such shifts.

However, a lot of websites don't have the *agile marketing* abilities to take advantage of shopping day opportunities.

Here are some common mistakes:

- Not updating page titles, descriptions and headings to include event-related modifiers.

- Not updating page titles, descriptions and headings to include event-related modifiers until just a few days before that event. This is too late from a business point of view and an SEO one. Google Insights research[15] suggests that Black Friday searches can come as early as July.

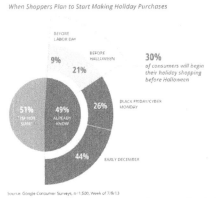

Figure 76 30% of shoppers plan their Christmas shopping list before Halloween.[16]

- Creating year-specific pages (e.g., Christmas 2014) but removing them without proper redirects once the holiday/event ends.

- Not planning for a "flash" link building campaign to target event-specific modifiers.

- Not targeting (or improperly targeting) last-minute buyers by adding free or next-day shipping in the page titles.

Figure 77 55% of consumers expected free shipping.[17]

Additionally, very few ecommerce websites will create content (e.g., guides, ideas, how-to's) specifically targeting such retail dates. That's a shame, since this type of content can capture potential customers during their research stage, when they use informational searches queries, like "Halloween costumes ideas", "Christmas gift guides" or "Easter egg decorating pictures".

Using keyword modifiers to update titles, descriptions, headings and possibly copy

How consumers search online before shopping events is different from how they do so the rest of the year. They add keyword *modifiers* to their usual search queries to better define their intent. Shopping event keyword modifiers can be words like "Christmas", "Cyber Monday" or "Boxing Day", but also "same day shipping", "next day shipping" and even "gifts".

Take a look at the spikes associated with the "next day shipping" keyword modifier. The spikes reach the maximum a few days before Christmas. You should be agile enough to capitalize on this search pattern change.

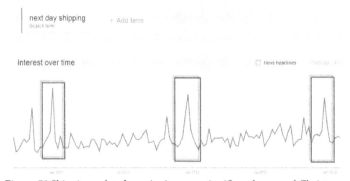

Figure 78 Shipping-related queries increase significantly around Christmas.

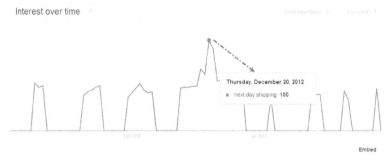

Figure 79 Adding "same-day shipping" or "next-day shipping" to your titles by December 15 may prove wise.

Let's say you want to capitalize on searches that contain the keyword "Christmas".

Add the word "Christmas" in the title of the category or product detail pages immediately after Cyber Monday is over. You can consider altering descriptions and page content as well. Be sure to check the rankings associated with these pages in a couple of days, and regularly after that, to see whether there's a big drop in traffic. You can expect some fluctuations, but as you get closer to the Christmas, you should see an increase in traffic.

If there's a drop, revert back to the usual titles. If there's an increase, change all category, subcategory and product detail page titles.

As you get closer to Christmas (e.g., December 15), change the title to "Free same-day Christmas shipping" since "free shipping" tops the list of the strongest incentives for visitors to buy goods online.

Get any page crawled and indexed by Google in less than one minute

Use the "Fetch as Google" functions in Google Webmaster Tool to achieve this.

Figure 80 Once you hit the Fetch button, Googlebot will crawl the URL. If the page passes Google's filters, it will be indexed in minutes.

```
66.249.71.244 - - [23/May/2012:14:00:37 -0700] "GET
/sem/how-to-use-facebook-ads-to-grow-your-ecommerce-sales
HTTP/1.1" 200 12333 "-" "Mozilla/5.0 (compatible; Googlebot/2.1;
+http://www.google.com/bot.html)"
```

Figure 81 Use the 500 requests per week limit wisely.

Once Christmas is over, change the titles to target the next Holiday, e.g., *Boxing Day*.

If there's a gap of more than three to four weeks between shopping events, you can default to the usual titles.

You may want to use an automated system that allows event-specific titles, descriptions and headings to be updated on certain dates. If that's not possible, then at least set up calendar reminders a month before the less important shopping events, and two months before the most important ones. Refer to this article[18] for consumer trend data and the importance of each consumer holiday.

Create holiday-specific landing pages

Seasoned marketers create holiday/promotion-specific landing pages to drive targeted traffic with PPC, email and catalogs. During the year, they will create pages for "Christmas 2014 Promotion", "Father's Day Specials" or "Valentine's Day Two-for-One Deals". You've probably noticed this implemented by big brands (or small, but smart, competitors).

By creating these landing pages, which are visually themed in accordance with the event they target, marketers make ecommerce websites more relevant to visitors. These pages can get natural links from deals/coupons websites if your brand is recognizable or if you push the pages with an outreach campaign.

Usually, when ecommerce websites create specific event and holiday pages, those pages will have their own URLs—e.g., *mywebsite.com/Boxing-Day-Sale*. But improper handling (e.g., no 301 redirects, or any 301 redirects to the wrong pages) may lead to *link juice* loss at the end of the event (link juice is a colloquial term that refers to the equity passed to a page via links).

A couple of tips for those using separate URLs for each holiday:

- It's better not to include years or other dates in the URLs. It's okay (and recommended) to include the year in page titles and headings.

- When the shopping event is over, redirect the dedicated page to the most appropriate section of the website.

- In the following years, you can "revive" the promotion-specific URLs weeks before the event.

A mixed tactic

I like another tactic, which is to update a mix of titles, descriptions, headings and custom landing pages.

Choose the most important categories on your website (or the categories that will be promoted during a specific consumer holiday), and customize their look and feel to match the shopping holiday. Customization can be as simple as displaying a banner at the top of the main content area or adding a background image for the entire page, or it can be as complex as creating a totally new themed layout.

The difference is that you will not publish this new layout under a different URL. Instead, this customized "look and feel" (LAF) and message will be published under the regular category page URLs.

For example, let's say your Christmas 2014 promotion includes a 25% discount on all Cleansing and Digestion products.

Rather than creating the URL *mywebsite.com/Christmas-Deals* for this holiday, you will use its usual URL, *mywebsite.com/Cleansing-Digestion/* but with the themed layout.

The main benefit of customizing the current category pages for shopping events instead of creating dedicated event URLs is that you will be able to build backlinks to those pages more easily. Another benefit is that there will be no future redirect headaches. If other websites want to link to your promotions, they will have to link to your category pages.

Once the holiday/promotion is over, go back to the usual, non-themed layout. You will also have to update the titles, descriptions and page copy a bit.

Tip: If your website gets SERP image-rich snippets, you can "theme" the image thumbnails with an event/holiday-specific icon. Once the shopping event/holiday is over, revert back to the usual image.

For instance, if you sell cameras, instead of this video thumbnail:

Canon EOS 60D DSLR 18MP Camera w/ Lens, Bag, 16GB Card ...
www.qvc.com/**Canon-EOS-60D-DSLR-18MP**-Came... ▾
Jun 2, 2013
The best moments happen in an instant. Capture them like a pro with the **EOS 60D DSLR** camera from **Canon** ...

Figure 82 Video listing in search results.

use:

Canon EOS 60D DSLR 18MP Camera w/ Lens, Bag, 16GB Card ...
www.qvc.com/**Canon-EOS-60D-DSLR-18MP**-Came... ▾
Jun 2, 2013
The best moments happen in an instant. Capture them like a pro with the **EOS 60D DSLR** camera from **Canon** ...

Figure 83 Personalizing the video thumbnails can lead to a better CTR.

Optimize for "gift card" related keywords

Last-minute shoppers often choose to buy e-gift cards instead of real products, to avoid shipping delays. Consider these points:

- 26.7% of the gift cards sold during December 2011 were sold between December 21 and 24, according to Giftango Corp.[19]

- 57.3% of shoppers planned to buy a gift card in 2011.[20]

- Gift cards were the most requested gift in 2012, with 59.8% of US shoppers wanting one.[21]

- E-gift cards reach their recipients instantly (no delays, no shipping and no hassle).

It makes sense to offer both e-gift cards (perfect for last-minute shoppers) and gift cards (for those who don't know what to buy).

Figure 84 When you optimize your pages for Christmas, don't forget to target "gift card" keywords as well.

Target long-tail keywords

For ecommerce websites (especially those new on the market) it is more viable to start by targeting long-tail search queries and gradually progress towards more competitive head terms. Usually, long-tail search queries tend to generate more qualified traffic and have less competition, but those that contain brand names may sometimes prove to be competitive.

Targeting search queries that assist with conversion is a good tactic (make sure you track assisted conversions with your web analytics software). Often such search queries require content (interactive tools, comprehensive guides, etc.), but this content is an investment. For example, targeting the search query "how to choose a digital camera" may require creating a camera finder tool. If you target "how to choose shaving cream" you will need to create an extensive (eventually interactive) and visually appealing resource specifically for that.

Here are just a few benefits of targeting long-tail keywords:

- Better organic search results.

- Gather insights into your customer.

- Improved paid search results.

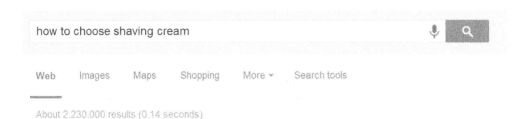

Figure 85 None of the top 10 results for this search query has a shaving cream finder tool. There's your opportunity.

In addition to targeting long-tail search queries, you may need to avoid targeting head terms with very vague user intent. For example, let's say you sell greeting cards. Would it be useful to rank for a keyword like "greeting" or "cards"? No, because you won't be able to clearly identify the user intent behind these keywords. You will invest a lot to brand your business for those terms, and you will get a ton of traffic if you manage to rank at the top, but generic terms generate very few conversions, at a very high cost per conversion. Instead, you can start targeting keywords like "40th birthday greeting cards for dad", perhaps on a blog post, or, if it's a popular search query, with a content-rich subcategory page.

As you can see, keyword research is far from being simple or fast. It's a process that can't be fully automated, and human review is irreplaceable, especially when bucketing keywords for relevance to your business. After reading this chapter, you hopefully understand that performing keyword research without user context (intent) is a bad idea.

During the next chapters, we'll find that keywords are part of almost every on-page SEO factor, from page titles to URLs and internal anchor text to product copy. But for search engines to find and analyze keywords, they first have to find and reach the pages where those keywords are featured.

Since ecommerce websites are a challenging crawling task for search engines, you need to optimize how search engines discover important URLs. This process is called crawl optimization.

CHAPTER FOUR

Crawl Optimization

Crawl optimization is aimed at helping search engines discover URLs in the most efficient manner. Important pages should be easy to reach, while less important pages should not waste *crawl budget* or create crawler traps. This is a key SEO focus for large websites like ecommerce websites.

Search engines assign a crawl budget to each website, depending on its authority. The authority of a website is somehow proportional to the PageRank. The concept of crawl budget is important for ecommerce websites because they usually comprise a huge number of URLs—from tens of thousands to millions.

If the technical architecture puts the search engine crawlers (aka robots, bots or spiders) in infinite loops or traps, the crawl budget will be wasted on pages that are not important for users or search engines, which may lead to important pages being left out of search engines indices.

Crawl optimization is where very large websites can take advantage of the opportunity to have more important pages indexed and low PageRank pages crawled more frequently.[1]

It's true that the number of URLs Google can index at the time of the crawl increased dramatically after the introduction of Google's powerful Percolator[2] architecture, with the "Caffeine" update.[3] However, it is still critical to monitor where search engine bots spend time on your website and to prioritize crawling accordingly.

Before we begin, it is important to understand that crawling and indexing are two different processes. Crawling means just fetching files from websites. Indexing means analyzing the files and deciding whether they are worthy of inclusion. So, even if search engines crawl a page, they won't necessarily index it.

Several factors can influence crawling, such as the website's structure, internal linking, domain authority, URL accessibility, content freshness, update frequency, and use of product and category feeds, and the crawl rate setting in the webmaster accounts.

Before detailing these, let's talk about tracking and monitoring search engine bots.

Tracking and monitoring bots

Googlebot, Yahoo! Slurp, Bingbot and Baiduspider are *polite bots,*[4] which means that they will first obey the crawling directives found in *robots.txt* files before they request resources from your website. Such bots will identify themselves to the webserver, so you can control them as you wish. All the resources bots request are stored on your web logs and are available for your analysis.

Webmaster tools (such as the ones provided by Google and Bing) only uncover a small part of what bots do on your website—e.g., how many pages they crawl or their bandwidth usage data. That is useful in some ways but is not enough.

For really useful insights, you have to analyze your traffic log files. From these you will be able to extract information that can help identify large-scale issues.

Traditionally, log file analysis is performed using the *grep* command line with regular expressions. Your sys admin should know how to use grep pretty well. But there are also desktop and web-based solutions that will make this type of geek analysis easier and more accessible to marketers.

On ecommerce websites, monthly log files are usually huge—gigabytes or terabytes of data. But you don't need all the data inside the log files to track and monitor Googlebot (or other bots). You just need the lines generated by Googlebot requests.

Using the following command line will extract all the lines containing "Googlebot" (case sensitive) from one monthly log file (*weblog_jan_2014.log*) to another, smaller log file (*googlebot_jan_2014.log)*:

grep "Googlebot" weblog_jan_2014.log > googlebot_jan_2014.log

To extract similar data for Bing and other search engines, replace *Googlebot* with other bots' names.

You can significantly reduce the size of the log files by extracting only the data generated by search engine requests and then uploading them on your desktop or web-based log analyzer.

Figure 86 The log file was reduced from 162Mb to 1.4Mb.

You can import up to one million rows in Excel; if you need to import more than this, use MS Access.

Open the bot-specific .log file with Excel, then go to *Data* → *Text To Columns* and use *Delimited with Space* to enter the log file data into a table format like the one below:

	A	B	C	D	E	F	G	H	I	J	K	L	M	N
1	IP	Date	TimeZone	Get	Status	Size	Referr	Bot						
45	37.59.44.19	[03/Nov/2013 -0800]		GET /blo	404	6025	http://pit	Googlebot/2.1 (+http://www.google.com/bot.html)						
88	66.249.73.18	[12/Oct/2013 -0700]		GET /sen	404	11513	-	Mozilla/5.0 (compatible; Googlebot/2.1; +http://www.google.com/bot.html)						
131	66.249.73.18	[12/Oct/2013 -0700]		GET /sen	404	11496	-	Googlebot-Image/1.0						
132	66.249.73.18	[12/Oct/2013 -0700]		GET /sen	404	11513	-	Mozilla/5.0 (compatible; Googlebot/2.1; +http://www.google.com/bot.html)						
156	66.249.73.18	[12/Oct/2013 -0700]		GET /sen	404	11484	-	Googlebot-Image/1.0						
160	66.249.73.18	[12/Oct/2013 -0700]		GET /sen	404	6588	-	Googlebot-Image/1.0						
177	66.249.73.18	[12/Oct/2013 -0700]		GET /sen	404	11491	-	Mozilla/5.0 (compatible; Googlebot/2.1; +http://www.google.com/bot.html)						
234	66.249.73.18	[13/Oct/2013 -0700]		GET /sen	404	11489	-	Mozilla/5.0 (compatible; Googlebot/2.1; +http://www.google.com/bot.html)						
759	66.249.73.18	[14/Oct/2013 -0700]		GET /sen	404	11425		Mozilla/5.0 (compatible; Googlebot/2.1; +http://www.google.com/bot.html)						
793	66.249.73.18	[14/Oct/2013 -0700]		GET /sen	404	6025	-	Googlebot-Image/1.0						
796	66.249.73.18	[14/Oct/2013 -0700]		GET /sen	404	6610	-	Mozilla/5.0 (iPhone; U; CPU iPhone OS 4_1 like Mac OS X; en-us) AppleWebKit/5						
814	66.249.73.18	[14/Oct/2013 -0700]		GET /sen	404	6611	-	Mozilla/5.0 (iPhone; U; CPU iPhone OS 4_1 like Mac OS X; en-us) AppleWebKit/5						
871	66.249.73.18	[14/Oct/2013 -0700]		GET /sen	404	6612	-	Mozilla/5.0 (iPhone; U; CPU iPhone OS 4_1 like Mac OS X; en-us) AppleWebKit/5						

googlebot

Figure 87 The data is filtered by the *Status* column to get a list of all 404 Not Found errors encountered by Googlebot.

For example, to quickly identify crawling issues at the category pages level, chart the Googlebot hits for each directory. (This is where the advantage of category-based navigation and URL structure comes in handy.)

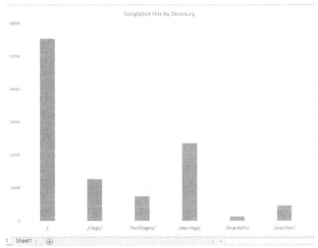

Figure 88 It looks like the */bracelets/* directory needs some investigation, as there are too few requests compared to the other directories.

By pivoting the log file data by URLs and crawl date, you can identify content that gets crawled more or less often:

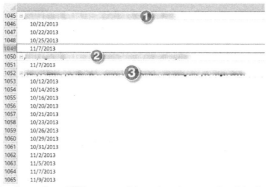

Figure 89 Although the above three URLs are positioned at the same level in the website architecture, URL number three gets crawled much more often than the other two.

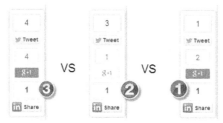

Figure 90 More external links and social media mentions may result in increased crawl frequency.

Here are some issues and ideas you should consider when analyzing bot behavior using log files:

- Analyze server response errors and identify what generates those errors.

- Discover unnecessarily crawled pages and crawling traps.

- Correlate days since the last crawl with rankings.

- Discover whether products listed at the top of category listings are crawled more often and get better rankings than products listed on component pages (paginated listings). Consider moving the most important products to the first page, rather than having them on component pages.

- Check the frequency and depth of crawl.

One interesting test you can run is to check whether pages crawled less frequently could generate more traffic or better rankings if Googlebot crawled them more often. Choose a page that is important but doesn't get crawled frequently, and use *Fetch as Google* in Google Webmaster Tools to get Google to crawl that page at regular intervals (e.g., every day for two to four weeks). Do rankings improve?

The goal behind tracking bots is to:

- *Establish* where the crawl budget is used.

- *Identify* unnecessary requests (e.g., "Write a Review" links that open pages with the exact same content except for the product name, e.g., *mysite.com/review.php?pid=1, mysite.com/review.php?pid=2* and so on).

- *Fix* the leaks.

Instead of wasting budget on unwanted (e.g., duplicate) URLs, focus on sending crawlers to low PageRank pages that matter for you and for users. This is because low PR pages require more frequent crawling to rank better.

Another useful application of log files is to evaluate backlinks. Rent links from various external websites and point them at pages with no other backlinks (product detail pages or pages that support product detail pages), then analyze the spider activity on your pages. If the crawling frequency increases, then that link is more valuable than a link that doesn't increase spider activity at all. An increase in crawling frequency on your pages suggests that the page you got the link from also gets crawled often, which means it has good authority. Once you've identified good opportunities, work to get a natural link from that website.

For those who want to take log file analysis to higher levels, enterprise platforms like Splunk® Enterprise can help with better slicing and dicing of the data:

Figure 91 Screenshot from Splunk® Enterprise.

Flat website structure

If there are no other technical impediments to crawling large websites (e.g., crawlable facets or *infinite spaces*[5]), a flat website architecture can help crawling by allowing search engines to reach deep pages in very few hops, therefore using the crawl budget very efficiently.

Pagination—or, to be more specific, de-pagination—is one way to flatten your website architecture. We will discuss pagination later, in the *Pagination* section of the chapter on *Listing Pages.*

For more information on flat website architecture, please refer to the section titled *The concept of flat architecture* in the *Website Architecture* chapter.

Accessibility

During this chapter I will refer to accessibility in terms of optimization for search engines rather than optimization for users.

Accessibility is probably the critical factor for crawling. If the technical architecture of your website makes it impossible for search engine bots to access URLs, then those URLs won't be indexed. URLs that are not accessible after a few unsuccessful attempts will be removed from search engine indices.

So, what prevents URLs and content from being accessible?

DNS and connectivity issues

Use *http://www.intodns.com/* to check for DNS issues. Everything that comes in red and yellow needs your attention (even if it's an MX record).

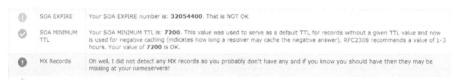

Figure 92 Report from intodns.com.

Using Google and Bing webmaster accounts, fix all the issues related to DNS and connectivity:

Figure 93 Bing's Crawl Information report.

Figure 94 Google's website Errors report.[6]

One DNS issue you may want to pay attention to is related to wildcard DNS, which means the webserver responds with a 200 OK code for any subdomain request, even ones that did not exist—or even more severe, unrecognizable hostnames (DNS lookup failed).

One large retailer (500k+ visits per month) had another strange misconfiguration. Two of its country code top-level domains (ccTLDs)—the US (.com) and the UK (.co.uk)—resolved to the same IP. If you have multiple ccTLDs, host them on different IPs (ideally from within the country you target with the ccTLD), and check how the domain names resolve.

Needless to say, if your web servers are down, no one (including search engine bots) will be able to access the website. You can keep an eye on the availability of your website using a server monitoring tool like Monitor.Us, Scoutt or Site24x7.

Host load

Host load represents the maximum number of simultaneous connections a web server can handle. Every page load request from Googlebot, Yahoo! Slurp or Bingbot generates a connection with your web server. Since search engines use distributed crawling from multiple machines at the same time, you can theoretically reach the limits of the connections, and your website will crash (especially if you are hosting on a shared server or if you have a horde of simultaneous users).

Use *http://loadimpact.com/* to see how many connections your website can handle. (Be careful, your website can become unavailable or even crash during this test.)

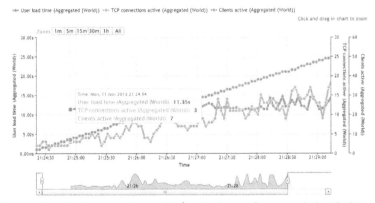

Figure 95 If your website loads reasonably quickly (under three to four seconds, but the lower, the better) when used by a large number of visitors, you should be fine. Graph generated by *loadimpact.com*.

Page load time

Page load time is not only a crawling factor, but also a ranking and usability factor. Amazon reportedly increased their revenue by 1% for every 100ms of load time improvement,[7] and Shopzilla increased revenue by seven to 12% by decreasing the page load time by five seconds.[8]

There are plenty of articles about page load speed optimization, and they can get pretty technical. Here are a few pointers to summarize how you can optimize load time:

- Use content delivery networks for media files and other files that don't update too often.

- Implement database and cache (server-side caching) optimization.

- Enable HTTP compression and implement conditional GET.

- Optimize images.

- Use expires headers.[9]

- Ensure fast and responsive design to decrease the *time to first byte* (TTFB). Use *http://webpagetest.org/* to measure TTFB. (There seems to be a clear correlation between lower rankings and increased TTFB.[10])

- Defer loading of images until they are needed for display in the browser.

Figure 96 Amazon uses CSS sprites to minimize the number of requests sent to your server.

Figure 97 Apple used sprites for main navigation.

If your URLs load really slowly, search engines may interpret this as a connectivity issue, meaning they may give up crawling the troubled URLs.

The time spent by Google on a page seems to directly influence the number of pages it crawls. The less time to download a page, the more pages are crawled.

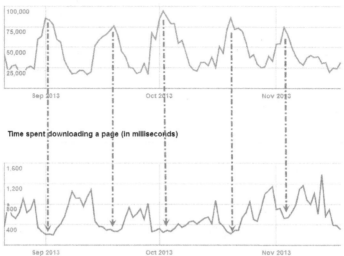

Figure 98 The correlation seems pretty obvious.

Broken links

This is a no-brainer. When your internal links are broken, crawlers won't be able to find the correct pages. Run a full crawl on the entire website with the crawling tool of your choice and fix all broken URLs. Also use the webmaster tools provided by search engines to find the broken URLs.

HTTP caching with Last-Modified/If-Modified-Since and E-Tag headers

In reference to crawl optimization, the term "cache" refers to a temporarily stored page in a search engine, proxy-cache or web browser. Note that caching is a highly technical issue, and improper caching settings may make search engines crawl and index a website chaotically.

When a search engine requests a resource on your website, it first makes a request to your web server to check the status of that resource. The server will reply back with a *header response.* Based on the header response, search engines will decide to download the resource or to skip it.

Many search engines check whether the resource they requested has changed since they last crawled it. If it has, they will fetch it again—if not, they'll skip it. This mechanism is referred to as *conditional GET.* Bing confirmed that it uses the *If-Modified-Since* header,[11] and Google does as well.[12]

Below is the header response for a newly discovered page that supports the *If-Modified-Since* header when a request is made to access it.

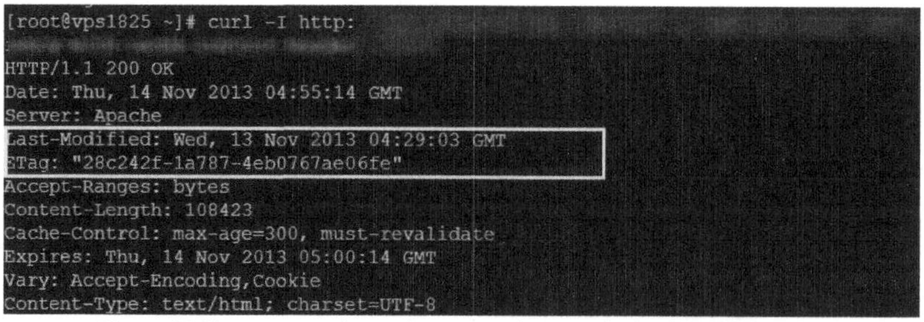

Figure 99 You can use the curl command to get the last modified data.

When the bot requests the same URL the next time, it will add an *If-Modified-Since* header request. If the document has not been modified, it will respond with a 304 status code (*Page Not Modified*):

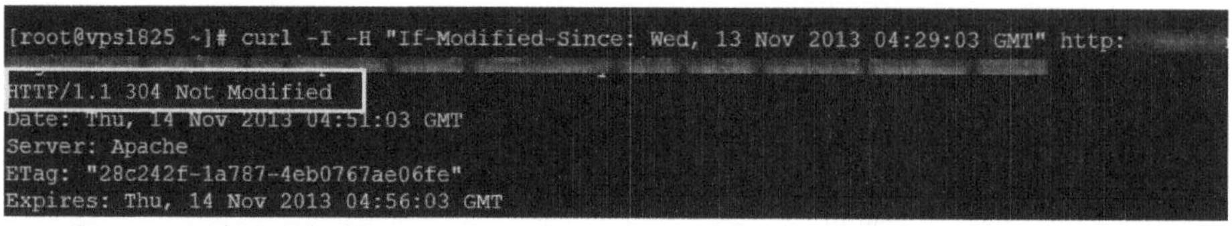

Figure 100 If-Modified-Since will return *304 Not Modified* if the page hasn't been changed.

If it has been modified, the header response will be 200 OK, and the search engine will fetch the page again.

The E-Tag header works similarly but is more complex to handle.

If your ecommerce platform uses personalization, or if the content on each page changes frequently, it may be more challenging to implement HTTP caching, but even dynamic pages can support *If-Modified-Since*.[13]

Site maps

There are two major types of site maps:

- HTML site maps.

- XML Sitemaps (or TXT, RSS, mRSS).

If you experience crawling and indexing issues, keep in mind that site maps are just a patch for more serious problems, such as duplicate content, thin content or improper internal linking architecture. Creating site maps won't fix those issues.

HTML site maps

HTML site maps are a form of *secondary navigation*. They are usually accessible to people and bots through a link placed at the bottom of the website, in the footer. A usability study on a mix of websites, including ecommerce websites, found that people rarely use HTML maps. In 2008, *only 7% of the users turned to the site map when asked to learn about a site's structure,*[14] down from 27% in 2002. In 2014, the percentage is probably even less.

Still, HTML site maps are very useful for sending crawlers to pages at the lower levels of the website taxonomy, and for creating a flat internal linking infrastructure.

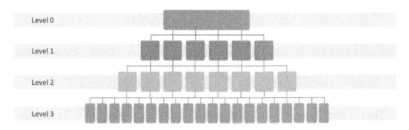

Figure 101 Sample flat architecture.

Below are some HTML site map crawl optimization tips:

Use segmented site maps

When optimizing HTML site maps for crawling, it's important to remember that PageRank is divided between all the links on a page. Splitting the HTML site map into multiple smaller parts is a good way to create more user and search engine friendly pages for large websites, such as ecommerce sites.

Instead of a huge site map page that links to almost every page on your website, create a main site map index page (e.g., *sitemap.html*) and link from it to smaller site map component pages (*sitemap-1.html, sitemap-2.html*, etc.).

The number of links you can list on the site map index page depends on its PageRank. If the PageRank of the site map index page is 5, you can afford to link 150 to 200 component pages, but if you are at PageRank 2 or 3, you should limit links to 100.

You can split the HTML site maps based on topics, categories, departments or brands. Start by listing your top categories on the index page. The way you split the pages depends on the number of categories, subcategories and products your catalog has. It also depends on the PageRank of each page, as described in the previous paragraph.

You can use the "100 links per page" rule below as a guideline, but don't get stuck on this number, especially if your website has good authority.

- If you have more than 100 top-level categories, you should display the first 100 of them on the site map index page and the rest on additional site map pages. You can allow users and search engines to navigate the site map using previous and next links (e.g., "see more categories") to next.

- If you have fewer than 100 top-level categories in the catalog/store, you will have room to list several important subcategories as well, as depicted below:

Home » SiteMap

SiteMap

▪ Photography	▪ Computers & Solutions	▪ Pro Audio
Digital Cameras	Laptops	Recording
Film Cameras	iPads & Tablets	Computer Audio
Lenses	Desktops	ENG, EFP & Broadcast
Batteries & Power	Drives & Storage	Live Sound

Figure 102 The top-level categories are Photography, Computers & Solutions and Pro Audio. Since this business has a limited number of top-level categories, there is room for several subcategories (digital cameras, laptops, recording).

Don't link to redirects

The URLs linked from site map pages should land crawlers on the final URLs, rather than going through URL redirects.

Enrich the site maps

Adding a bit of extra info by annotating links with info is good for users and can provide some context for search engines as well. You can add data, such as product thumbnails, customer ratings or the manufacturer, on site maps that list products.

You can add brief snippets of info for the most important categories on the categories and subcategories site map pages.

These are just some suggestions for HTML site maps so that you can make the pages easier for people to read and very lightly linked for crawlers.

XML Sitemaps

Most ecommerce platforms will auto-generate XML Sitemaps, but many times the default file is not optimized for crawling. It's therefore important to manually review and optimize the automated output, or to generate the Sitemaps on your own.

It's preferable to include the path of the XML Sitemap file within the *robots.txt* file. This condition is mandatory if you use a Sitemap index file (when you submit more than 50,000 URLs). *Robots.txt* is requested, crawled and cached by search engines every time they start a crawling session on your website (except if the header responds with *Not Modified*). If you don't specify the location of your XML Sitemap inside *robots.txt*, then search engines won't know where to find it—unless you submit it within the webmaster accounts. Doing this allows access to more insights, such as how many URLs have been submitted, how many are indexed, and what eventual errors are present in the Sitemap.

Figure 103 If you have an almost 100% indexation rate, you probably don't need to worry about crawl optimization.

Using XML Sitemaps seems to have an accelerating effect on crawl rate:

"At first, the number of visits was stabilized at a rate of 20 to 30 pages per hour. As soon as the sitemap was uploaded through Webmaster Central, the crawler accelerated to approximately 500 pages per hour. In just a few days it reached a peak of 2,224 pages per hour. Where at first the crawler visited 26.59 pages per hour on average, it grew to an average of 1,257.78 pages per hour which is an increase of no less than 4,630.27%."[15]

Here are some tips for optimizing XML Sitemaps for large websites:

- Add only URLs that respond with 200 OK. Too many errors, and search engines will stop trusting your Sitemaps. Bing has a "1% allowance for dirt in a Sitemap. Examples of dirt are if we click on a URL and we see a redirect, a 404 or a 500 code. If we see more than a 1% level of dirt, we begin losing trust in the Sitemap."[16]

- Have no links to duplicate content and no URLs that canonicalize to different URLs—only to "end state" URLs.

- Place videos (use mRSS rather than XML), images, news and mobile in separate Sitemaps.

- Use separate Sitemaps for each topic/category and subtopic/subcategory (sitemap_camping.xml, sitemap_cycle.xml, sitemap_run.xml, etc.). This will help identify indexation issues at granular levels.

- Create separate Sitemap files for product pages.

- Fix Sitemap errors before submitting your website to search engines. You can do this within your Google Webmaster Tools account, using the Test Sitemap feature:

Figure 104 You can test the Sitemaps directly from your Google Webmaster Tools account.

- Keep language-specific URLs in separate Sitemaps.

- Don't assign the same weight to all pages (your scoring can be based upon update frequency or other business rules).

- Auto-update the Sitemap whenever important new URLs are created. For instance, users could create pages and URLs by using filters in the faceted navigation. Make sure you include only URLs that contain essential and important filters (see chapter eight, *Product Detail Pages*).

You probably noticed a commonality within the tips above: *segmentation*. It's a good idea to split your XML files as much as you can without overdoing it (e.g., just 10 items per file), so you can identify and fix indexation issues more easily.[17]

Keep in mind that site maps, either XML or HTML, should not be used as a substitute for poor website architecture or other crawlability issues, but only as a backup. Make sure that there are other paths (e.g., contextual links) for crawlers to reach all the pages on your website.

Below are some factors that can influence the crawl frequency:

Deep linking

Crawlers will request pages more frequently if they find more external and internal links pointing to them. Most ecommerce websites experience challenges building links to category and product details pages, but this has to be done. Guest posting, giveaways, link bait, evergreen content, outright link requests within confirmation emails, ambassadors programs, and perpetual holiday category pages are just some of the tactics that can help with link development.

Crawl rate settings

You can alter (usually decrease) the crawl rate of Googlebot using your Google Webmaster Tools account. However, changing the rate is not advisable unless the crawler slows down your web server.

With Bing's *Crawl Control* feature you can even set up day parting.

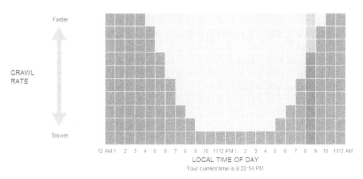

Figure 105 Bing's Crawl Control Interface.

Fresh content

Updating content on pages and then pinging search engines (e.g., by creating feeds for product and category pages) should get the crawlers to the updated content relatively quickly.

If you update fewer than 500 URLs per week, you can use the *Fetch as Google* feature inside your Google Webmaster Tools account to get the updated URLs re-crawled quickly. As well, you can regularly (e.g., weekly) create and submit a new XML Sitemap just for the updated pages.

There are several ways to keep the content fresh. For example, you can include an excerpt of about 100 words from related blog posts on product detail pages. Ideally, the excerpt should include the product name. Every time you mention a product in a new blog post, update the excerpt of the product details page, too.

You can even include excerpts from articles that don't directly mention the product name, if the article is related to the category in which the product can be classified.

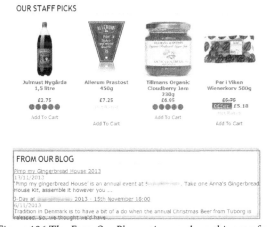

Figure 106 The *From Our Blog* section can keep this page fresh.

Another great tactic to keep the content fresh is to continuously generate user reviews, product Q&As or other forms of user-generated content.

Figure 107 Ratings or reviews are a very smart way to keep pages alive.

Domain authority

The higher your website's domain authority, the more visits from crawlers it will get. Your domain authority increases by pointing more external links to your website—easier said than done.

RSS feeds

RSS feeds are one of the fastest ways to notify search engines of new products, categories or other types of fresh content on your website. Here's what Duane Forrester (Bing's Webmaster senior product manager) says about RSS feeds:

"Things like RSS are going to become a desired way for us to find content ... It's a dramatic cost savings for us."[18]

You can get search engines to crawl the new content within minutes of publication with the help of RSS. For example, if you write content that supports category and product detail pages and link smartly from these supporting pages, search engines will request and crawl the linked-to products and categories as well.

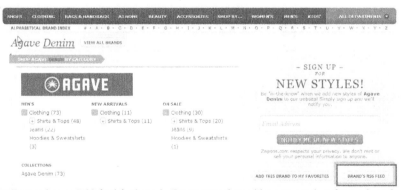

Figure 108 Zappos has an RSS feed for brands. Every time they add a new product from a brand, users and search engines are notified.

Guiding crawlers

The best way to avoid wasting crawl budget on junk pages is to avoid creating links to those pages in the first place. But that's not always an option. For example, you have to allow people to *Email to a Friend* from the product detail pages. Or you have to give visitors the option to write product reviews. If you create unique URLs for *Email to a Friend* links, for example, you create duplicate content.

10/26/2013 /	email-friend.php?pid=21
10/26/2013 /	email-friend.php?pid=24
10/26/2013 /	email-friend.php?pid=26
10/26/2013 /	email-friend.php?pid=30
10/26/2013 /	email-friend.php?pid=31
10/26/2013 /	email-friend.php?pid=32
10/26/2013 /	email-friend.php?pid=34
10/26/2013 /	email-friend.php?pid=40
10/26/2013 /	email-friend.php?pid=50
10/26/2013 /	email-friend.php?pid=60
10/26/2013 /	email-friend.php?pid=70
10/26/2013 /	email-friend.php?pid=71
10/26/2013 /	email-friend.php?pid=75
10/26/2013 /	email-friend.php?pid=76

Figure 109 The URLs above create near-duplicate pages. These URLs don't have to be accessible to search engines.

These *Email to a Friend* URLs will most likely lead to the same web form, and search engines will unnecessarily request and crawl hundreds or thousands of such links, depending on the size of your web inventory. You will waste crawl budget by allowing search engines to discover and crawl these URLs.

You should control which links are discoverable by search engine crawlers and which are not. The more unnecessary requests for junk pages a crawler makes, the fewer useful pages it will fetch.

Crawler directives can be defined at various levels, in this priority:

1. Site-level, with *robots.txt*.

2. Page-level, with meta tags (e.g., noindex) and HTTP headers.

3. Element-level, with the nofollow microformat.

Site-level directives overrule page-level directives, and page-level directives overrule element-level directives. It is important to understand this priority, because for a page-level directive to be discovered and followed, the site-level directives should allow access to that page. The same applies to element-level and page-level directives.

On a side note, if you want to keep content as private as possible, one of the best ways is to use server-side authentication to password protect areas—but even that is not a hundred percent safe.

Robots.txt

Although *robots.txt* files can be used to control crawler access, the disallowed URLs within *robots.txt* may end up in search engines' indices because of external backlinks pointing to the "robotted" URLs. This suggests that URLs blocked by *robots.txt* can accumulate PageRank. However, URLs blocked with *robots.txt* won't pass PageRank (unless the URLs were previously indexed), since search engines can't crawl and index the content (links) on such pages.

It's interesting to note that pages with Google+ buttons may be visited by Google when someone clicks on the plus button, ignoring the *robots.txt* directives.[19]

One of the biggest misconceptions about *robots.txt* is that it can be used to control duplicate content. The fact is, there are better methods for controlling duplicate content, and *robots.txt* should only be used to partially control crawler access. That being said, there may be cases where one doesn't have control over how the CMS platform generates content, or can't make changes to pages generated on the fly. In such situations, one can try as a last resort to control duplicate content with *robots.txt*.

Every ecommerce website is unique, with its own specific business needs and requirements, so there's no general rule for what should be crawled and what should not. For example, most websites don't need the print versions of pages to be crawled, but if you're selling content such as user manuals, you may need to let crawlers access the print pages. You will also need to manage the duplicate content generated by the print pages, using rel="canonical".

While tier-one search engines won't attempt to "add to cart" and won't start a checkout process or a newsletter sign-up, smaller search engines may. Considering this, below are some common types of URLs you can consider blocking access to:

Shopping cart and checkout pages

"Add to Cart", *"View Cart"* and other checkout URLs can safely be added to *robots.txt*.

If the *View Cart* URL is *mysite.com/viewcart.aspx*, you can use the following lines to disallow crawling:

User-agent: *

 # Do not crawl view cart URLs

Disallow: *viewcart.aspx

 # Do not crawl add to cart URLs

Disallow: *addtocart.aspx

 # Do not crawl checkout URLs

Disallow:/checkout/

The above directives mean that all crawlers (the wildcard in user-agent line) are forbidden to crawl any URL that contains *viewcart.aspx* or *addtocart.aspx*. All URLs under the */checkout/* directory are off-limits as well.

Robots.txt allows limited use of regular expressions (* - anything, $ - ends with, ^ - starts with) to match URL patterns, so your programmers should be able to play with a large spectrum of URLs.

User account pages

Account URLs (e.g., *Account Login* or *WishList*) can be blocked as well:

User-agent:*

 # Do not crawl login URLs

Disallow:/store/account/*.aspx$

All pages within the */store/account/* directory will not be crawled.

Resource	Sample URL	Directive
Session IDs	mysite.com/Gold-s-Gym-Trainer-410.php?SID=87alkdshks	Disallow: /*?SID=
Search results	mysite.com/search/results.php?q=Gold's%20Gym%20Trainer-410	Disallow: /search/
Newsletters signup	mysite.com/newsletter/	Disallow: /newsletter/
Product review invite URLs	mysite.com/review/	Disallow: /review/
Tell a friend	mysite.com/sendfriend/	Disallow: /sendfriend/
Tags	mysite.com/tag/	Disallow: /tag/
Whishlist	mysite.com/wishlist/	Disallow: /wishlist/
Includes	mysite.com/includes/	Disallow: /includes/
Scripts	mysite.com/scripts/	Disallow: /scripts/
Libraries	mysite.com/lib/	Disallow: /lib/
Site admin page	mysite.com/admin/	Disallow: /admin/
Email landing pages	mysite.com/email_promo/	Disallow: /email_promo/
Printable coupons	mysite.com/print/coupons/	Disallow: /print/coupons/
Pop-ups	mysite.com/annoy-to-win/	Disallow: /print/annoy-to-win/

Figure 110 Above are some other types of URLs that you can consider blocking.

You're probably asking yourself why SEO issues like pagination, sorting and faceted navigation are not on the list; that's because such issues are not optimally addressable with *robots.txt.*

Before you upload the *robots.txt* file, I recommend testing it against your existing list of URLs. You could use the "Blocked URLs" feature of Google Webmaster Tools, but you have other choices, too.

Generate the list of URLs on your website:

- Ask your programmers to generate a list of URLs on your site.

- Run a crawl of the entire website with your favorite crawler.

- Use weblog files.

Open this list in a text editor that allows searching by regular expressions. Software like RegexBuddy, RegexPal or Notepad++ (use the last one for large files) are good choices. Test the patterns you used in the *robots.txt* file using these tools. You will need to rewrite the regex pattern you used in the *robots.txt,* depending on the software you use.

Let's say that you use the disallow command below to block crawlers' access to email landing pages:

> *User-agent:* *
>
> *# Do not crawl view cart URLs*
>
> *Disallow: / ads/*

Using RegexPal, you can test the URLs list using this simple regex:

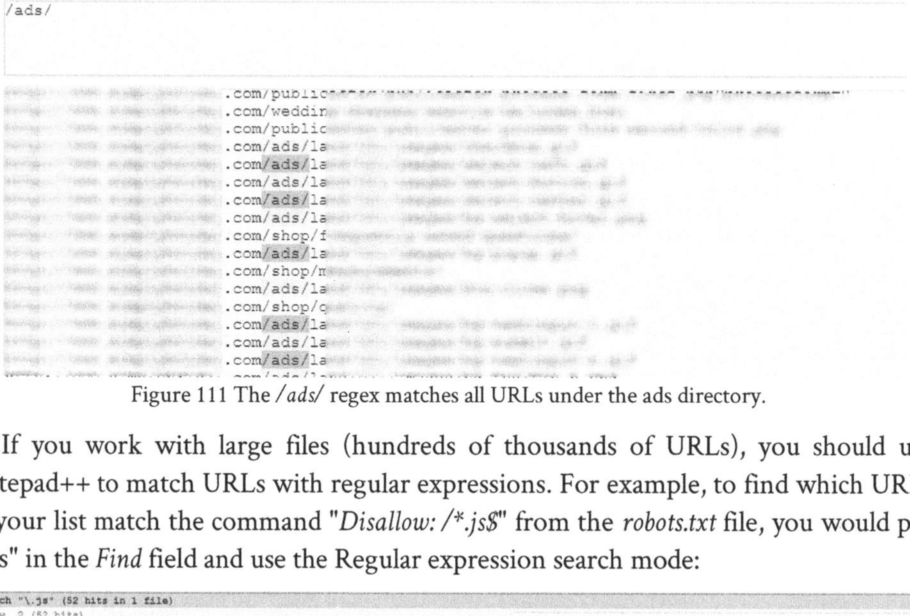

Figure 111 The */ads/* regex matches all URLs under the ads directory.

If you work with large files (hundreds of thousands of URLs), you should use Notepad++ to match URLs with regular expressions. For example, to find which URLs in your list match the command "*Disallow: /*.js$*" from the *robots.txt* file, you would put "\.js" in the *Find* field and use the Regular expression search mode:

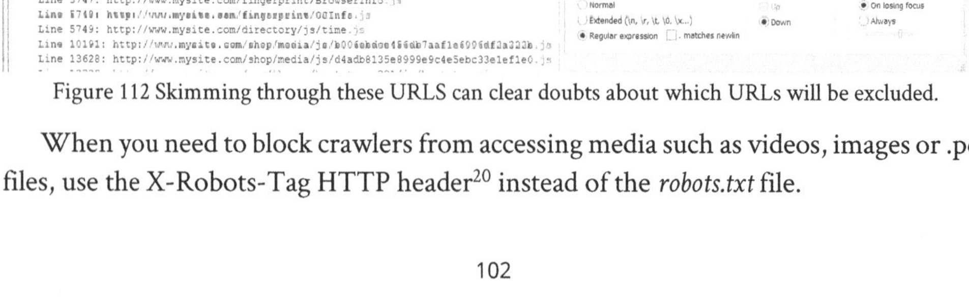

Figure 112 Skimming through these URLS can clear doubts about which URLs will be excluded.

When you need to block crawlers from accessing media such as videos, images or .pdf files, use the X-Robots-Tag HTTP header[20] instead of the *robots.txt* file.

But remember, if you want to address duplicate content issues for non-HTML documents, use rel="canonical" headers.[21]

The exclusion parameter

With this technique you *selectively* add a *robots.txt* excluded parameter (e.g., *crawler="no"*) to the URLs you want to be inaccessible. (Credit goes to Jaimie Sirovich,[22] who seems to be one of the first to have mentioned and implemented this method.)

First, decide which URLs you want to block. Let's say you want to control the crawl of the faceted navigation by not allowing search engines to crawl URLs generated when applying:

- More than one filter from the same facet (multiple selection facets). In this case, you will add the *crawler=no* parameter to all URLs generated when a second filter is added for the same facet.

- More than two filters from different facets. In this case, you will add the *crawler=no* parameter to all URLs generated when a third filter is added, no matter which filtering options were chosen.

Here's a scenario for the second option:

1. The crawler is on the *Accessories > Battery Chargers* subcategory page.

The page URL is: *mysite.com/accessories/motorcycle-battery-chargers/*

2. The crawler "checks" one of the *Brands* facet values: *Accessories > Battery Chargers > Brand*

This is the first filter applied, and therefore you will let the crawler fetch the page.

The URL for this facet doesn't contain the exclusion parameter:

mysite.com/accessories/motorcycle-battery-chargers/?brand=noco

3. The crawler now checks one of the *Style* facet filters: *Accessories > Battery Chargers > Brand > Style*

Since this is the second filter applied, you will still let the crawler access the URLs.

The URL is still free of exclusion parameters:

mysite.com/accessories/motorcycle-battery chargers/?brand=noco&style=cables

4. The crawler checks one of the *Pricing* options: *Accessories > Battery Chargers > Brand > Style > Price*

Since this is the third filter, you will append the *crawler=no* parameter to the URL.

The URL becomes:

mysite.com/accessories/motorcycle-battery-chargers/?brand=noco&style=cables&pricing=1&crawler=no

To block the URL at point four, the *robots.txt* will contain:

User-agent:*

Disallow:/*crawler=no

The above method prevents the crawl of facet URLs when more than N filters have been applied, but it doesn't allow specific control over which filters are going to be crawled and which ones are not. For example, if the crawler checks the *Pricing* option first, the link containing the pricing parameter will be crawled.

URL parameters handling

URL parameters can cause crawl efficiency problems as well as duplicate content issues.

For example, if you implement sorting, filtering and pagination with parameters, then you are likely to end up with a large number of URLs, which will waste crawl budget. In a video about parameters handling, Google shows[23] how 158 products on *googlestore.com* generated an astonishing 380,000 URLs for crawlers.

Controlling URL parameters within Google's and Bing's webmaster accounts can improve crawl efficiency, but it won't address the root causes of duplicate content. You will still need to fix canonicalization issues at the source.

In some cases, controlling URL parameters with webmaster tools can be a testing ground to support programming changes. But since ecommerce websites use multiple URL parameters, controlling them correctly with webmaster tools may prove tricky and risky. Unless you know what you're doing, you are better off using either a conservative setup or the default settings.

An advantage of handling URL parameters within webmaster accounts is that page-level directives like *rel="canonical"* or *meta noindex* will still apply as long as the pages containing such directives are not blocked with *robots.txt* or other methods. However, while it is possible to use limited regular expressions within *robots.txt* to prevent the crawling of URLs with parameters, *robots.txt* will overrule page-level and markup/element-level directives.

URL Parameters

Currently Googlebot isn't experiencing problems with coverage of your site, so you don't need to configure URL parameters. (Incorrectly configuring parameters can result in pages from your site being dropped from our index, so we don't recommend you use this tool unless necessary.)

⚠ Use this feature only if you're sure how parameters work. Incorrectly excluding URLs could result in many pages disappearing from search.

From parameters that Googlebot discovered on your site here is a list of parameters that appear not to change the content of your pages. Google will ignore these. (If you're certain that this is incorrect, you can specify how you want these parameters to be handled.)

edsmi

Configure URL parameters »

Figure 113 If Google can crawl the entire website without difficulty, you can leave the default settings as they are.

If you want to set up the parameters, click on the *Configure URL parameters* link.

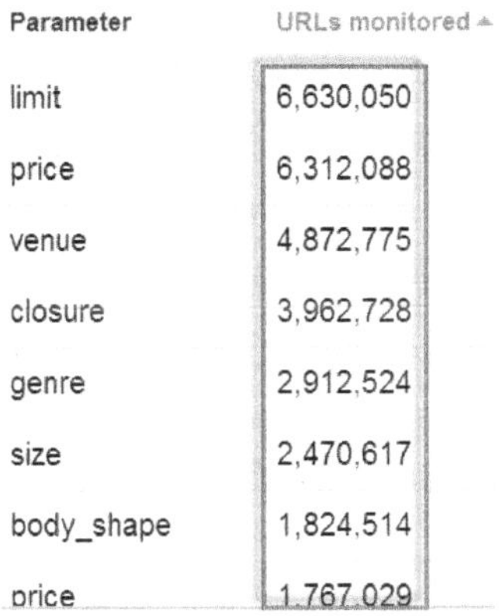

Parameter	URLs monitored ▲
limit	6,630,050
price	6,312,088
venue	4,872,775
closure	3,962,728
genre	2,912,524
size	2,470,617
body_shape	1,824,514
price	1,767,029

Figure 114 In the above image (this is for an ecommerce website with fewer than 1,000 SKUs), the website navigation generated millions of URLs.

For example, the *limit* key, which is used for changing the number of items listed on the category listing page, generated 6.6 million URLs when combined with all other possible parameters. Because this website has a strong authority (PageRank 6), it gets a lot of attention from Googlebot and doesn't have crawling and indexing issues.

When handling parameters, the first thing you want to decide is which parameters change the content and which ones don't. You're best to do this with your programmers.

The parameters that don't affect how content is displayed on a page (e.g., user tracking parameters) are a safe target for exclusion from crawling. Although Google by itself does a good job of identifying parameters that don't change content, it's still worthwhile to set them manually.

Click *Edit* for the parameter you want to exclude:

Parameter	URLs monitored ▲	Configured	Effect	Crawl	
utm_source	93	Oct 9, 2012	None	Representative URL	Edit / Reset
utm_medium	93	Oct 9, 2012	None	Representative URL	Edit / Reset

Figure 115 Then, choose "No: Doesn't affect page content (ex: track usage)."

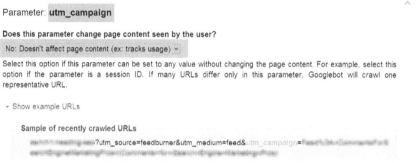

Figure 116 Tracking parameters can be safely excluded.

Some other common parameters that you may consider for exclusion are session IDs, UTM analytics tracking parameters (*utm_source, utm_medium, utm_term, utm_content* and *utm_campaign*) and affiliate IDs.

"Configuring site-wide parameters may have severe, unintended effects on how Google crawls and indexes your pages. For example, imagine an ecommerce website that uses storeID in both the store locator and to look up a product's availability in a store:

/store-locator?storeID=123

/product/foo-widget?storeID=123

If you configure storeID to not be crawled, both the /store-locator and /foo-widget paths will be affected. As a result, Google may not be able to index both kinds of URLs, nor show them in our search results. If these parameters are used for different purposes, we recommend using different parameter names."

This recommendation comes straight from Google.[24] In the above scenario, you can probably keep the store location in a cookie.

Controlling parameters gets more complicated when a parameter changes how the content is displayed on a page.

One safe setup for content-changing parameters is to only suggest to Google how the parameter affects the page (e.g., sorts, narrows/filters, specifies, translates, paginates, others) and use the default option *Let Google decide*. This will allow Google to crawl all the URLs and will provide more insights into what each parameter does.

Parameter: **mid** ←·—·—·—

Does this parameter change page content seen by the user?

Yes: Changes, reorders, or narrows page content ✓←·—·—·—·—

How does this parameter affect page content?

Sorts ✓←·—·—·—·—·—·—·—

Sorts content as specified by the parameter. For example, displays product listings sorted by name, by brand, or by price.

Which URLs with this parameter should Googlebot crawl?

- ◉ Let Googlebot decide ⑦ (Default) ←·—·—
- ○ Every URL ⑦ (the page content changes for each value)
- ○ Only URLs with value [   ] ▼ ⑦ (may hide content from Googlebot)
- ○ No URLs ⑦ (may hide content from Googlebot; overrides settings for other parameters)

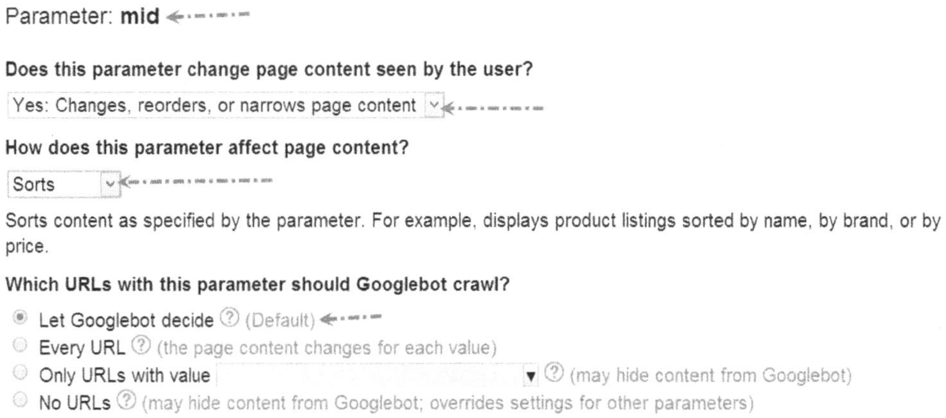

Figure 117 You can suggest what each parameter does, but let Google decide what to do.

The reason I recommend letting Google decide on the version of canonical URL is because of the way Google identifies canonical URLs: it groups duplicate URLs into clusters based on internal linking and link popularity, and it finds the best URL to display in search results. Since Google doesn't share the complete link graph of your website, you won't know which duplicate URL gets the most links, so you may not be able to choose the right URL.

I suggest experimenting with one parameter at a time, evaluating the impact on crawling and indexing (using segmented Sitemaps will come in handy). Based on the test results, you can decide either to fix the URL parameter at the source (get rid of those internal links or hide them from crawlers), or to keep the settings in the webmaster accounts.

Next, we'll look into internal linking optimization.

CHAPTER FIVE

Internal Linking

The importance of external links for rankings is a well-documented SEO fact, as well as being part of conventional SEO wisdom. However, internal links can also impact rankings.

Links, either internal or from external websites, are the primary way that website visitors and search engines discover content.

If a page does not contain internal links (e.g., products are accessible only after a website search, or the entire catalog is available only to logged in members), not only may that page not be accessible to search engines for crawling and indexing, but even if it does get indexed, the page will be deemed as less valuable (unless a lot of external links point to it).

Conversely, if you have a page that doesn't link out to other pages, you send search engine robots into a dead-end.

In between these two extremes, internal links can lead crawlers into traps or unwanted URLs that contain "thin", duplicate or near-duplicate content, or put them into circular referencing and other crawling challenges.

When optimizing the internal linking, SEOs have to remember that websites are for users as well, not just for search engines. The reason links exist in the first place is to help users navigate and find what they want, quickly and easily. Consider an approach that balances which links are available to crawlers and which should be available to users. Build your internal linking for users, and then accommodate the search engines.

Ecommerce websites come with an interesting advantage: the large number of pages allows a large number of internal links to be created. The larger the website and the more links pointing to a page, the more influential that page is. Strangely enough, although SEOs typically know that the more links you point to a page, the more authority the page receives, many SEOs still focus on getting links from external websites first.

But why not optimize the lowest hanging fruit, the internal links, first? When you optimize your internal linking architecture, you don't need to hunt for backlinks. You need to increase the relevance and authority of key pages on your own website by creating quality content (which attracts organic traffic and possible links) and interlinking pages thematically.

Let's see how ecommerce websites can take advantage of internal linking to boost relevance, avoid or mitigate duplicate content issues and build long-tail anchor text to rank for natural language search queries.

Note: Do not blindly implement any of the techniques discussed below. Decide which solution best suits your website, based on your business needs and specific situation. If in doubt, get professional SEO help from an experienced consultant before attempting to make changes.

Crawlable and uncrawlable links

A crawlable link is one that is accessible to search engine crawlers when they request a resource from your web server.

An uncrawlable link is one that search engines can't discover when they parse a page, but that is still accessible to users in a browser. Uncrawlable links are implemented with technologies such as JavaScript or AJAX, which generate the link client-side (i.e., in the browser). Uncrawlable links are created on purpose and are not the same thing as broken links, which occur accidentally. It's also worth noting that uncrawlable links are not the same as hidden links (e.g., off-screen text with CSS, white text on white background, etc.).

Because the main goal of ecommerce websites is to sell online, they have to be usable and present information in an easy to find manner—imagine an ecommerce website that doesn't allow consumers to sort or narrow 3,000 items in the same category. But this sorting and filtering generates URLs that present no value for search engines and, arguably, limited value for users. Since the current crawling and browsing technologies are so dependent on clicks and links, these issues are here to stay for a while.

But why do ecommerce websites generate trouble-making URLs, and why are search engines able to access such URLs? Well, URLs with internal tracking parameters are generated for personalization or for web analysis, or URLs with A/B testing data are created to improve conversion rates.

A compromise for offering a great user experience while helping search engines crawl complex websites is to make the trouble-making links uncrawlable for robots but available to users.

For example, a link that is important for users but not important for search engine robots can be created with uncrawlable JavaScript or within an iframe. Before we look at examples, here are a couple of notes:

- Decide whether there's an indexing or crawling issue to be addressed in the first place. Are 90%+ of your URLs indexed? If yes, then maybe you just need to build some links to the other 10% of pages, or add more content to get them indexed.

- Would you hinder user experience by blocking content with JavaScript?

- Hiding links from robots may qualify as cloaking, depending on the reason for the implementation.

"If the reason [for cloaking] is for spamming malicious, or deceptive behavior—or even showing different content to users than to Googlebot—then this is high-risk."[1]

- Are there any other methods to improve internal linking (e.g., better website architecture)?

Please note that from an SEO point of view, I advocate using uncrawlable links only for creating better crawl paths to help search engines reach important pages on your website, and for not wasting bandwidth on internal linking traps. I don't endorse this method if you want to hide spam content or to mislead unsuspecting visitors.

Here are a couple of methods for keeping crawlers away from unwanted links:

iframes

While the HTML *<iframe>* element has been/is used by spammers to game search engines, this is still one of the legitimate applications of *<iframe>* for content flow and crawl optimization. Let's say you don't want **any** links generated by faceted navigation to be visible to search engines.

You can embed the faceted navigation in an iframe and block the spider's access with robots.txt. The advantage of the iframe is that it is fast to implement—and to remove if the results are not satisfactory. One disadvantage is that you can't granularly control which facets can be indexed; once the iframe source is blocked with robots.txt, no facet will be crawled.

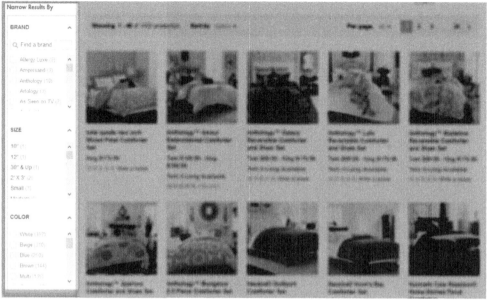

Figure 118 Faceted navigation often creates bot traps.

Intermediary directory/file

This requires redirecting through a file or directory that is blocked in *robots.txt*. Using the same example as above, let's say the facet URLs are:

/bedding/?CatalogId=110504+423949610&CatRefId=105024&pagSort=0

Instead of linking to the above URL, you can link through an intermediary directory, which is then disallowed by *robots.txt*:

/facets/bedding/?CatalogId=110504+423949610&CatRefId=105024&pagSort=0

> *User-agent: **

> *# Do not crawl faceted URLs*

> *Disallow: /facets/*

Instead of a directory, you can use a file:

/bedding/facets.php&CatalogId=110504+423949610&CatRefId=105024&pagSort= 0

> *User-agent: **

> *# Do not crawl faceted URLs*

> *Disallow: /facets.php**

JavaScript and AJAX

JavaScript (or AJAX) is another way to hide links, to silo the website and to eventually avoid duplicate content issues at the source. Search engines can execute JavaScript (e.g., "document.write" statements) and AJAX to discover content and URLs, but only to some extent,[2] and there are limitations to what they can understand.

While SEOs want to make AJAX content more accessible to search engines most of the time, in this case you will actually try to achieve the opposite. You can use JavaScript or AJAX to generate the link in the browser rather than at the back end. Therefore, those URLs won't exist when the crawler requests the content from your web server.

One application of this method is to generate clean internal tracking URLs at the back end and modify them on demand in the browser.

Let's say you have three links on your home page that point to the same URL, but each link is in a different location—one is in the primary navigation, another is on a product image and the last one is in the footer—so that your analytics can track where people clicked. Tag each URL with tracking parameters (campaigns, link position, affiliates, referrers, etc.). The three links will look like:

mysite.com/watches/?trackingkey=hp-watches-primary_nav

mysite.com/watches/?trackingkey=hp-watches-body_image

mysite.com/watches/?trackingkey=hp-watches-footer

The *trackingkey* parameter in the first link tells the web analytics tool that the click came from the home page (*hp*), in the watches category located in the primary navigation (*primary_nav*). The other two are similar, except that the link location is different. When you add these tracking parameters, you create three duplicate URLs.

Here's one way to use JavaScript to avoid generating duplicate content URLs and still use URL parameters.

At the front end, in the browser, your anchor element will look similar to:

<a href="http://www.mysite.com/watches/" param-string="trackingkey=hp-watches-primary_nav">Watches</a>

The href link is clean of parameters, which is great for SEO.

The page featuring this link includes a JavaScript code that "listens" when users click the tracked link. When the mouse is pressed, the href is updated in the browser by appending the content of the *param-string* attribute.

<a href="http://www.mysite.com/watches/?trackingkey=hp-watches-primary_nav" param-string="trackingkey=hp-watches-primary_nav">Watches</a>

You can get a sample code on this book's companion website at *http://www.ecommercemarketingbooks.com/companion-files/*.

If you decide to hide links with JavaScript, keep in mind that Google has the ability to read a link (or something that looks like a link) even if it's in JavaScript. *OnClick* events that generate links are the most likely to be crawled. I've seen cases where Google requested and tried to crawl virtual page view URLs for Google Analytics.[3]

Note that hiding links with JavaScript can be challenging for IT and may hinder the user experience for those visitors who don't have JavaScript enabled. If your existing website doesn't work with JavaScript off, you should be fine using AJAX links. However, don't sacrifice user experience for SEO.

Selective user agent delivery

This method is the most controversial because it delivers content based on who's accessing the page (user agent-based delivery). The principle behind this method is simple. When there's a request for a URL, find the user agent behind the request and identify whether it's a search engine or a browser. If it's a browser, you can add parameters to URLs; if it's a search engine bot, you deliver clean URLs.

Think this method is too close to cloaking? Let's see how Amazon uses it to add internal tracking parameters. If you go to their *Call of Duty: Ghosts - Xbox 360* page[4] while using your browser's default user agent and mouse over the *Today's Deals* link, you will get a URL that contains the tracking parameter *ref*:

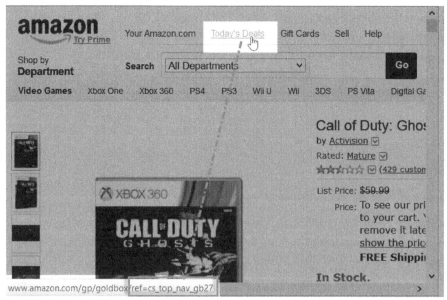

Figure 119 Internal tracking parameter.

Now, change the user agent to Googlebot (use one of the many browser extensions to accomplish this), reload the page, and mouse over the same link. This time, it is a clean URL:

Figure 120 No parameters now.

Here's their HTML code:

Googlebot user agent

```
<ul id='nav-cross-shop-links' >
        <li class='nav-xs-link nav_first'><a href='/gp/yourstore/home' class='nav_a' id='nav-your-amazon'>Yo
            <li class='nav-xs-link '><a href='/gp/goldbox' class='nav_a'>Today's Deals</a></li>
            <li class='nav-xs-link '><a href='/gift-cards/b?ie=UTF8&node=2238192011' class='nav_a'>Gift Card
            <li class='nav-xs-link '><a href='/gp/seller-account/mm-product-page.html?ie=UTF8&ld=AZSOAUSCSNa
            <li class='nav-xs-link '><a href='/Help/b?ie=UTF8&node=508510' class='nav_a'>Help</a></li>
    </ul>
```

Brower's default user agent

```
<ul id='nav-cross-shop-links' >
        <li class='nav-xs-link nav_first'><a href='/gp/yourstore/home/ref=topnav_ys' class='nav_a' id='nav-y
            <li class='nav-xs-link '><a href='/gp/goldbox/ref=cs_top_nav_gb27' class='nav_a'>Today's Deals</
            <li class='nav-xs-link '><a href='/gift-cards/b/ref=topnav_giftcert?ie=UTF8&node=2238192011' cla
            <li class='nav-xs-link '><a href='/gp/seller-account/mm-product-page.html/ref=mm_soa_csnavt1?ie=
            <li class='nav-xs-link '><a href='/Help/b/ref=topnav_help?ie=UTF8&node=508510' class='nav_a'>Hel
    </ul>
```

Figure 121 This is an example of "white-hat cloaking".

Assessing internal linking

The first step towards internal linking optimization is diagnosis. Analyzing whether pages are linked properly or whether there are problems such as broken links can reveal technical and website taxonomy issues.

One of the fastest, easiest ways to ascertain which pages are the most interlinked and deemed the most internally important by search engines is to use your Google Webmaster Tools account.

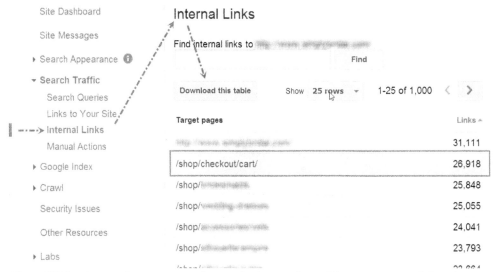

Figure 122 Are the most important pages for your business at the top? For ecommerce websites, those are usually the categories listed in the primary navigation.

In the above example, the */shop/checkout/cart/* URL is the second most linked page on the website. This makes sense from a user standpoint because this link has to be present on most pages.

However, the cart link is not important for search engines. You can add the */checkout/* directory in *robots.txt* to prevent it being crawled.

```
<a href="https://www.        .com/shop/onestepcheckout/" rel="nofollow">Checkout</a></li>
<a href="https://www.        .com/shop/customer/account/login/" rel="nofollow">Login</a>
<a href="https://www.        .com/shop/customer/account/" rel="nofollow">Account</a>
<a href="https://www.        .com/shop/wishlist/" rel="nofollow">Wishlist</a>
<a href="https://www.        .com/shop/checkout/cart/">Shopping Cart</a>
                                                                    followed link
```

Figure 123 The shopping cart link is the one link that is followed.

Next, let's see how each page is linked, anchor text wise. For this we'll use one of the best (if not the best) and most underestimated desktop SEO crawlers and on-page SEO audit tools. Meet IIS SEO Toolkit.[5]

Search Engine Optimization

The IIS Search Engine Optimization (SEO) Toolkit provides a set of tools that you can use to make your Web site relevance of your Web site in search engine results.

Site Analysis

Use this feature to analyze your Web site so that you can optimize it for search engine crawlers. The structure, and URLs, and help you discover and fix the identified problems.

Create a new analysis | View existing reports
Recently used:

Sitemaps and Sitemap Indexes

Use this feature to manage the sitemap and sitemap index files for your Web site. The sitemaps help content is most relevant to users.

Create a new sitemap | Create a new sitemap index | View existing sitemaps and sitemap indexes

Figure 124 An indispensable, on-demand desktop crawler.

You don't hear SEOs talking about this tool much (probably because it is Microsoft technology), but the flexibility and extended functionalities of the IIS SEO Toolkit make Xenu and similar tools pale by comparison (no offense intended to Xenu, which is also great).

There are virtually thousands of ways to analyze your website with this toolkit:

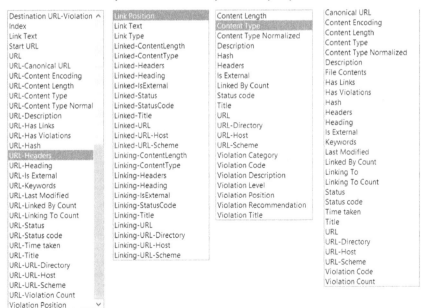

Figure 125 You can slice and dice the SEO data in almost any way you can imagine.

Install it[6] and run your first crawl (it's pretty simple to set up). Now let's see how we can use the toolkit to identify some major internal linking issues.

Broken links

Finding broken links is a breeze, and the tool reports such issues in several places.

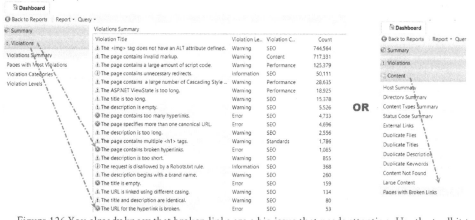

Figure 126 You already know that broken links are a big issue that needs attention. Use the toolkit to identify and take care of them.

Link depth

The general SEO wisdom is that any page should be accessible in as few clicks as possible. Four levels deep is ok and acceptable, but any more becomes problematic.

Figure 127 Having URLs 24 levels deep is not a good sign.

Too many links on a page

Use the *Pages with Most Links* report to quickly identify the number of outgoing links from each page on your website. Sort data by *Count* to get a quick idea of where the problems are.

Figure 128 Having 936 links on a page is something you need to investigate.

This report is also available under the *Violations* section:

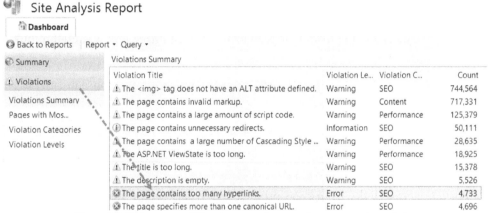

Figure 129 This report will list the pages that contain too many hyperlinks.

Identify hubs

The *Most Linked Page* report can help you identify internal hubs. In terms of website taxonomy, a hub is a parent with lots of children linking back to it. Usually the largest link hubs on ecommerce websites are the home page and the category pages linked from the primary navigation. If you see other pages at the top, that may be a sign of internal linking issues. If your primary navigation has secondary navigation that lists subcategories (e.g., menu fly-outs), then you should see those subcategory pages at the top of the list as well.

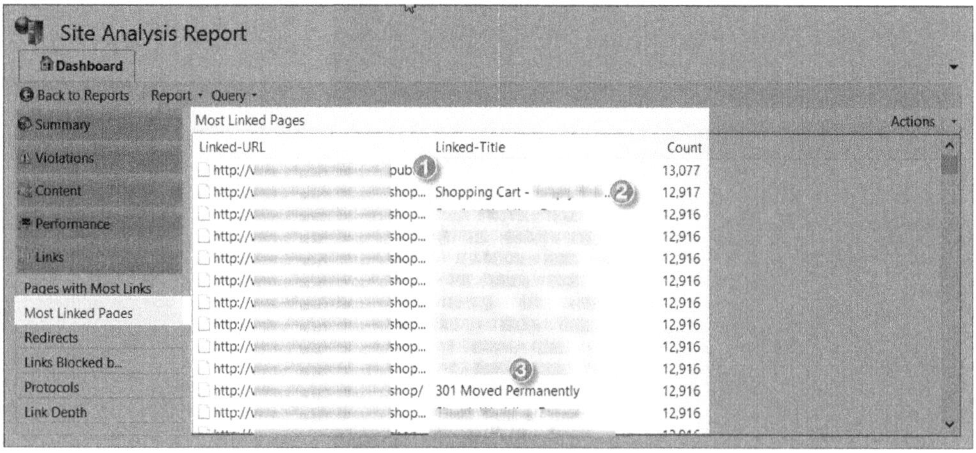

Figure 130 The Most Linked Page report is very similar to the Internal Links report in Google Webmaster Tools.

The numbers in the above image highlight three issues:

1. The most linked page doesn't have a <title>. This might be either because the title is missing from that page or because an image link was used to link to the home page instead of a text link.

2. The shopping cart URL gets too many internal links; consequently, it gets crawled too many times.

3. A significant number of internal links point to 301 redirects. If possible, link directly to a final URL.

Although the above screenshot doesn't show this, the tool also found a large number of *Email to a Friend* links, from every product details page on the website. Generally, you don't need to allow such links to be crawled, so make sure you block their URLs with *robots.txt* (or another method).

To dig more deeply and get additional details on how each URL is linked, right click the URL you would like to analyze (listed in the *Linked-URL* column) and then click on *View Group Details in New Query*.

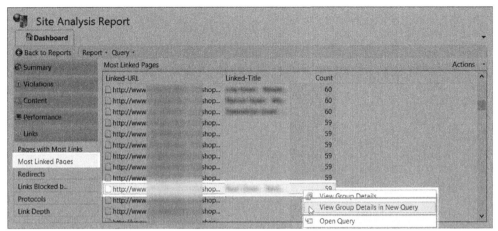

Figure 131 View Group Details in New Query report.

Then click on *Add/Remove Columns* and add the *Link Text* column (click on *Execute*, at the top left, to update the report):

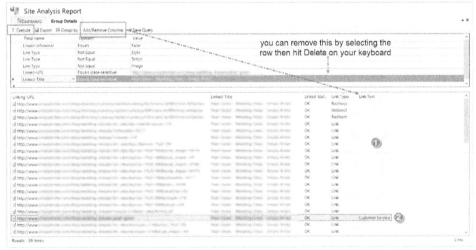

Figure 132 You can remove/add columns to your reports.

Notes:

- If a page is linked using an image link, the tool does not report the alt text of the image (this is one big downside to the Toolkit).

- This page is linked with the "customer service" anchor text, which is wrong; the linked page is not the customer service page.

Now let's group by anchor text to see aggregate anchor text data:

- Click on *Group by*.

- Select *Link Text* in the *Group by* tab, then hit *Execute*.

- You get a count of each anchor text pointing to that particular URL.

- To analyze a different URL, simply change the value in the *Linked-URL* field.

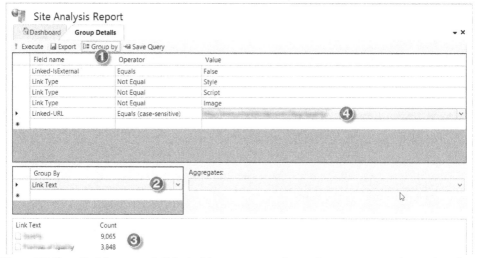

Figure 133 If you find that a page is linked with too many varying anchor texts, you need to evaluate how close the anchor texts are semantically and taxonomically.

Ideally, you will link to category pages consistently using the category name, but a few variations in the anchor text are acceptable. For example, you can link to the *Office Furniture* category with "office furniture" as the anchor text, but you can also link with "furniture for office". When you link to product pages, use the product name as the anchor text. If you interlink blog articles, you have room to play with the product's name.

To get an overall picture of the website-wide anchor text distribution, you need to create custom reports (aka *queries*). This is where the enormous flexibility of the tool comes in handy.

Go to the *Dashboard*, click on *Query* and select the *New Link Query*:

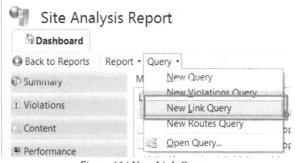

Figure 134 New Link Query.

Then:

1. Select the highlighted field names.

2. Click on *Group by Link Text.*

3. Click *Execute.*

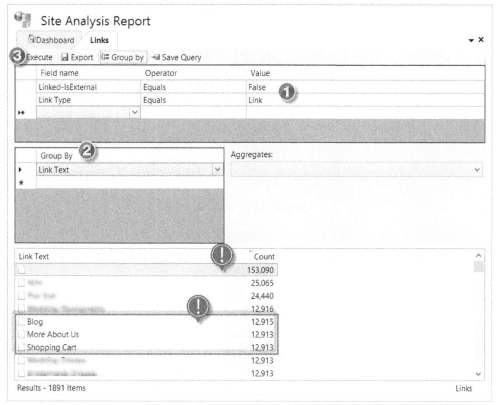

Figure 135 There you have it! The internal anchor text distribution for the entire website.

You can already notice a couple of things that need to be investigated further:

- Missing anchor text for the most linked page.

- Do you really need a link to your blog from so many pages?

- How about blocking the crawl of the shopping cart link, or consolidating the About Us and Blog into a single URL?

If you want a fancy visualization of your hub pages, you can use the *Export* function of the IIS SEO Toolkit to generate the list of all URLs and import it to a data visualization tool.

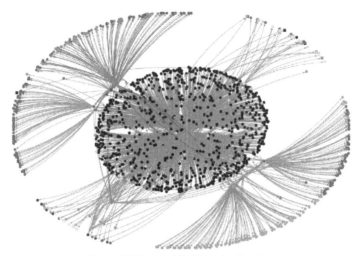

Figure 136 Internal linking visualization.

You can find three tutorials on Google's Fusion Tables,[7] NodeXL[8] and Gephi.[9]

Problematic redirects

Using this report will help identify internal PageRank leaks through 302 redirects, unnecessary 301s or other bad response codes. To make the analysis easier, I prefer to sort by *Linking URL*, to see the issues grouped by page.

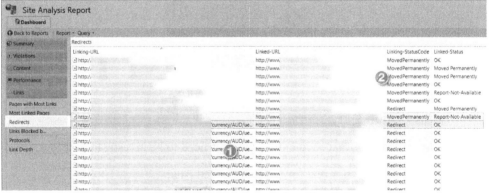

Figure 137 Sort by Linking-StatusCode to identify issues.

Notes:

- Use cookies if possible rather than keeping the currency in URL parameters. For this website, each currency switch generated a unique URL on almost every single page of the website.

- Instead of linking to a URL that returns a 301, link directly to the final destination.

The unnecessary redirects reporting is also available in the *Violations* section:

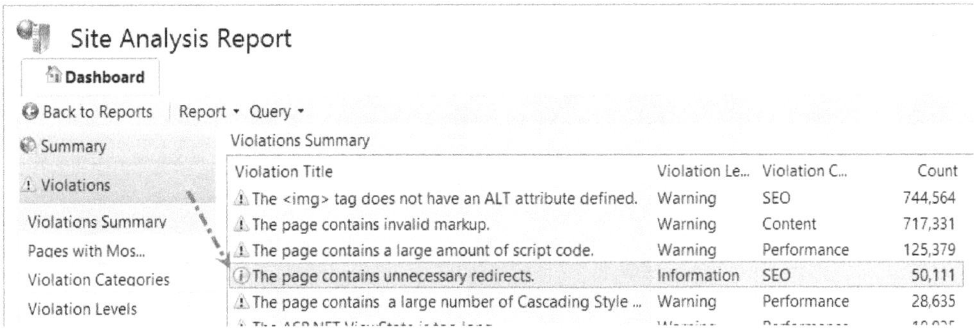

Violation Title	Violation Le...	Violation C...	Count
⚠ The <img> tag does not have an ALT attribute defined.	Warning	SEO	744,564
⚠ The page contains invalid markup.	Warning	Content	717,331
⚠ The page contains a large amount of script code.	Warning	Performance	125,379
ⓘ The page contains unnecessary redirects.	Information	SEO	50,111
⚠ The page contains a large number of Cascading Style ...	Warning	Performance	28,635

Figure 138 Links blocked by *robots.txt*.

Use this report to check whether *robots.txt* blocks unwanted URLs.

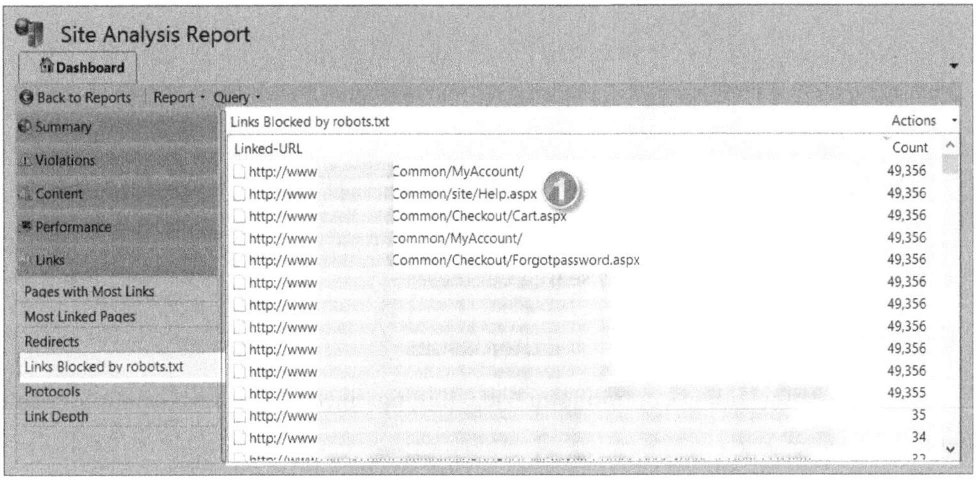

Linked-URL	Count
http://www Common/MyAccount/	49,356
http://www Common/site/Help.aspx	49,356
http://www Common/Checkout/Cart.aspx	49,356
http://www common/MyAccount/	49,356
http://www Common/Checkout/Forgotpassword.aspx	49,356
http://www	49,356
http://www	49,356
http://www	49,356
http://www	49,356
http://www	49,356
http://www	49,355
http://www	35
http://www	34

Figure 139 The *Help.aspx* page is blocked with *robots.txt*.

Does the Help.aspx page need to be blocked with a page-level meta robots tag? Probably not, but because the page is located under the */Common/* directory(which is blocked with *robots.txt*) search engines won't be able to access it.

```
User-agent: *
Disallow: /
Disallow: /Common
Disallow:
Disallow: /common
Disallow: /checkout
```

Figure 140 All pages under /Common will be blocked.

Protocols

This report displays the various protocols used for linking to other resources:

Figure 141 If your website is non-secure (http), do you link to secure pages (https), or vice versa? If you do, what happens when visitors go back and forth between http and https? Are the URLs consistent?

In most cases, shopping carts, logins or checkout pages are https secure, and such pages don't need to be indexed by search engines.

Other issues

Here are some other common internal linking mistakes, apart from the issues highlighted above:

- Linking inconsistency happens when linking to the same page with multiple URL variations: *http://mysite.com/*, *http://www.mysite.com/* or *http://www.mysite.com/index.php*. When you link internally, be consistent—link to one consolidated URL only.

- Default page dispersal, which is linking to index files rather than to a root directory. For example, many use *href="/index.php"* when linking to home pages. Instead, you have to link to *href="/"*.

- Case sensitivity that leads to 404 Not Found errors. Apache is case sensitive, and if you link to "/Product-name.html" with upper-case "P" instead of lower-case, the server may generate errors.

- Mixed paths when linking to the same file with both absolute and relative paths. This is not an SEO issue per se, but adopting standardized URL referencing (I prefer absolute paths) will help with troubleshooting. If you use absolute paths, when content scrappers steal content they may still leave the absolute links to your URLs.

Tip: When you assess your competitors' links from an SEO perspective, compare the source code when you access the website with Googlebot as your browser's user agent (and with JavaScript disabled) with the source code when you browse as a normal user. Are there any differences in the URLs? You should also analyze the differences between their cached versions of the links and the links in the live website.

Nofollow on internal links

The nofollow microformat[10] is a Robot Exclusion Protocol (REP) that applies at the element level (link) and prevents PageRank and anchor text data from being passed on to the linked page.

Some SEOs use the nofollow attribute believing it will prevent the indexation of the linked-to URL. Often, we find statements along the lines of: "Simply nofollow the admin, account and checkout pages to prevent these pages being indexed."

However, *nofollow does not totally prevent crawling and indexing*.

rel="nofollow" Action	Google	Yahoo!	Bing	Ask.com
Uses the link for ranking	No	No	No	?
Follows the link	Yes	Yes	?	No
Indexes the "linked to" page	No	Yes	No	No
Shows the existence of the link	Only for a previously indexed page	Yes	Yes	Yes
In results pages for anchor text	Only for a previously indexed page	Yes	Only for a previously indexed page	Yes

Figure 142 "Nofollow" behavior according to Wikipedia.

Matt Cutts, head of Google's Webspam team, says that Google doesn't crawl nofollow links:

"At least for Google, we have taken a very clear stance that those links are not even used for discovery." [11]

However, Google's Content Guidelines state this a bit differently:

*"How does Google handle nofollowed links? **In general**, we don't follow them."* [12]

A test I performed in December 2013 with internal nofollow site-wide footer links showed that although it took about a month, Googlebot, msnbot/2.0b and bingbot/2.0 did crawl and index nofollowed links. Yahoo! Slurp still hadn't requested the URL as of February 2014.

My recommendation is to use nofollow *not* as a method to keep search engines away from content, but just as a secondary method to prevent crawling. If you nofollow links that search engines previously discovered, those links may still be indexed. Also, if there are external links pointing to the nofollowed URLs, they will be indexed as well.

You will often see the nofollow tag applied to links such as shopping carts, checkout buttons, account logins, etc.:

Figure 143 Search engines won't add to cart and initiate checkouts.

A few years ago, nofollow was used to funnel PageRank to important pages, a tactic named "PR sculpting". But nowadays, the vast majority of SEOs know that PageRank sculpting with nofollow no longer paid off,[13] and many ecommerce websites stopped nofollowing internal links. However, some still continue doing it:

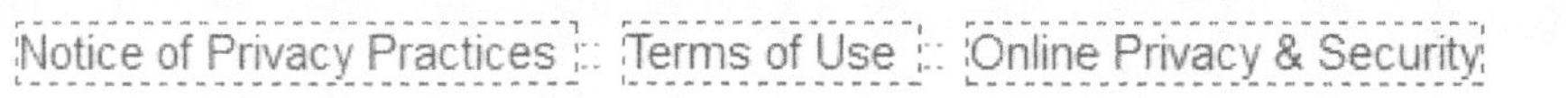

Notice of Privacy Practices :: Terms of Use :: Online Privacy & Security

Figure 144 Instead of nofollowing these links, consolidate them into a single page.

When you nofollow a site-wide URL like "Terms of Use", you take that page out of the internal link graph completely.[14] This means that the page won't receive internal PageRank, but it also means *it won't have internal PageRank to pass*.

The above example brings us to a more important issue: nofollowing links in primary and/or secondary navigations. Depending on what links you nofollow in the primary navigation, you could be making a big mistake.

PageRank is a renewable resource, which means that it flows back and forth between pages that link to one another, with a decay/damping factor between 10% and 15% at each iteration to avoid infinite loops[15] (according to the original PageRank formula).

Let's say that page A below is the home page and it links to category pages B and C from the primary navigation menu. To simplify, let's assume that pages B and C don't have any external links.

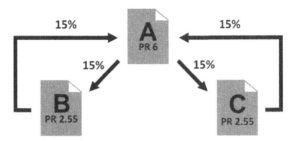

Figure 145 A simple PageRank flow diagram.

The above is an overly simplified flow of PageRank, but the most important thing to understand is that page B and page C each return PageRank to page A, increasing its value.

Let's see what happens when you add rel="nofollow" to the Page C link in the primary navigation:

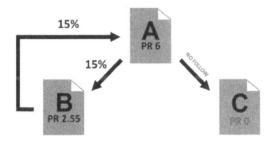

Figure 146 The nofollow attribute stops sending PR to page C.

What happens is that page C doesn't send internal PageRank back to page A, because it doesn't receive any internal PageRank.

Toyota surprises me by adding nofollow to all model links (Yaris, Corolla, etc.).

Figure 147 The outlined model name links are nofollowed.

Toyota's home page has a PageRank 7, and the Yaris page (which is a nofollowed link in the primary navigation) has PageRank 5. My guess is that the PageRank 5 is because of the large number of external links, rather than because of the internal linking flow:

URL Information

External Backlinks	Referring Domains	Referring IPs:	Referring Subnets:
43,457	2,579	1,544	1,272

Figure 148 The Yaris page gets a lot of external backlinks.

However, the situation is different on jtv.com. This time, the category pages linked from their primary navigation don't get too many backlinks from external sources.

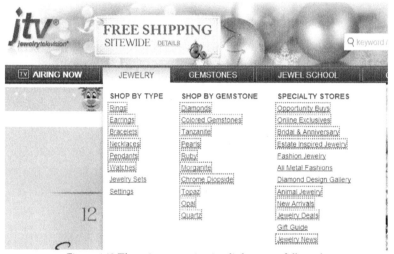

Figure 149 The primary navigation links are nofollowed.

Their home page has PageRank 5, but all "shop by type" pages have a "not ranked" PageRank. These are all pages linked from the primary navigation and should get at least some authority (e.g., PageRank 3 or 4). The nofollow attribute doesn't mean that those pages won't show in SERPs (as a matter of fact, they are all cached by search engines), but their authority has been significantly decreased.

If some links are not important for users, remove them from the navigation completely. Not every category needs a link in the primary navigation menus.

If you want to send link juice only to specific pages, here are some alternatives to nofollowing:

- Have fewer links on the page, and move important links to prominent places.

- Make those links that you don't want to pass link juice uncrawlable.

- Block search engine robots from crawling the unwanted links.

Keep in mind that *nofollow is not a solution for duplicate content*.

Because nofollow is incorrectly used to prevent indexing, it may also be inadvertently used to prevent duplicate content issues. However, adding nofollow to links is not the best approach for controlling duplicate content. Since nofollow is not 100% crawling and indexing failproof, how can it be used to prevent indexation of duplicate content?

Internal linking optimization

Users navigate from one page to another by clicking on links. That's one of the core principles of the Internet, and it hasn't changed since the Web's inception. But while links are simply a way for people to navigate websites, search engines will use links as an authority and relevance signal.

For search engines, though, all links are not equal, and they assign some links more power based on various and undisclosed criteria. For example, links surrounded by text are considered more important than links in a menu list or links in the footer, as Matt Cutts states in a video.[16] Links surrounded by text are called *contextual text links*, while links created to structure a website (e.g., links in the primary/secondary navigation, or breadcrumbs) can be named *structural* or *hierarchical links*. One of the reasons contextual text links receive more search engine weight is related to the fact that users often ignore structural links to go straight to the content,[17] and rarely scroll to click on footer links.

Figure 150 Contextual internal text links are still very important for search engines.

Large websites such as ecommerce ones have the advantage of generating an incredible number of links, but unfortunately, most of those are structural links that don't carry the same power as contextual text links. And in some cases, Google might even ignore boilerplate links:

> "We found that boilerplate links with duplicated anchor text are not as relevant, so we are putting less emphasis on these."[18]

There are several ways to optimize internal linking, and there is no excuse for ecommerce websites not to capitalize on SEO issues that are under their direct control. Theoretically, numerous factors could influence the value of an internal link,[19] but we are going to limit them to the following:

- Position in the page layout.

- Contextual VS structural links.

- Text in the anchor.

- Type of link (an image's alt text seems to pass less ranking value than text links).[20]

- Page authority and the number of outbound links on the page.

Link position

The positioning of the link in the page layout (e.g., in primary navigation, footer or side bar) influences how much PageRank flows out to the linked-to page.[21]

Microsoft has the VIPS patent—*VIPS: A Vision-based Page Segmentation Algorithm*[22]—which talks about breaking down page layouts into logical sections, and a paper that talks about *Block-Level PageRank.*[23] Google has the patents for *Document ranking based on semantic distance between terms in a document*[24] and *Reasonable Surfer,*[25] which discuss similar concepts. All these papers indicate that links placed in prominent places will pass more PageRank than links in less important sections of the page.

Generally speaking, contextual text links are assigned more weight than primary and secondary navigation links, which in turn are deemed more important than footer links. However, the large number of occurrences of the same anchor text in the primary navigation can compensate for relevance and compete with the powerful contextual text links.

Unfortunately, you can have only a limited number of anchor text in the primary or secondary navigation, which means you have to choose carefully. But with contextual links, you can implement a large number and variety because you're not limited by space (design) or by strict anchor text labeling. For example, you may be restricted to using the anchor text "hotels" in your structural navigation, but on content-rich pages you can use contextual text links such as "5 star hotels in San Francisco" or "San Francisco's best 5 star hotels".

Related to the link position, it's worth mentioning the concept of the *First Link Rule*. This rule says that when multiple links on the same page point to the same URL, only the first anchor text matters to search engines.[26]

Figure 151 Multiple links to the same URL happen often on ecommerce websites.

Notes:

- In this particular case, linking back to the home page with the anchor text "home" may confuse search engines. This is because the anchor text "home" conflicts with the anchor text "home products".

- *Children's Bedroom Furniture* should be a subcategory page on its own at a separate URL.

- The *Decorating with Metal Beds* link points to a shopping guide, which is great, but *modern metal beds* should point to a *Modern Metal Beds* category page if the keyword research shows this is an important category.

If you want to make search engines count multiple anchor texts,[27] one of the best options is to add the hash sign (#) at the end of the URLs:[28]

First link: *http://www.mysite.com/metal-bed-guide.htm*

Subsequent links: *http://www.mysite.com/metal-bed-guide.htm#value*

However, if you link to the same URL with varied (but related and relevant) anchor text, you don't need the hash tag in the URL. For example, you can link to the same product page once with the product name, and a second time using the product name plus the manufacturer name.

Very often you will encounter multiple URLs pointing to the home page—once on the logo and once on breadcrumbs.

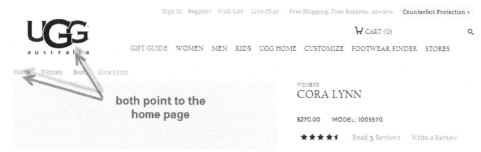

Figure 152 Both links point to the same page.

The logo's alt text is "UGG Australia", but the text link anchor is "Home". While having a "Home" link is good for usability, I am not a big fan of the "home" anchor text. I would either:

- Use the brand name in the breadcrumb, because UGG is very short. So, instead of "Home", I would use "UGG Australia".

- Replace the word "Home" with a small house icon that will have the alt="UGG Australia".

Multiple same-page linking (i.e., page A contains multiple links to page B) on ecommerce websites also frequently arises when links point to product detail pages from listing pages. One link can be on the clickable image thumbnail and another on the product name text:

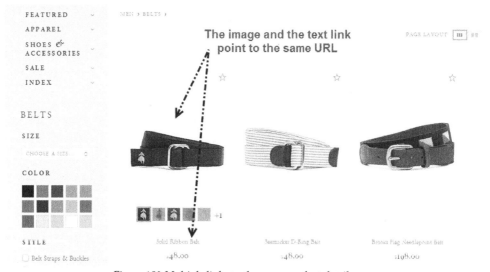

Figure 153 Multiple links to the same product details page.

In the above image, both links (image thumbnail and product name) point to the same product details page URL. The image's alternate text is "black", while the product anchor

134

name text is "Solid Ribbon Belt". This sends confusing relevance signals and is not optimal:

Figure 154 This is the image thumbnail link.

- The *<A>* element has an alt attribute attached to it, but it's in the wrong place. The alt attribute is not allowed on the *<A>* element. This alt attribute was probably intended to be a title attribute.

- The alt text used in alt text #1 should actually be used with alt text #2, and alt attribute #1 should be removed.

Figure 155 This is the product name text link.

Below are several options for addressing multiple links generated by image thumbnails and product names:

- Repeat the product name text in the image's alt (the easiest way to tackle this). In our example, the thumbnail's alt text will become "Solid Ribbon Belt".

- Wrap the image and text in a consolidated link (not always possible and not good for accessibility).

- Use the hash sign (#) if you need to use totally unrelated anchor text for the same URL.

- Place the product name above the image (this is against the usability conventions).

- Code the page so that the text link is above the image link in the HTML code, then use CSS to display the anchor text below the image (a bit complex to implement; not a very good idea).

Keep in mind that while the anchor text information will send confusing relevance signals, authority will pass through both links.[29]

Now that you know contextual text links are important, let's see how you can have more of them with user-generated content, product descriptions, brand pages and blog posts.

Contextual links on ecommerce websites

User generated content

User generated content (UGC) is one of the best ways to feed search engine robots, send engagement signals and help users make purchasing decisions.

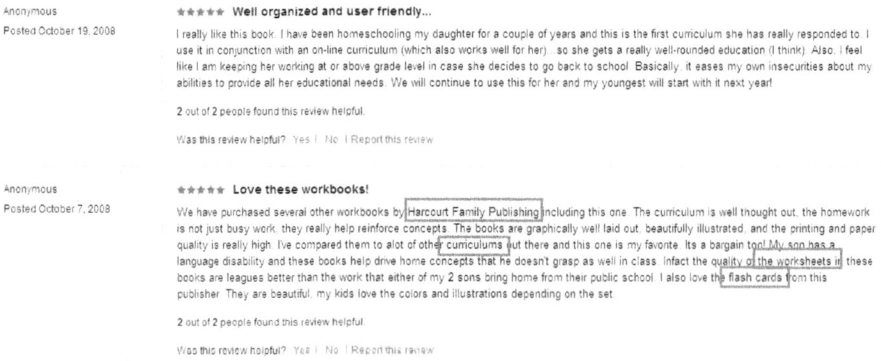

Figure 156 Reviews are a form of UGC. Highlighted are potential internal links.

Product reviews form one type of content-heavy UGC and represent a huge opportunity for generating contextual links. But not many ecommerce websites are taking full advantage of them.

While researching this topic I was surprised to find that only one of the top 50 online retailers was adding contextual links on user reviews. For whatever reasons (e.g., poor SEO implementation, vendor restrictions, fear of linking out from product detail pages and losing conversions, etc.), the others didn't. In fact, very few of the top 50 online retailers deployed SEO-friendly reviews (we'll discuss this in detail in the chapter dedicated to product detail pages).

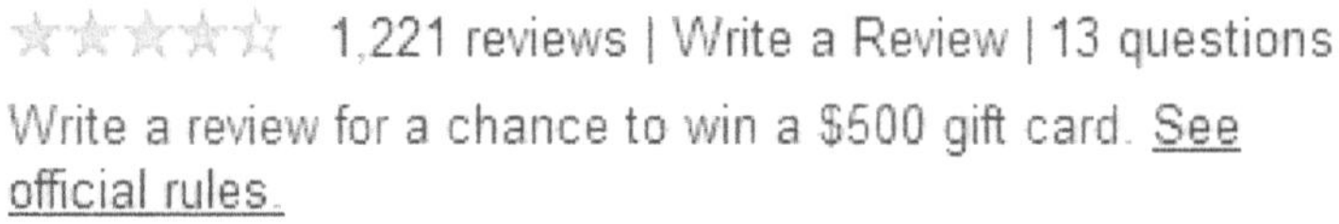

Figure 157 This product has 1,221 reviews. If you add one contextual link on 10% of them, those will be 120 very powerful links.

Other types of UGC that you can use to create contextual links are blog comments, user and customer support Q&A, user guest posts, product images with captions, user images and curated rich media.

Product descriptions

Many ecommerce pages contain text-rich sections. Take product details pages, where each product has a description. These content-rich sections are great places to link up to parent categories and brand pages:

Details & Care

A dramatic, wrap-style cardi is cut with an asymmetrical hem and secured with a single button at the neckline.

- 32" regular length to longest point; 26" back length (size Medium).
- 30" petite length to longest point; 24" back length (size Medium P).
- White, Wild Ruby, Spruced, Ivory, Heather Festival, Heather Creekside, Heather Spruced, Heather Wild Ruby, Heather Pink Rose and Heather Ginger are 68% polyester, 27% rayon, 5% spandex.
- All other colors are 61% polyester, 33% rayon, 6% spandex.
- Hand wash cold; line dry.
- By Bobeau; made in the USA or imported.
- Point of view and Petite Focus.

Figure 158 The highlighted text could be a link to Bobeau's brand page.

When you link from product descriptions, it's important to link to the parent category and, optionally, to other highly related categories.

Brand pages

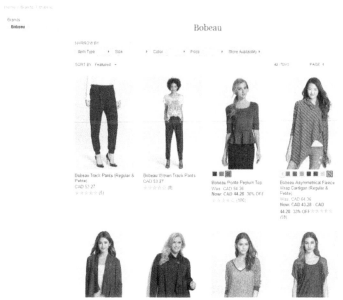

Figure 159 Most of the time, brand pages are nothing but a listing page.

To build relevant and valuable contextual text links that send more PageRank authority to product lines and products, the brand pages have to be content rich (with text, media and social signals). Be creative with the content and link smartly. Add a paragraph about the brand's history and link to the brand's top sellers, or add interesting facts about the brand and a couple of useful reviews. Get the brand's owners interviewed and publish the interview (you can even ask for a link/mention from their Press or News section). Yes, you can list a brand's products, but make this page valuable worthy as well.

Take a look at how Zappos improved the internal linking on their brand pages:[30]

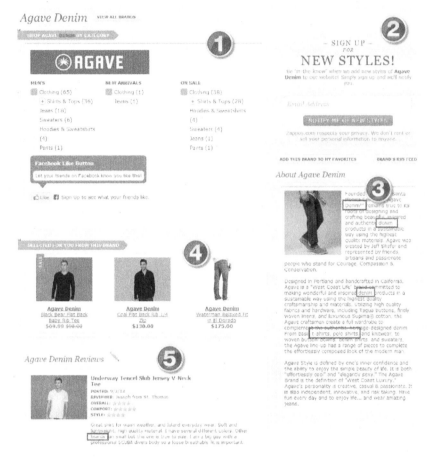

Figure 160 Zappos carefully interlinks thematically related pages.

Notes:

1. It uses section 1 as a site map.

2. It implements brand-specific RSS feeds; when a brand adds a new product to its online catalog, search engines will be notified instantly.

3. It uses text-rich content for contextual linking.

4. It links to a brand's featured products.

5. It has contextual links within user reviews.

Blogging

As mentioned in the *Information Architecture* chapter, blogs can be used to support and increase authority for category and product pages. As of 2014, very few ecommerce websites take full advantage of blogging. However, Google's Hummingbird update might change their mindset.

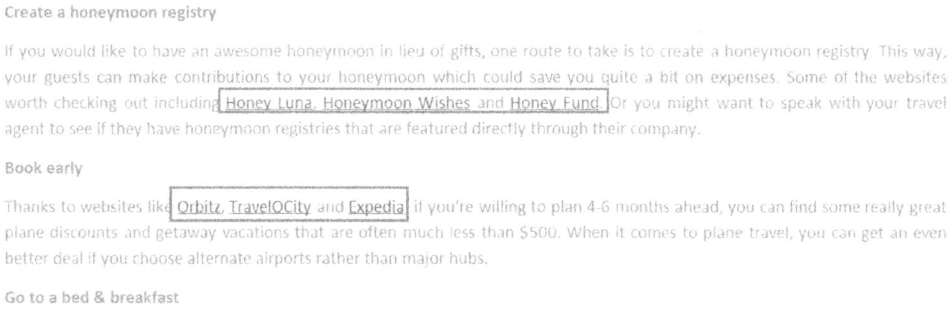

Create a honeymoon registry

If you would like to have an awesome honeymoon in lieu of gifts, one route to take is to create a honeymoon registry. This way, your guests can make contributions to your honeymoon which could save you quite a bit on expenses. Some of the websites worth checking out including Honey Luna, Honeymoon Wishes and Honey Fund. Or you might want to speak with your travel agent to see if they have honeymoon registries that are featured directly through their company.

Book early

Thanks to websites like Orbitz, TravelOCity and Expedia if you're willing to plan 4-6 months ahead, you can find some really great plane discounts and getaway vacations that are often much less than $500. When it comes to plane travel, you can get an even better deal if you choose alternate airports rather than major hubs.

Go to a bed & breakfast

Figure 161 The above article contains links (underlined text), but unfortunately all those links are external.

When you write blog posts, link internally contextually to several pages on your website, ideally to product and category pages:

Ready for Spring Sports Season

Posted by Walgreens on March 19, 2013 at 8:57 am

Play ball! The sun is out and it's time to get active. Soccer, baseball, lacrosse, track—whatever sport you're gearing up for, make sure you have all the outdoor sport essentials to have a happy and healthy sports season:

Pack a first aid kit. You never know when you'll need it, but you know you don't want to be without it. You'll want your basic bandages for small scrapes and cuts, but also pack medicated cleansing wipes and antibiotic ointment to stop infection. Other things that will be helpful for sport injuries may be self-wrap bandages, ice packs, and pain relievers.

Figure 162 As long as you don't overdo it, exact anchor text match is still important.

At the risk of becoming annoying, I need to stress this: if you're not blogging, you're missing a huge amount of long-tail search queries typed by possible customers in the early buying stages.

Remember, you write articles not to sell or promote something, but to grab long-tail traffic for informational search queries. The amount of content you need to create to support the category/subcategory/products depends on how competitive each main target keyword is.

Anchor text

The anchor text optimization principle is simple: the text used in the anchor sends relevance clues to search engines, and it has to be relevant to the linked to pages.

For example, if the anchor text is "suitcases" and the linked-to page includes the phrase "suitcases" and other related words (e.g., synonyms, variations, singular, etc.), then the anchor text in the incoming link is given more weight.

But if you were to use "click here" on internal anchor texts pointing to hotel description pages, then search engines would assign less relevance to those links. Instead, you should use the hotel names in the anchor text.

A Conductor study of more than 3,000 ecommerce and non-ecommerce websites with 280,000 internal links identified the most common words used in internal anchor text:

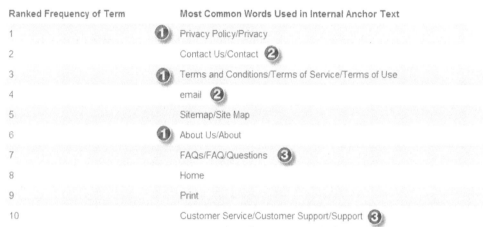

Ranked Frequency of Term	Most Common Words Used in Internal Anchor Text
1	① Privacy Policy/Privacy
2	Contact Us/Contact ②
3	① Terms and Conditions/Terms of Service/Terms of Use
4	email ②
5	Sitemap/Site Map
6	① About Us/About
7	FAQs/FAQ/Questions ③
8	Home
9	Print
10	Customer Service/Customer Support/Support ③

Figure 163 Conductor shows how 3,000 websites use anchor text in internal linking.[31]

Seven out of 10 anchor text links could be logically consolidated into three groups (represented by the numbers in the image). This technique is called *link consolidation*, and it is a better alternative to link sculpting with nofollow. However, if the links you consolidate are in the footer, the value of doing this is minimal.

First, let's find out whether there are generic anchor texts (e.g., "click here" or "here") on your website. Use IIS SEO Toolkit to check whether the *The link text is not relevant* violation is reported in the *Violations Summary:*

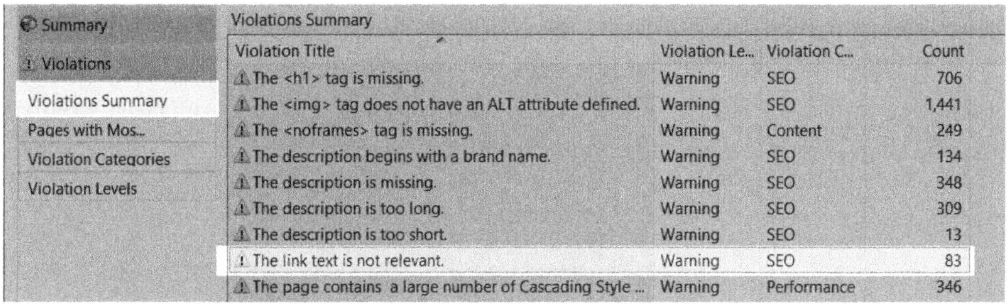

Violation Title	Violation Le...	Violation C...	Count
⚠ The <h1> tag is missing.	Warning	SEO	706
⚠ The <img> tag does not have an ALT attribute defined.	Warning	SEO	1,441
⚠ The <noframes> tag is missing.	Warning	Content	249
⚠ The description begins with a brand name.	Warning	SEO	134
⚠ The description is missing.	Warning	SEO	348
⚠ The description is too long.	Warning	SEO	309
⚠ The description is too short.	Warning	SEO	13
⚠ The link text is not relevant.	Warning	SEO	83
⚠ The page contains a large number of Cascading Style ...	Warning	Performance	346

Figure 164 Double click the warning message to get more details about each error.

There are situations where it is ok to use "click here" as anchor text—for example, when you link to a page that is not important for rankings, or when you use it as a call to action ("click here" is a powerful *call to action*, or CTA).

By default, the IIS SEO Toolkit searches for the words "here" and "click here" in text anchors. In practice, there are more generic anchors that you should pay attention to.[32] If you want to be exhaustive, you need to export the list of anchor texts from the Toolkit and use Excel for a deeper analysis.

Figure 165 In IIS SEO Toolkit, go to *Dashboard -> Query -> New Link Query*

Use the field settings below for sections 1 and 2 and then click on *Export* (section 3):

Figure 166 This will generate the aggregated link text report.

Alternatively, you can download the XML file that generates the same report from *http://www.ecommercemarketingbooks.com/companion-files/*. After downloading the file, import it into the IIS SEO Toolkit: *Dashboard* → *Query* → *New Link Query*; then right click on the gray area and select *Query* → *Open Query*:

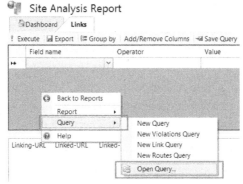

Figure 167 Export the data to a .csv file.

Open the file with Excel to get the list of all anchor text along with the occurrence count. Add a header and an empty column, *Presence*:

anchor	▼	Occurei ▼	Presence	▼↓
\		25,065		
F		24,440		
V		12,916		
A		12,913		
Auunu, un weuunig υιcssc>		12,913		

Figure 168 The *Presence* column will be filled later using a *VLOOKUP* function.

In a separate spreadsheet (name it *generic anchors*), add the generic keywords list and add a header and a *Presence* column:

Generic Words	▼↓ Presence ▼
a fantastic read	1
a knockout post	1
about his	1
additional hints	1
additional info	1
additional reading	1
additional resources	1

Figure 169 Fill the *Presence* column with 1's.

Now, go back to the first spreadsheet (named, say, *anchors)* and add the following VLOOKUP formula *=VLOOKUP(A2,'generic anchors'!A:B,2,FALSE)*:

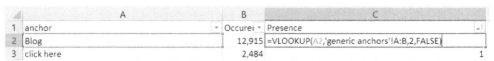

	A	B	C
1	anchor	Occurei ▼ Presence	▼↓
2	Blog	12,915 =VLOOKUP(A2,'generic anchors'!A:B,2,FALSE)	
3	click here	2,484	1

Figure 170 Copy the *VLOOKUP* formula all the way down.

If there's an exact match between the anchors used on the website and the generic keywords list, the cell value will be "1". You will get "#N/A" when there's no match. Sort or filter by "1" and you will get the list of generic anchors on your website:

	A	B	C
1	anchor	Occurel	Presence
2	Blog	12,915	1
3	click here	2,484	1
4	Home	1,495	1
5	here	10	1
6	Website	2	1
7		25,065	#N/A

Figure 171 The *Blog* anchor is the most used anchor on this website.

To make things easier, I made the sample Excel file available for download from *http://www.ecommercemarketingbooks.com/companion-files/*. You will need to replace the anchors text with your own.

We found that the "blog" anchor text is heavily used; it's probably a site-wide link.

Now we will use the IIS SEO Toolkit to see which pages link to the blog section:

Figure 172 Use the settings in the above image (left), hit *Execute*, and then double click on "Blog" to get a detailed list of Linking URLs. Repeat the process for all generic anchor text.

You have to be more creative and replace "blog" with something more appealing to search engines. Even "CompanyName Blog" is a better choice, but you could *theme* this anchor text even more. For example, if you sell fishing/hunting equipment, use "CompanyName's Fish & Hunt Blog". If you sell running shoes, use "Mad Runner's Blog".

Exact internal anchor text match still matters a lot for ecommerce websites, as long as you don't go overboard (e.g., with website-wide footer links). When you link to category pages or product details pages, use the category/subcategory and product names in the anchor. If you sell books, you will link to the product details page with the book's name. When you sell products, you can vary the anchor text a bit—for instance, by adding the brand's name to the product name.

Usually, it's a good idea to match users' search queries with your internal anchor text as closely as possible. So how do you know which anchors to use to link to a page that lists ignition systems for a *2004 Audi A3*? By doing keyword research.

For example, if you sell auto parts, you can break down the data by year, make, model and product names. Collect keyword data from as many sources as you can (user testing, Google Analytics, AdWords, webmaster accounts, competitor research, etc.) and put all of the keywords in a master spreadsheet. Remove duplicates using Excel.

Add search volume data and other metrics that you want to take into consideration:

ID	Keyword	Avg. monthly search	Conversio
1	chevy silverado grille	50	1
2	chevy silverado grill	260	1
3	chevy silverado grilles	70	2
4	chevy silverado grills	110	1
5	2004 chevy silverado grill	70	0
6	2005 chevy silverado grill	50	1
7	2007 chevy silverado grill	70	1
8	chevy silverado	60500	3
9	silverado grill	720	1
10	2002 chevy silverado grill	50	0
11	2013 chevy silverado	18100	4

	custom grille inserts		1.02
798	blacked out chevy silverado for sale	40	
799	2013 silverado reviews	70	1.28
800	ford grille emblem	110	0.87
801	chrome billet grille	70	0.81

Figure 173 Conversions is a good metric, but search volume is also important.

Now you need to identify search patterns by replacing each word with its corresponding product attribute. For example, you will replace "2007" or any other year with {year}, "Chevy" or any other make with {make}, "grill" or any other category name with {category} and so on:

	Keyword	Avg. monthly searches	Conversions
1	{make} {model} {category}	50	1
2	{make} {model} {category}	260	1
3	{make} {model} {category}	70	2
4	{make} {model} {category}	110	1
5	{year} {make} {model} {category}	70	0
6	{year} {make} {model} {category}	50	1
7	{year} {make} {model} {category}	70	1
8	{make} {model}	60500	3
9	{model} {category}	720	1
10	{year} {make} {model} {category}	50	0
11	{year} {make} {model}	18100	4

Figure 174 Help from your programmers can save a lot of time.

Once you've replaced all the words with product attributes, identify the most used patterns using pivot tables:

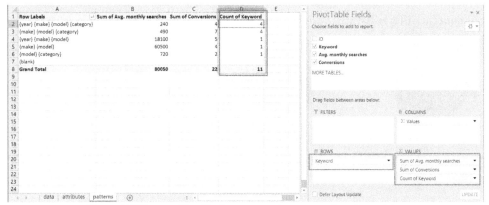

Figure 175 You can identify the most used patterns using pivot tables.

There you have it! The most used pattern in this particular case is *{year}{make}{model} {category}*. By mimicking user search patterns in your internal linking, you will increase the authority of the linked-to pages for those patterns.

Anchor text variation

It's a good idea to slightly vary the internal anchor text pointing to the same page. In the case of ecommerce websites, the category and subcategory pages will allow only some room for keyword variations. For example, when you link to the *Vancouver Hotels* page, you can use "hotels in Vancouver". When you link to a specific product (e.g., Rebel XTi), you can add the brand name ("Canon Rebel XTi") or the product line the product belongs to (e.g., "Canon EOS Rebel XTi").

Keyword (by relevance)		Avg. monthly searches ?
canon eos digital rebel xti		720
canon eos rebel xti 400d		170
canon digital rebel xti		720
canon eos rebel xti manual		170
canon rebel xti manual		590
canon rebel xti review		320
canon rebel eos xti		210

Figure 176 If you link from blog posts, you have even more opportunities to vary the anchor text.

Contextual text links allow more anchor text variation than structural links (related products and navigation) because structural links are often based on business rules, such as product attributes.

For product variations (e.g., model numbers or different colors), the item name link can contain differentiating product attributes:

Figure 177 In the above screen-cap, all products represent various SKUs for "Canon Digital Rebel XTi".

Remember to link using text that makes sense for users, without forcing keywords. When you use a plural in anchor text (e.g., "digital cameras"), consider linking to a listing page, because search queries that contain a plural usually denote that users want to see a list of items.

Related links

Merchandising and online marketing teams needed to cross-sell online; that is how ecommerce websites started featuring *related items* sections that link to *related* products. Related linking can be found under various names and implemented in various ways, such as *people who purchased this also purchased, you may also like, people also viewed, related products, tags* or *related searches*. This concept was originally introduced as a way to increase the number of items added to the cart and the average order value, and to help users navigate to related products.

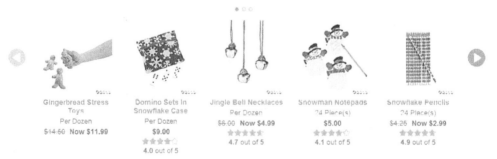

Figure 178 Presenting related products/categories is very common on ecommerce websites.

But SEOs realized that related items sections can also be used to:

- Optimize internal linking by interconnecting deep pages that were otherwise impossible to connect within other types of navigation (e.g., breadcrumbs).

- Flatten the website structure.

- Silo the website architecture by linking to siblings and parent categories (siloing with related products requires very strict business rules).

Related links can be used to boost the authority of certain pages whenever needed:

- If you add a new product under the *Bathing* category, you can boost its crawling, indexing and, eventually, ranking by linking directly from the category listing page or even from the home page.

- If there are products that have very high value for your business, linking from the home page will send more authority signals to those products.

- On a page that lists all houses for sale in a particular district, you can also link to houses in nearby neighborhoods.

- Link to recently reviewed hotels in a particular city listing page.

If you have a lot of data to rely on, you can implement related products with the help of recommendation engines. Such engines are used to optimize the shopping experience on-the-fly, but often they are implemented with uncrawlable JavaScript.. One way of tackling JavaScript related items is to define a set of default related products that are accessible to search engines, then replace them with AJAX once the page loads in the browser.

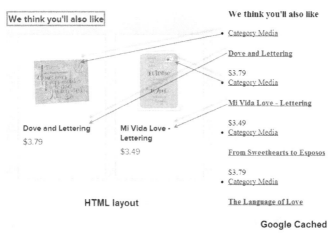

Figure 179 Hallmark's related items section is accessible to search engines. The content of the recommendation engine is indexed, but the alt text of the images could definitely be improved.

On the other hand, on Crocs's website the AJAX implementation prevents search engines from finding the recommended products:

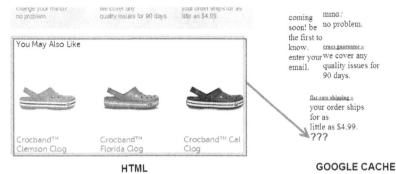

HTML   **GOOGLE CACHE**

Figure 180 The "You May Also Like" section should show up in the cached version, but it doesn't.

Here are a few things to consider when implementing the recommended actions:

- If you need to add tracking parameters to recommended item URLs, do so in the browser, at mouse down or click.

- Keep the number of recommended items low and focus on quality (three to five products should be enough).

- If you want to provide even more recommended items, you can use carousels.

Figure 181 Saks Fifth Avenue links to a sweater and sandals because they are related. You can interlink such items even if they are in different silos (e.g., link from a skirt to the sandals that complete the look)

Popular searches is another type of related links that can be implemented on ecommerce websites. Run a search on Google and Bing and see which keywords they suggest at the bottom of the results.

Internal linking over optimization

While internal links with exactly matching anchor text typically don't hurt,[33] try not to overdo it.

Let's take a look at a few scenarios that can raise over-optimization flags.

Unnatural links to the home page

It doesn't seem to help too much if you replace the anchor text "home" with your primary keyword.[34]

online pharmacy > medicine & health > **stop smoking aids**

Figure 182 If your domain or your business name is "online pharmacy", then it may be fine to use the keyword-rich anchor text to point to the home page.

Too many contextual text links

A high ratio of internal anchor text links to content is not advisable. For example, if your category description is 100 words and you place 15 anchor texts in it, that's too much.

The Christmas holiday season is coming soon which means lots of great holiday gear including ornaments, stockings and gnomes. Grab some officially licensed college football and NCAA basketball apparel, or get ready for 2014 with Super Bowl, Winter Classic, and USA Sochi apparel. With hot items like sweatpants, slippers, gloves, scarves, beanies and pajamas to choose from, we're sure you'll find the perfect item this holiday season. Check out our other great product categories like lanyards and camo gear, and get your gift shopping done early.

Figure 183 Contextual links are great, but that doesn't mean you have to abuse them.

Contextual text links like the ones above are either created automatically or added manually by copywriters or SEOs. In both cases, you need to define rules to avoid over-optimization.

Let's exemplify with a set of rules for category descriptions:

- First, add links to other products in the parent category. Maximum products linked per 100 words is two.

- Second, add links to related categories. Maximum related categories linked per 100 words is two.

- Maximum consecutive anchor text links is two.

- Maximum number of links with the same anchor text is one (my personal preference).

- Minimum number of links per 100 words is two.

The above rules are just an example—you should customize based on your own circumstances.

Below is an example of decently safe internal linking:

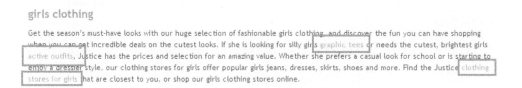

Figure 184 The text in the paragraph above flows naturally, and the anchors are natural.

Keyword-stuffed navigation and filtering

Some ecommerce websites try to enhance rankings for head terms, like category or subcategory names, by stuffing keyword-rich anchor text links in the primary navigation, similar to:

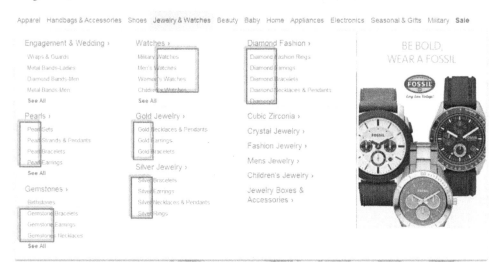

Figure 185 It is not necessary to repeat keywords over and over again in the navigation.

If your website architecture is properly built, search engines will be able to understand that if the category name is *Watches*, all the links/products found under it belong to the *Watches* category.

The same applies for other forms of navigation, such as faceted navigation.

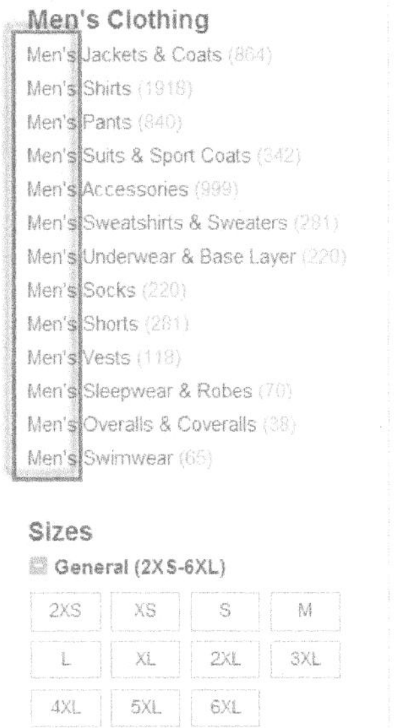

Figure 186 Use properly nested list items to help search engines understand categorization, so that you don't need to repeat the category name over and over again.

External link reinforcement

Because PageRank is a renewable metric, having external links to category and subcategory pages not only provides ranking authority to the target pages, but also increases the amount of PageRank that flows throughout your website.

It's not economically feasible to build links to individual product pages for ecommerce websites with large inventories. Therefore, the link-earning efforts should be focused on category and subcategory pages. Keep in mind that link development is complex and outside the scope of this book.

Focusing your link building towards just a few top-performing category pages is a good idea for new websites or websites with limited marketing budgets, but generally you need to diversify the targets. Once you build enough links to a category page, that page becomes a hub: it will pass link equity to subcategory and product pages downwards and upwards in the website hierarchy. The more hubs you build, the more natural your website will look and the more PageRank will flow throughout it.

Identify existing link hubs using Google Webmaster Tools, and use them to your advantage. Anytime you want to boost a new page, you can tap the power of the hubs. For example, let's say you find that the women's apparel subcategory is a hub. If you want to boost the women's sleepwear category, link to it from the hub page, contextually, from the main body content.

CHAPTER SIX

The Home Page

Of all the pages on a website, home pages usually have the highest authority. I say *usually* because the internal linking architecture can sometimes have issues—or other pages may receive more external links—and in such cases, those pages could have the highest internal authority.

Every department—including marketing, merchandising, information architecture, SEO, design and executive—wants a piece of the home page. Hence, home pages are often cluttered with links to tens or even hundreds of categories, calls to action, marketing banners, etc., making these types of pages unfriendly for users and for search engines.

The biggest advantage of home pages is that they pass a lot of authority downwards on the website taxonomy. Pages linked directly from the home page get more search engine love. Do you need a boost for a new product line? Link to it from the home page. It's a simple concept. If, for example, you want to increase authority for the most important, profitable or best converting cities/hotels you sell rooms in, then link from the home page.

Tip: If you want to push authority to categories or product pages but don't want to crowd the home page, add a *featured categories* section on the index page of the HTML site map.

Site map

Figure 187 *New Top Products* and *Top Ink Families* will create shorter crawler paths and send more authority.

Before getting into the details, remember that when optimizing home pages (and all other pages, for that matter) for search engines, it's highly important to balance SEO with user experience and business goals. Generally, you don't want too many links on the home page, and you want important links in prominent places. Also, the decision to add, remove and/or consolidate links on the home page needs to take users into account first, and only then accommodate search engines.

Let's identify the sections that appear most frequently on ecommerce home pages, and discuss SEO tactics specific to each:

- Logo (e.g., graphic logo, tag line).

- User account (e.g., register, sign in, my account and order tracking).

- Site personalization (e.g., country/currency selector, store locator).

- Search field.

- Primary navigation.

- Cart (shopping cart, checkout).

- Marketing area (e.g., sliders, promotional banners, featured products, top categories, most popular deals, brands, etc.).

- Promotional area (e.g., wish list, gifts).

- Help (e.g., FAQ, live chat, contact us, help center).

- Footer.

Primary navigation

Theoretically, any HTML link is a navigation element, but for our present purposes we'll refer to navigation in the context of primary (aka global) and secondary (aka local) menus that users click to browse items.

Primary navigation usually appears horizontally at the top of a web page, or sometimes vertically as a sidebar on the left side of the page. Primary navigation is easy to identify, as it consistently appears in the same position across the website.

The labels in primary navigation systems represent major groups of information and can be organized by departments, topics, top-level categories, target market, alphabetical order or other ways, depending on how the IA, marketing and usability team structures the website.

Figure 188 The label on Walmart's vertical primary navigation lists departments.

Figure 189 On this website, the horizontal primary navigation lists top-level categories.

Figure 190 On Crocs, the primary navigation is represented by the main target market segments.

Tip: Use vertical navigation when you have a lot of menu items and horizontal when you can fit all of the important topics at the top of the design.

Number of links in primary navigation

Displaying the primary navigation horizontally limits the number of links that can be placed at the top of the layout to between five and twelve, depending on how long the labels are. Don't worry, these are reasonable numbers for both users and search engines. A vertical navigation bar is more versatile and allows for more categories and subcategories.

On ecommerce websites, however, the primary navigation is often accompanied by sub-navigation menus such as dropdowns, fly-outs or mega menus, which can substantially increase the number of links on any given page. Usually triggered by mouse hover dropdown and fly-out menus present some substantial usability issues.[1] However, mega menus seem to perform better.[2]

Figure 191 The *Clothing* dropdown menu lists several topical links.

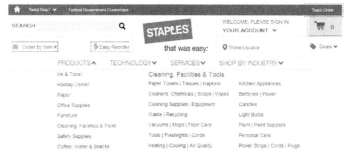

Figure 192 Mega menus can include more than just a list of links.

Figure 193 Staples handles dropdown menus in a more user-friendly manner. They gave up the standard mouse hover implementation; the sub-menu expands at click only. Additionally, notice the down arrow icon, which suggests the dropdown menu.

There isn't a hard limit on how many links to list in sub-menus. I recommend using as few or as many as make sense for users; don't think about SEO too much. Let me explain why you don't need to worry about the number of links in sub-menus.

Often, SEOs suggest limiting the number of links on a page (or removing them altogether) to send more PageRank to more important pages. And many times, this recommendation disregards user experience and usability. There is also a widely accepted SEO best practice that *all* menus have to be SEO friendly, meaning search engines should be able to crawl all the links in the menus. However, this is not totally true.

In practice, many ecommerce websites could actually benefit more from *not allowing* robots to crawl just about any link in sub-menus. No doubt you should present to users as many links as you want, but you can also make some of them *uncrawlable*.

This search engine "unfriendliness" can't be categorized as cloaking as long as it is not done for cloaking purposes. After all, even Amazon successfully uses this technique to push authority to products and categories listed in the body of the page:

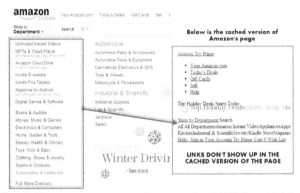

Figure 194 The *Shop by Department* mega menu has more than 100 links, which is useful for users to navigate the website, but the entire mega menu is uncrawlable for search engines.

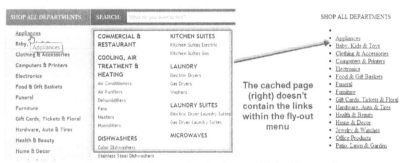

Figure 195 Other retailers in the top 100 do this as well.

Figure 196 Primary navigation links are cached, but sub-menu navigation links aren't.

Making links uncrawlable may sound strange and against SEO common sense, but it's a great way to balance usability and SEO: users get the info they need, and search engines only have access to prioritized links.

The number of links in the primary navigation also depends on how many categories and subcategories your taxonomy has. If you have only five top category pages, each with three to five subcategories, then you can list all of them (assuming that the rest of the page is not stuffed with other links). If you have twenty categories with 10 subcategories each, you need to give the primary navigation more consideration.

Another, more radical, technique for limiting the number of links in the navigation is to get rid of the sub-menus completely (no dropdowns, no mega menus, maybe just a *dropline menu*). Instead of linking to every subcategory, provide links to top categories only. Then provide links to relevant subcategories from within the top category.

Figure 197 Ann Taylor uses a *dropline menu* with carefully chosen labels.

Figure 198 Aéropostale uses a minimalist approach, with just four links in the primary navigation.

If you decide to keep a minimal number of links, make sure that the navigation helps users find content quickly and is not actually making their task more complex.

Going back to PageRank basics, we know that the more links on a page, the less authority flows through each link. Thinking in terms of user experience, the more cluttered a page is, the more complex content *findability*[3] is, and the higher *shopper anxiety*.[4] It therefore makes sense to reduce the number of options and improve user experience by minimizing *decision paralysis*.[5]

This is where click tracking/analysis plays an important role. You identify which links are helpful for users (using metrics such as the most-clicked links) and remove the ones that are not. If you have multiple links pointing to the same URL, you can decide either to leave only one link or to implement browser-side URL tracking parameters.

You have several tools at your disposal to track clicks and click paths. For example, Google Analytics allows visual click analysis with reports like *Visitor Flow* and *Behavior Flow* (under *Behavior → Behavior Flow):*

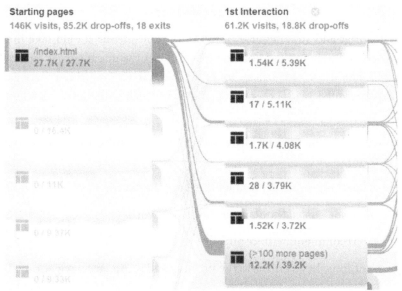

Figure 199 Google Analytics Visitor Flow report.

Using the *Navigation Summary* report under (*Behavior* → *Site Content* → *All Pages*), you get up to 500 data points that you can export and analyze further with Excel:

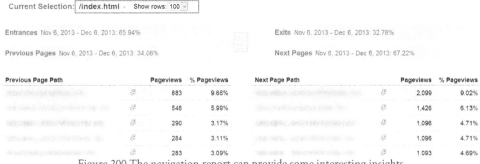

Figure 200 The navigation report can provide some interesting insights.

Other tools, such as CrazyEgg or ClickTale, can do click analysis as well, but no matter which tool you use, the goal is to identify links that can be either:

- Removed from the navigation or

- Consolidated into logical groups.

In many cases, home pages link to top-selling and high-margin products, categories or subcategories, and this is good for users and search engines. But you can easily consolidate the links to About Us, Contact Us, Terms of Use and Privacy pages.

I advise testing to see whether the uncrawlable links approach or the reduced number of links approach works best for you, as each website is different in its own vertical.

Navigation labels

The categories and subcategories listed in the sub-menus should take into account business goals and user testing. For example, if 20% of your categories generate 80% of the revenue, then those categories should be linked from the primary navigation. You should also experiment with other decision metrics, such as the most-searched terms on site search, the most-visited pages and so on.

Regarding the labels present in the navigation text links, there are two schools of thought in terms of SEO:

- The labels *should not* contain the target keyword.

- The labels *should* contain the target keyword.

What I can recommend with confidence is to:

- Not force keywords into the primary and secondary navigation labels.

- Focus on avoiding clever labeling;[6] this makes navigation easier for users to understand and enables them to find the information they want quickly and easily.

- Design the navigation to pass the trunk test[7]—make it very intuitive and use clear labels. SEO should not be the focus when labeling primary and secondary navigation.

Sometimes, keywords can show up in the navigation naturally. For example, if an ecommerce website sells musical instruments and wants to rank for the keyword "guitars", having the "guitars" label in navigation is natural and may help. There is an alternative for those who want to push longer keywords in the primary navigation menus: you can use images to design the menu with short text labels for users, while adding keywords (without spamming) in the alternate text of the images for search engines (or implementing image replacement[8]).

For example, the short labels in the image below ("shoes", "handbags", "watches", "jewelry" and "dresses") are image links:

Figure 201 Short labels allow people to scan them easily.

However, the alt text of each image label contains longer keywords:

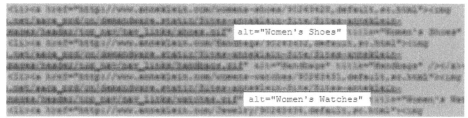

Figure 202 The end goal is to create navigation menus that meet user needs and reflect their behavior on the website.

Menu labels can represent a single category, but they can also represent multiple categories grouped into a single label. Whenever you group categories into a single label, you need to create separate URLs for each category. For example, if you group "Pharmacy", "Beauty" and "Health" into one label, as in the image below, you need to create a URL for the *Pharmacy* landing page, another for *Beauty* and another for *Health*.

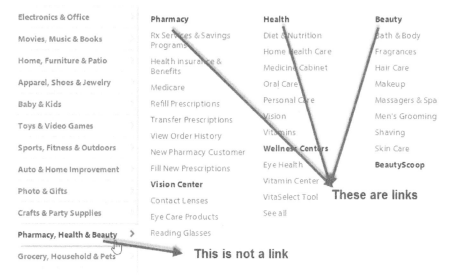

Figure 203 If you want to rank for "Pharmacy", "Health" or "Beauty" separately, you need separate category pages for each term.

Grouping categories works best when you plan a new website, or if the current website is fairly new and you can make changes easily. It can be more complicated to split URLs if your website has already been online for a while and you grouped categories under a single URL. In the latter case, one option is to leave the grouped category as is and create new pages for each subcategory in the group.

From primary navigation you should link to canonical categories. For example, if *Video Games* is cross-categorized in both *Games* and *Electronics*, and *Games* is the default category for *Video Games*, then the primary navigation should link to *Games* → *Video Games*. This creates short, unique crawl paths for search engine robots.

Search field

The internal site search on ecommerce websites is often enhanced with an autocomplete functionality that suggests items from a list of popular searches, or from product and category names. While autocomplete may be great for users, it is implemented with AJAX, and the suggested links are not accessible to search engines.

You can help improve findability for users and for search engines by adding plain HTML links to popular searches, directly under the search field. You will need to track internal site searches with your web analytics tool:

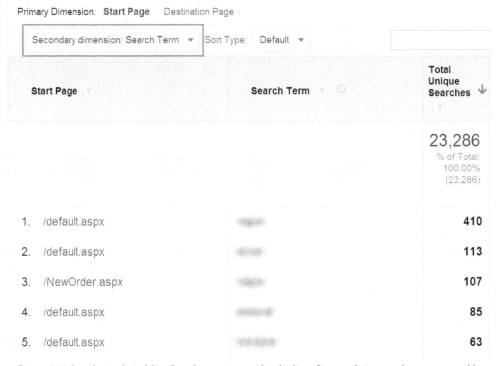

Figure 204 Google Analytics' Site Search report provides the list of internal site searches, segmented by Start Page, and the Search Term as a secondary dimension.

You can also add links to product attribute patterns (size, narrow, wide, etc.) or a link to a *popular searches* page:

Figure 205 The *Search By* links are entry points for search engines.

To improve the user experience, the popular searches vary from page to page, to match:

- Top searches performed on a page.

- Top products or categories visited immediately after landing on the page (using visitor flow data to identify those pages).

If you use the HTML *<label>* element for the search field, bear in mind that its content is indexable:

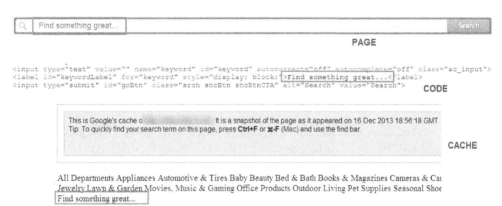

Figure 206 If you use the HTML *<label>* tag along with the *<input>* element, consider improving the wording. Instead of "finding something great", use something that's more relevant to users, e.g., "search for shoes" (or clothing, bags, etc.).

Tip: It is not a good idea to create HTML links for the search button, since search engines will unnecessarily try to crawl anything that looks like a link.

Figure 207 The above implementation creates an additional link to the root document. Avoid doing this.

Text content

Usually, home pages don't allow too much room for plain text content, so you find very few contextual text links going out from most home pages. Many ecommerce websites try to get around this challenge by adding text at the bottom of the page, somewhere close to the footer section, as exemplified on the next page:

LOOKING FOR OFFICE SUPPLIES? WORK WITH US.

At OfficeMax®, we have the office supplies you need to manage your workload and your day, so you can be at the front line of business. We're here to help you succeed with top, trusted brands of office products, technology and office furniture that deliver the performance and quality that you deserve.

From "green" office solutions to back-to-school essentials, we'll help you maintain a more organized office, classroom or home. Whether you shop online or in one of our 900+ office supply store locations, you'll find great deals on office supplies for your unique needs.

Discover how we can help you stay on budget and on schedule with our expansive office supply selection, and count on OfficeMax to be with you every step of the way. Work with us today.

OFFICE SUPPLIES

Take advantage of a wide variety of office supplies built to help you succeed—no matter what the job. Stock up on printer paper, file folders, calendars and planners, as well as a premium selection of pens, pencils and markers that deliver superior performance.

OFFICE TECHNOLOGY

Work more productively with office technology solutions equipped to help you stay ahead of the game. From affordable ink and toner to the latest software choices and brand name PCs to essential computer accessories, we have the latest technology to keep you moving forward.

OFFICE FURNITURE

Outfit your workspace with stylish office furniture that guarantees comfort and performance. Our ergonomic office chairs and functional desks come in a variety of shapes and sizes, so you'll quickly find reasonably-priced furniture options for any office type.

Figure 208 This is a common approach on many websites.

Some websites use CSS to position text sections such as the one above at the top of the source code, while the text is at the bottom of the page visually.

This might have worked in the past to overcome the 100Kb indexing limit, but nowadays you don't need it.

The so-called "text to code ratio" can be altered by using tabbed navigation or SEO-friendly carousels like the one below:

Top Selling Auto Accessories

Deflectors
Deflect and redirect the ambush of sticky bugs, flying debris and whipping winds with a custom-fit bug deflector or vent visor. With our huge selection of deflectors, rain guards, sunroof visors and more—plus name brands like WeatherTech, EGR and the famous AVS bug deflector, AutoAnything is your number-one source for deflection.

Car Covers
Once you park your prized ride—indoors or out—it's vulnerable to the bird squeeze, sun rays, dust & dirt seeking to smatter its paint. Stop fading, scratches and dings dead with indoor & outdoor car covers from AutoAnything. With a huge selection of Coverking & Covercraft car covers, and over 5,000 car covers reviews, finding the perfect Corvette car cover, or any car cover is easy.

Lights
Take your ride to the cutting-edge of style and light up the night with our brilliant selection of automotive lights. Featuring a full spectrum of Euro & led tail lights, replacement headlight bulbs, off-road lamps and more—plus the brightest names in the biz like Anzo headlights, Spyder headlights and PIAA lights—lighting up with AutoAnything is an illuminating experience.

Products for Top **Makes** and **Models**

Ford F-150 Accessories
Introduced way back in 1983, the Ford F-150 has become the undisputed king of trucks. And, with our vast selection of custom-fit Ford F150 seat covers, protective Ford F150 floor mats, more than one secure & stylish F150 bed cover, paint-protective F150 fender flares and much more, AutoAnything has become the undisputed king of Ford F150 accessories.

Chevy Silverado Accessories
Like a rock, standing arrow straight, your Chevy Silverado is the heartbeat of all your work & play activities. And, when it comes to Chevy Silverado accessories, AutoAnything is an American revolution—which makes us the place for sturdy step bars for Chevy Silverado, secure Silverado bed cover, a powerful Silverado exhaust system, custom Silverado seat covers and all your truckin' stuff.

Dodge Ram Accessories
In a world of Fords and Chevys, only one truck stands out from the crowd—the mighty Dodge Ram. And, in the world of Dodge Ram accessories, only one retailer stands out from the crowd—AutoAnything. With a huge selection of Dodge Ram floor mats, Dodge Ram seat covers, Dodge Ram running boards and a custom Dodge Ram brush guard, we help you put the 'tough' in Ram Tough!

Figure 209 Carousels will allow you to add much more text content. In the above image, not only that there's plenty of plain text for search engines but there are good internal links.

Another method for creating more contextual text links from a home page is to use *tabbed navigation*:

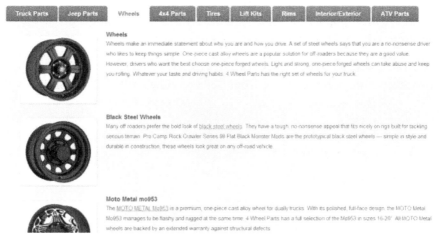

Figure 210 Using tabbed navigation, you can add a lot of plain text content in a relatively limited design space.

This is text content that search engines can read and analyze.

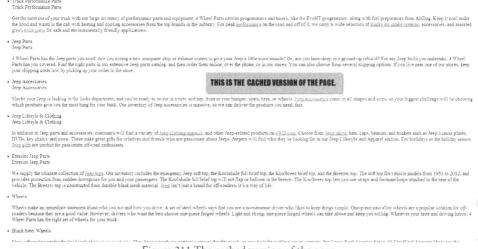

Figure 211 The cached version of the page.

If you want to add even more content, use the expand/collapse feature to show/hide more content, but remember not to fill that content with spam.[9]

If you decide to use tabbed navigation in the main body content, it's worth mentioning that users easily overlook tabs, so you need to provide strong design clues to help them understand that there is more content behind this type of navigation.

Marketing and merchandizing area

Sliders (aka *carousels*) and static banners are some of the most used marketing elements on home pages. Frequently used merchandizing sections are featured products, top categories, most popular deals, or brands. These areas are not controlled by SEOs, but many times there is nonetheless room for improvement.

While carousels seem to have several usability and conversion issues,[10, 11, 12] they are still present on ecommerce websites, from Dell and Hewlett Packard to SMBs:

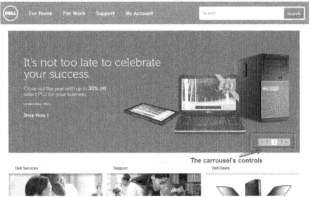

Figure 212 Carousels can pose some usability and conversion issues.

From an SEO perspective, there are usually two major issues with carousels:

1. The entire carousel is built with unfriendly JavaScript.

2. The text content and the links are embedded in images.

Unfriendly JavaScript

Custom-made carousels may use AJAX or JavaScript to dynamically populate content in the carousel, and that's when you can get into indexing issues. Carousels can be tested from an SEO point of view by placing them on a test domain, subdomain or page. Once Google crawls and caches the URL, analyze the cached version of the page. If you see something along the lines of "loading" or "waiting for content", or if the content of the carousel is totally missing, it means that the carousel's implementation prevents it from being indexed.

LOADING... LOADING...

Figure 213 The content of this carousel is not indexed.

If you want to send more authority to specific items and index the links in carousels, you have to correct the coding so their content gets crawled and indexed.

166

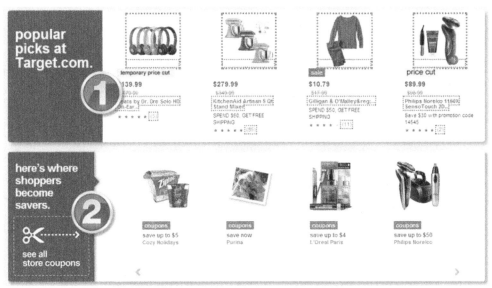

Figure 214 Neither section above is cached by search engines.

The items linked from section 1 above are nofollowed, which suggest that this online retailer doesn't want those links to be crawled and indexed. But the links inside section 2 *are* followed, which may suggest that those items are supposed to be indexed. However, section 2 is implemented with JavaScript, which blocks access to those URLs.

Embedded text and links

Use CSS positioning and image replacement whenever you can to overlay text on background images, or else create the carousels and featured banners with simple HTML:

Figure 215 This carousel on HP's home page is built mostly with CSS and HTML.

Figure 216 The text on the banner above (*complete your list with great holiday gifts*) is overlaid with CSS and HTML (it whitens out when selected in the browser).

If the imagery is more complex and you can't implement image replacement or simple CSS/HTML carousels, then use image alt attributes and *<area>* with *<map>* tags to create the links on calls to action.

For example, the image below embeds three call-to-action links:

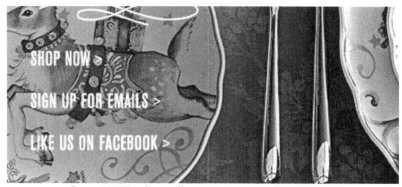

Figure 217 The three calls to action are actually area maps.

It deploys the HTML *<map>* element with three areas, each with its own alt text, to make the links clickable:

```
<map name="intl-hero">
  <area shape="rect" coords="0,305,200,349" href="http:/
  cm src=hphero&cm re=International- -Hero- -Email alt="Sign Up for Emails">
  <area shape="rect" coords="0,350,200,400" href="http:/
  Facebook" alt="Like Us on Facebook" class="newWindow">
  <area shape="rect" coords="0,0,989,518" href="http:/
  cm src=hphero&cm re=International- -Hero- -Twas The Night TTop" alt="Shop Now">
</map>
```

Figure 218 The HTML source code.

If you think about it, maps inside images make sense for ecommerce websites in many cases. For example, online apparel catalogs that feature complete model looks on product pages could allow clicks on the hat, the pants or any other piece of clothing depicted in that image, to send users directly to the product page.

You can improve image maps a bit with SEO-friendly tooltips and hot spots that expand at click. Notice the + and $ signs in the carousel below:

Figure 219 The two hotspots can be used to add more text content.

When you hover the cursor, the + and $ expand to provide more details:

Figure 220 The text in the + tooltip is indexable.

Since *<map>* and *<area>* are not very commonly used for SEO, here are a couple of tips:

- Every area element should have an alt attribute, even if it's empty (alt=""). The alt text should describe the image in 150 characters maximum. The alt text should not start with the word "copyright" or with the copyright symbol [© or (c)][13].

- Avoid Flash area maps.

- Use XML or text files for tooltips, to allow the SEO or the copywriter to make changes easily.

- If a particular AdWords ad you tested worked well, it may also help with the CTR on tooltip links (since ad titles are usually fewer than 25 characters).

Merchandizing areas

Products and categories linked from the merchandizing areas of the home page (e.g., the areas called *hot deals*, *best sellers*, *top brand*, etc.) receive higher internal link authority than structural links. This is why you can use these areas to push more SEO value to the products and categories that are the most important for your business.

The image below depicts *Hot Deals* and *Best Sellers* merchandizing areas:

Hot Deals
$399.99
$399.00
$649.99
$149.99
Best Sellers

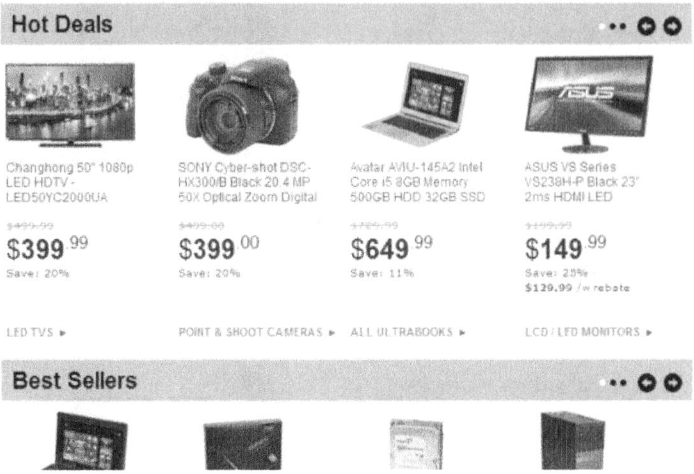

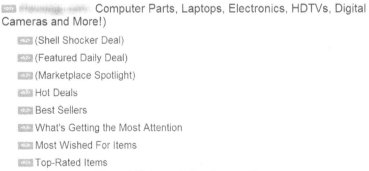

Figure 221 Merchandizing is a very common practice among online consumer electronics retailers.

Sometimes, the items listed in these areas are implemented with carousels (users will probably miss the black arrows and the dots that control the carousel in the above image). If you want the items to get PageRank authority, implement the carousel in an SEO-friendly way, as previously discussed. When you absolutely have to use AJAX to load the items, I recommend loading a default set of items in the first slide of the carousel (available in plain HTML) and loading the next ones with AJAX when the user clicks the controller buttons.

Here are some SEO tips to optimize the items listed in the merchandizing areas:

- It's not mandatory to wrap the merchandizing section name in an HTML heading, but it can be done. Since there will likely be more than one merchandizing area, I recommend using H2 (and above) headings. H1s are usually used on more important labels, and it is not best practice to have multiple H1s on the same page.

Computer Parts, Laptops, Electronics, HDTVs, Digital Cameras and More!)
(Shell Shocker Deal)
(Featured Daily Deal)
(Marketplace Spotlight)
Hot Deals
Best Sellers
What's Getting the Most Attention
Most Wished For Items
Top-Rated Items

Figure 222 A sample headings outline.

The product image thumbnails and the product names need to be optimized to send one consolidated signal to search engines (e.g., the image alt text and text anchor should be the same).

Figure 223 The image's alt text is the same as the anchor text.

▪ Add one to three links to manufacturers, brands or any other relevant attribute of the items, whenever you have the space to do so:

Figure 224 Amazon links to various subcategories from these areas.

▪ Avoid linking with generic anchor texts:

Figure 225 The *See Details* link in the image above is not optimal. It can either be removed completely or blocked from being crawled.

▪ Do you really need a "Buy Now", "Add to Cart" or "More Details" link on the items listed in these areas of the home page? Do visitors really add to cart directly from the home page? If not, consider either removing such strong CTAs all together or at least implementing them with uncrawlable links.

If you are keen on using add to cart buttons, implement them with either HTML *<button>* elements or JavaScript:

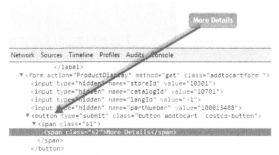

Figure 226 The "More Details" link is implemented as HTML *<button>* elements, so it won't be crawled.

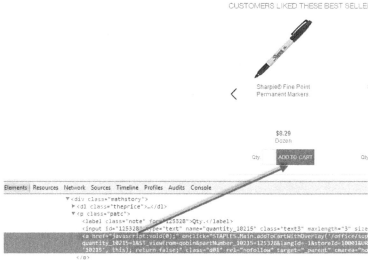

Figure 227 The "add to cart" link is implemented with JavaScript, which means it won't be followed by search engines.

- If you want to add even more content inside the merchandizing area, use the CSS expand/collapse features:

Figure 228 The "[+] more details" link displays more details about the product (note that I have added this link; it doesn't exist on the original website).

- Use alt text and image map areas for links whenever you use images to display promotional banners.

Logo

The vast majority of logos are implemented as images. Sometimes, the logos embed the company's tagline, slogan or unique selling proposition.

Alt text or image replacement?

There are online debates about how to implement logos properly, not only from an SEO point of view, but also as HTML markup. In terms of SEO, some argue that using the alt text on the logo image is enough; others recommend using image replacement techniques. In terms of HTML markup, some believe logos should be wrapped in H1, while others say it should be an H2, or have no heading at all.

No matter how you provide better context for a logo image (whether with alternate text or image replacement), that content won't provide a big lift in SERPs when it comes to competitive industries. For example, just because you use the primary keyword in the alt text of the logo (e.g. *SiteName - Digital Cameras*) doesn't mean that search engines will consider your website the online authority for digital cameras. It may help a bit, but not much.

If you can easily and safely implement image replacement for your logo, do it. Image replacement is not spam as long as you don't abuse it with keyword stuffing or other crazy stuff. *W3C* uses image replacement in their logo; *A List Apart* and *Smashing Magazine* do it too, and *MOZ* used it before their site redesign. But using alt text on the image logo will work, too.

That being said, let's look at a few options you can consider for the text describing the logo, whether it's implemented with alt text or image replacement:

1. Use just the company name (e.g., "Staples logo").

2. Use your company name plus two or three top categories (e.g., "Dell laptops, tablets and workstations").

3. Use dynamic text that includes the brand name plus category name—the text changes from one page to another. For example, on the *Home* page you use the alt text "Microsoft logo", but on the *Tablets* page you use the alt text "Microsoft logo – Tablets".

4. Use the company name plus the tagline/USP/slogan (e.g., "Walmart – Save Money. Live Better"). Ideally, the slogan is short, descriptive and contains some keywords.

Figure 229 Kohl's slogan.

5. Use the company name, followed by the company slogan in plain text:

Figure 230 HP's slogan clearly states the focus of the website and cleverly includes the keyword pattern "Printing Solutions". This improves relevance for keywords like "large format printing solutions", "commercial printing solutions" and "industrial printing solutions". Overall, this is a well thought out tagline.

I like implementing option #5 wherever possible, followed by #3, #2 and #1. In each case, the text has to be representative of the logo it describes and not be spammy.

You can provide context using the logo's alt text or with image replacement—both should be user friendly and ok for SEO as long as you don't spam. But there are also implementations that don't allow alternate text on logos (e.g., CSS backgrounds or CSS sprites).

Figure 231 Remember that the alt text on images is the equivalent of the anchor text on text links. In the above example, the alt text for the logo is missing, since the logo was implemented as a CSS background.

The logo should link using the home page's canonical URL to consolidate relevance signals. This ensures that internal reputation isn't split between multiple URLs. For example, don't link to the home page using both *index.php* and "/". Choose a canonical version (usually the root, "/") and link consistently through the entire website.

Semantic markup for logos

Google started[14] supporting schema.org markup for organization logos[15] in May 2013. This means that you can markup your HTML code to specify which image shows as the logo in the Google Knowledge Graph when someone searches for your brand name.

Simply wrap the logo using the Organization markup:[16]

```
<div itemscope itemtype="http://schema.org/Organization">

<a itemprop="url" href="http://www.example.com/">Home</a>

<img itemprop="logo" src="http://www.example.com/logo.png" />

</div>
```

This will help get more SERP real estate dedicated to your brand in the SERPs.

Should logos be wrapped in H1 or not?

Wrapping the logo in an H1 heading is highly contentious.[17] Additionally, the SEO influence of H1s is not significant enough.[18, 19]

My stance is that the logo should not be marked up with H1—or any other heading, for that matter. A heading is a textual element that should be marked up as text, while a logo is a branding image and should be marked up as an image.

Utility links

Site personalization, user account login, help and cart links can be labeled as what usability experts call *utilities* (Steve Krug[20]) or *courtesy navigation* (Jesse James Garret[21]) links.

Site personalization

These are the links used to personalize the shopping experience based on users' geolocation. Some of the best-known site personalization links are shipping destination, language and currency selectors:

Figure 232 Ship to country selector.

For example, someone vacationing in France can visit the Canadian website (.ca) to send a gourmet gift basket to their spouse in Canada. You identify the originating IP as French and decide to change (automatically or pop-up based) the ship-to country to France, the item currency to EUR and the website language to French. In our scenario, this would be wrong, so you need to give users the ability to change these settings.

Figure 233 The language is set to French, shipping destination is France and currency is EUR.

One of the common SEO mistakes with selectors such as *ship-to*, *language* and *currency* is that they create crawlable URLs (even if they are temporary 302 redirects). This happens because, in many cases, the user selection is kept in URLs:

```
<li class="current currency">
    <span>AUD</span>
</li>
                                    <li class="currency-GBP">
    <a href="http://www.                                                      ">GBP</a>
</li>
                        <li class="currency-CAD">
    <a href="http://www.                                                      ">CAD</a>
</li>
                        <li class="currency-USD">
    <a href="http://www.                                                      ">USD</a>
</li>
```

Figure 234 These crawlable URLs will create duplicate URLs for each page that has currency selectors.

The solution is straightforward: Don't create crawlable URLs for selectors, and keep user choices in cookies rather than URLs. Additionally, you can use AJAX to load the user choices and to set up the cookies.

Figure 235 When the "ship to" icon is clicked (top right), a modal window opens for users to make their selections. When "CONTINUE" is clicked, the choice updates are made using AJAX, and the users' choices are kept with cookies.

Store locator

These links are present in more or less prominent places in the page layout, depending on how important the web-to-store behavior is for each company. Sometimes, the link will be in the masthead, sometimes at the bottom.

Figure 236 Walmart puts a lot of emphasis on store locations.

Figure 237 The store locations don't seem too important to Nordstrom.

The *Store Locations* link positioned in the footer implies to a certain degree that the web-to-store traffic is not very important for Nordstrom. However, the mobile version of the same website displays the store location icon in the primary navigation:

Figure 238 The mobile version of Nordstrom's website.

The store locator link should *not* be nofollowed or otherwise blocked to search engines. The link should land users on a page that lists all store locations or that allows easy, quick location searches. Additionally, you should have a dedicated landing page for each store location and create a separate XML Sitemap for store location pages.

Cart links

These are the shopping cart and checkout links:

Figure 239 Most of the time, the shopping cart/bag icon is placed at the top right of the page. Amazon has trained shoppers to expect it here.

Perpetual mini-shopping[22] carts (called perpetual because they display the number of items in the cart while users navigate other parts of the website) are often implemented with AJAX and are not crawlable. That is fine because you don't need the shopping cart or checkout pages to be crawled or indexed.

Some prefer to nofollow these URLs as a way to preserve crawl budget. This won't hurt, but it is not necessary for SEO. Checkout pages can either be blocked in *robots.txt* or noindexed with meta robots at the page level.

Help links

These are the links to *Contact Us, FAQ, Live Chat, Help Center* and similar pages. If the *Live Chat* link is not JavaScripted, block it with *robots.txt*. Links such as *Help, FAQ and Contact Us* should be accessible to robots as plain HTML links.

You can consolidate many help links under a single menu (e.g., "Help") to list more links in a limited space:

Figure 240 The dropdown lists in the *Need Help?* section contains important links for users.

On many websites, these links also appear in the footer. If that's the case for you, implement the dropdown with "unfriendly" JavaScript so search engines don't find the same links twice.

User account links

These are links that allow users to perform actions such as creating or logging into their accounts, registering, tracking their order status, etc.:

```
# /robots.txt for Secure https://www-ssl.bestbuy.com

User-Agent: *
Disallow: /
```

Figure 241 Best Buy disallows the entire secure subdomain (https).

Usually, account links lead to secure (https) sections, and there is no need for search engines to index https pages (except when the entire website is secure).

You will notice that a lot of ecommerce websites nofollow the user account links:

Figure 242 Target nofollows several account pages.

Figure 243 OfficeMax does the same.

Google recommends leaving the nofollow off not only for account links but for all internal links.[23] This, they say, allows PageRank to flow freely throughout your website.

However, controlling the crawl, no matter how it's done (e.g., with nofollow, *robots.txt* or uncrawlable JavaScript) is tricky. Here's why:

- If you control crawling with *robots.txt*, PageRank *flows into* robotted URLs,[24, 25] but it *doesn't flow out* from those URLs.

- If you control crawling with nofollow, PageRank **doesn't flow into** the nofollowed URL,[26] but it **flows out** from the linked-to URL.

- If you control with uncrawlable links, then **no** PageRank **flows in**, but it **flows out**.

Do account pages give users any help if indexed by search engines? Do users really search for *My Account Login at {company_name}*? If not, is there any reason to have these pages indexed? If not, block access to them.

Paradoxically, if you want pages completely out of search engines' indices, you have to allow crawling (which means not blocking them with *robots.txt*) and add a noindex meta tag at page level.

If you're concerned about link juice flow, *robots.txt* might be a better crawl optimization alternative than nofollow. PageRank doesn't flow out of *robots.txt* blocked pages because Google is not able to crawl those pages to determine how PageRank should flow through each link. But if pages were indexed before being blocked by *robots.txt*, Google knows where and how to pass URLs. Theoretically, leaving those pages open for crawling once in a while until they get crawled should allow Google to crawl them temporarily and flow PageRank.

However, if you are not worried about the PageRank flow, there are a few alternatives to robotted and nofollowed account links.

- Consolidate links into groups and make them accessible with JavaScript:

Figure 244 The *Your Account* section (right) is a dropdown menu that consolidates several links.

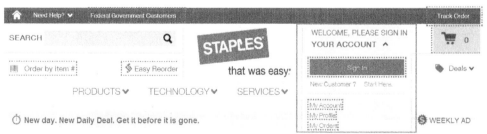

Figure 245 The account pages are accessible with JavaScript off.

- Deactivate some account links until the user signs in:

Figure 246 The above links (*Your Profile*, *Check Order Status*, etc.) are not active HTML links until you sign in.

Additionally, the *sign in | join for free | My Location* links are implemented with JavaScript and are not accessible to search engines:

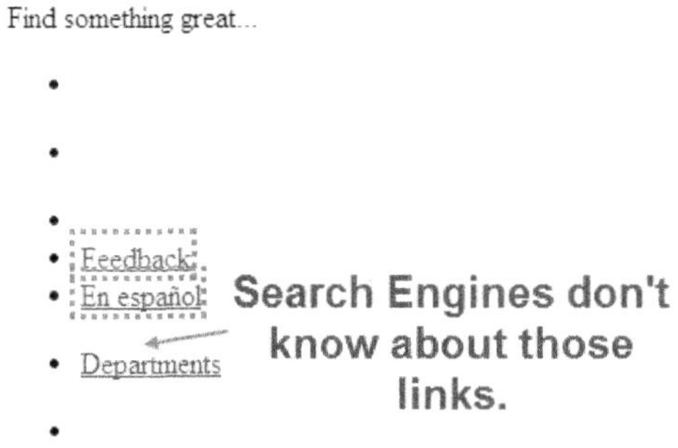

Find something great...

-
-
-
- Feedback
- En español **Search Engines don't**
- **know about those**
- Departments
- **links.**

Figure 247 Search engines can't find the links.

- Use modal windows to log in users:

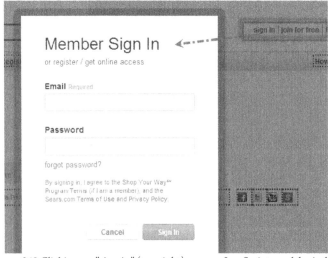

Figure 248 Clicking on "sign in" (top right) opens a JavaScript modal window.

Footers

Footers remain one of the most abused site-wide sections of websites. This is probably because footer links still work (at least for some websites), despite Google saying this strategy is not acceptable and doesn't work.

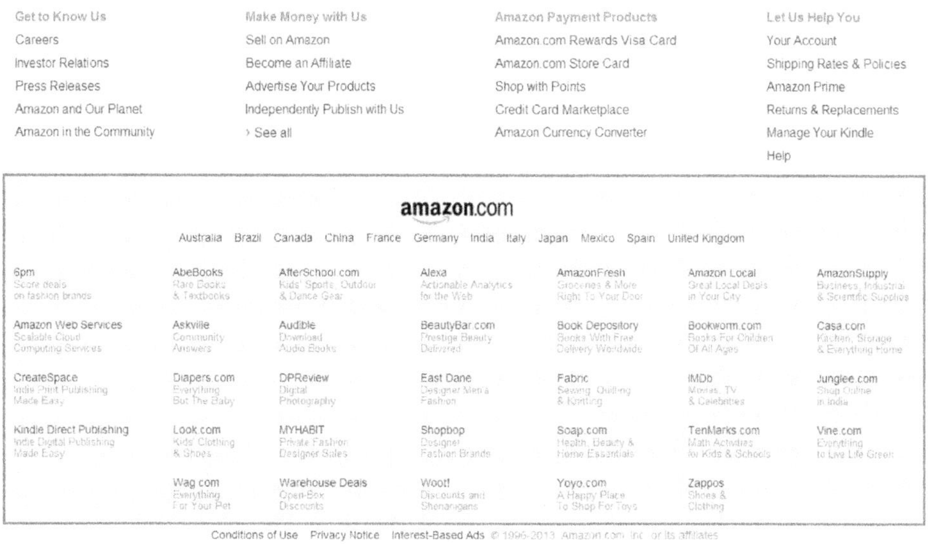

Figure 249 Look no further than Amazon to see risky use of keyword-rich footer links.

The footer is often the last section visitors check if they're unable to find the information they need anywhere else on the page. Frequently, they won't check the footer at all. It's thus important not to bury important links there.

Footers are usually implemented as boilerplate text and may send less link authority to the linked-to pages. Yahoo! has stated that they may devalue footer links:

> *"The irrelevant links at the bottom of a page, which will not be as valuable for a user, don't add to the quality of the user experience, so we don't account for those in our ranking."*[27]

Google sends contradictory signals to webmasters by (i) stating that site-wide links are outside their content quality guidelines, but at the same time (ii) not taking action against those who successfully spam with footer links.

Since footers are at the very bottom of web pages, the CTR on footer links is pretty low. However, footers can be great for user experience (this is why footers are a web design best practice), especially fat footers,[28] and they may be a pretty useful internal linking tool as well.

Let's discuss some ideas for improvement.

Don't repeat the primary navigation in the footer

If a link shows in the primary navigation or masthead, don't repeat it in the footer. The most important links for users should be somewhere in the masthead of the home page. Keep the footer for relevant but less important links.

Group links logically

If you want to reduce the number of links in the footer, consider consolidating multiple URLs in a single page. If space is a concern, you can implement JavaScript dropdowns:

Figure 250 Instead of creating unique URLs for each topic in the section "Your Orders", create just one main URL for "Your Orders" and include the content of all sections on that page (e.g., Order Status, Shipping & Handling, etc.).

Take a look at how Staples and YouTube handle this. Both are very good examples of footers:

Figure 251 The *Corporate Info* "drop-up" menu links to relevant pages, but it takes up less visual space.

- About Staples
- Corporate Responsibility
- Investor Information
- Media Information
- Community Relations
- STAPLES Center
- Accessibility Compliance
- Affiliate Program

- 20+ Employee Custom Program
- Federal Government Customers

- Shipping
- Return an Item
- Rebate Center
- Help Center
- My Account
- Request a Catalog

Figure 252 Staples leaves the links open for crawling.

Figure 253 The country listing is made available with AJAX only when the *Country* selector is clicked. Imagine if this list was available in plain HTML on every single page of the website.

Figure 254 The country links are not available to crawlers.

Walmart uses expand and collapse links to give users more subcategory options, but search engines don't have access to subcategory links:

Figure 255 A click on the small [+] signs opens us several subcategories.

While the top categories links (*Electronics, Bikes, Toys*, etc.) are crawlable, corresponding subcategories (*Laptops, Apple iPads, Tablets, TVs*) are not:

Figure 256 This approach combines user experience and SEO.

Remove useless links

Track clicks on the footer links either with parameters or with click tracking tools, such as CrazyEgg, to analyze whether users rely on those links. Are you really helping the user, or do you have an optimized footer just for search engines? If you find that people don't click on some links, or if you do not believe that a page is important, then don't link to it from the footer.

On the other hand, if a link in the footer gets a high number of clicks, consider placing it in a more prominent location on the page. Test having versus removing the links in the footer and measure how each affects conversions rates, SEO or usability.

Don't abuse them

We know for a fact that search engines don't like external site-wide footer backlinks.[29] Search engines also treat links in boilerplate sections differently from contextual links (the former don't pass as much link authority).

Footer links are not inherently bad; in fact, it may not be the links that cause problems, but the general abuse of footers.

women's boots
women's boots
women's casual boots
women's sandals
women's dress sandals
women's flip flops
women's casual shoes
women's casual shoes
women's casual flats
women's dress shoes
women's dress shoes
women's dress pumps
men's boots
men's boots
men's outdoor boots
men's sandals
men's sandals
men's casual sandals
men's flip flops
men's casual shoes
men's casual shoes
men's boat shoes
men's dress shoes
men's dress shoes
men's dress boots
boys' shoes
boys' dress shoes
boys' casual shoes
boys' sandals
girls' shoes
girls' dress shoes
girls' casual shoes
girls' sandals
kids' shoes
kids' shoes
infant shoes
toddler shoes
youth shoes
top brands
Crocs shoes
Naturalizer shoes
Volatile shoes
Steve Madden shoes
Easy Spirit shoes
Ecco shoes
Keen shoes
Anne Klein shoes
Merrell shoes
Clarks shoes
shoe size
women's wide shoes
women's narrow shoes
men's wide shoes
men's narrow shoes

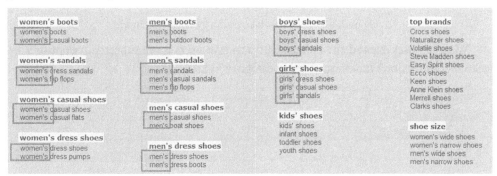

Figure 257 Footers seem to be one of the preferred sections for over-optimization. The extensive use of "women's" and "men's" here is totally unnecessary.

If you stuff exact anchor text keywords in the footer just because doing so still works, mind the Penguin penalty that may come with that strategy (see pointer number one in this video,[30] and see this comment[31]).

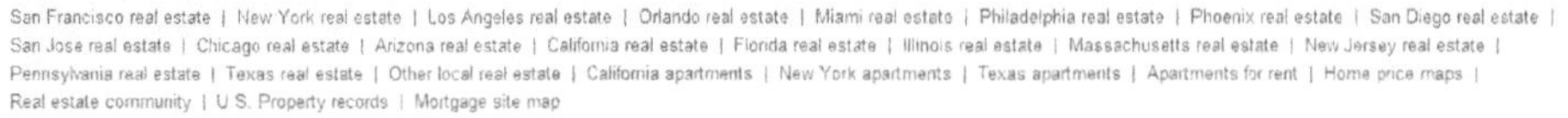

Residential Real Estate
San Francisco real estate | New York real estate | Los Angeles real estate | Orlando real estate | Miami real estate | Philadelphia real estate | Phoenix real estate | San Diego real estate |
San Jose real estate | Chicago real estate | Arizona real estate | California real estate | Florida real estate | Illinois real estate | Massachusetts real estate | New Jersey real estate |
Pennsylvania real estate | Texas real estate | Other local real estate | California apartments | New York apartments | Texas apartments | Apartments for rent | Home price maps |
Real estate community | U S. Property records | Mortgage site map

Figure 258 Site-wide links with exact anchor text across large websites will create problems

Another trick you must avoid is placing "SEO content" far below the footer, well below the "normal" view area. Maybe Google won't be able to penalize you algorithmically if you do this, but the ruse certainly won't pass a manual review.

Figure 259 The "SEO content" starts after the real footer ends, which is a foolish attempt to trick users. I wonder whether that's why this website has a gray toolbar PageRank.

Tabbed navigation

If you need to give users more links in the footer, tabbed navigation is another option:

Figure 260 Tabbed navigation will allow you to display more links.

Tabbed navigation can be further optimized by adding even more text in the footer. Take a look at how 1-800 Contacts does this:

Figure 261 Each link on the left side triggers a new slide.

Take a look at the *Our Commitment* tab:

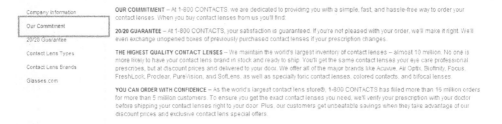

Figure 262 This is good content for a footer. Adding a few internal contextual text links would bring even more SEO value to this section.

Dynamic footers

Ecommerce websites can make the footers more appealing to search engines by dynamically updating the content and links in footers to be relevant to each section of the website (and even to each page). This approach works best when implemented with tabbed navigation that allows at least 150 words of content to be displayed in the footer.

Consider the same example from 1-800 Contacts. They could add a new tab to the page where the footer is displayed, featuring a relevant excerpt from a recent blog post. For example, on the *Avaira* brand page, the new tab's name could be something like *Avaira News,* and the blog post excerpt would contain the brand's name and, eventually, one or two linked Avaira products. The footer on the *Biomedics* brand page would be related to Biomedics products, and so on.

Just as properly related linking is helpful for users, adding page-specific links in the footer is also good for usability, as it customizes the shopping experience to meet users' expectations. You can even customize the links in the tabbed navigation. For example, on a product details page for Avaira lenses, you can dynamically change the link from "Contact Lens Brands" to "Avaira Contact Lenses" and list only products manufactured by Avaira.

Dynamic footers make sense if you keep in mind users' intent. These footers will not only help users by presenting content relevant to the page they are on, but will also help with varying the internal anchor text, thus reducing the occurrences of exact match anchor text and preventing the footer from generating site-wide links.

Currently, ecommerce websites don't use this concept. During the past 20+ years, footers—as compared to other areas of a page—have not evolved into something more helpful for users.

In terms of SEO, just imagine being able to link contextually and more relevantly from your footers.

Debugging and support

Footers are also valuable as debugging, development or customer-support features.

Tagging footers with unique text containing the year and month the page was last generated/updated (e.g., "page generated January 2015") will allow some basic crawl debugging a month or two later with a *site:mysite "page generated January 2015"* search.[32]

CHAPTER SEVEN

Listing Pages (Department, Category and Subcategory Pages)

Those involved in ecommerce in one way or another refer to product detail pages (also known as PDPs) as the "money pages". This seems to imply that many view PDPs as the most important pages for ecommerce. Because of this mindset, often the PDPs *do* get the most attention, at the expense of the listing pages: departments, categories and subcategories.

However, the listing pages are, in fact, the hubs for ecommerce websites, and have the ability to collect and pass the most equity to lower levels in the website hierarchy. Also, link development for ecommerce usually focuses on category and subcategory pages, not on PDPs.

Listing pages display a set of items, usually styled in a grid or a list. Sometimes, these pages are referred to as *product listing pages*, but this is inaccurate because they can actually list various types of items, such as categories, subcategories, products, cities, services, etc.

Two types of listings

Category and subcategory pages usually list one of two types of items on ecommerce websites:

1. *Products*, which are items belonging to the currently viewed category.

2. *Subcategories* under the currently viewed category or department.

Product listings

Product grids/lists usually display thumbnail images for all the items categorized in a certain category or subcategory. This means that all items listed there share a common *parent* in the hierarchy:

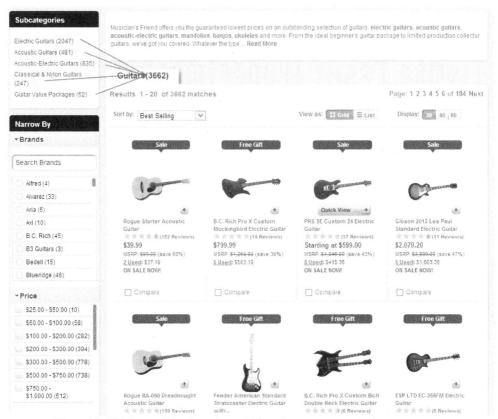

Figure 263 This is a traditional product grid found on category and subcategory pages.

The product grid/list approach has the advantage of sending more authority directly to the products in the list (especially for those on the first results page). However, these listings can give too many options to users, who may have to sift through hundreds or thousands of products:

Figure 264 Showing the entire list of products belonging to a top-level category often won't make sense to users. They need guidance in choosing a product, and thousands of items is too much and too generic.

Next, I will list some recommendations for optimizing product listings.

1. Deploy an improved SEO Quick View/Look functionality

Use this feature to provide even more content for users and search engines. This functionality is usually implemented with modal windows to quickly provide product summary information without going to the actual product detail page:

Figure 265 A click on "QUICK LOOK" brings up the overlaying modal window to the right, which can lead to a better shopping experience for users.

To make this functionality work to your advantage, implement it with SEO-friendly JavaScript whenever possible. For example, you can deliver more crawlable content by loading the static product description content in the source code but only displaying it on the browser when *Quick View* is clicked. Dynamic information (e.g., product availability, available colors, pricing) can be AJAXed.

Just as with any other method that displays content to users only at certain browser events, it's wise not to abuse "Quick Look". This means that the content should be super-relevant and brief (50 to 150 words for the product description is probably more than enough), and the internal linking should not go overboard (three to five links in the product description is enough). Also, you may want to consider the number of items you load in the default view (the one that gets cached by search engines). If you load 20 products, each with 100-word descriptions, that's already 2,000 words of content for that page. If you load 50, that's 5,000 words, which may be too much.

2. Create and improve internal algorithms to optimally display items in the grid/list

SEO is about increasing profits from organic traffic by optimizing for users coming from search engines. If a user lands on a category page and the first items in the grid don't generate enough profits, then you are missing opportunities. If you are a large retailer who owns a large set of data about your products, it's time to come up with your own product grid algorithm.

You may use an algorithm that assigns a *product rank* to each and every item, to organize products in the grid. The algorithm doesn't have to be complex. It can take into account a few different metrics—for example, percentage margin, sales statistics, stock availability and hand-picked items. The idea is to put the profit-maximizing items first in the grid/list.

Most sites have the *best-selling* or *most popular* items as the default view in the product grid, which is good for usability because most customers will be looking for the bestsellers. [1] But that doesn't mean you shouldn't try to optimize profits by experimenting with your own "custom" view listing that displays at the top the products most important to you.

3. *Add category-specific content*

Adding content to product listings can increase the chances of showing up higher in search result pages. This can apply to subcategory listings as well.

You are probably familiar with "SEO content" for category descriptions; many ecommerce websites have it nowadays, usually at the bottom of the page:

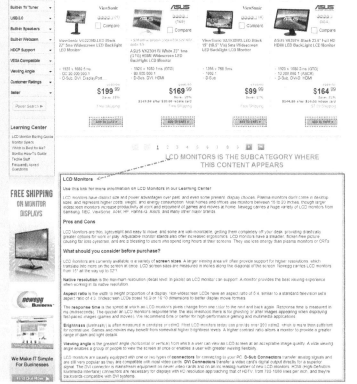

Figure 266 The "SEO" content here is displayed after the product grid, and its SEO influence could probably be improved by adding links to several internal pages.

Do you wonder whether this works for Newegg?

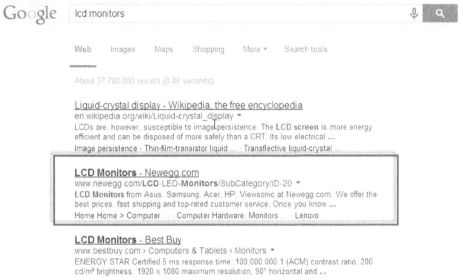

Figure 267 They rank #2 for "LCD monitors", above Best Buy.

Some websites prefer to place content above the listing, but this doesn't allow for much copy, as it will push down the listing:

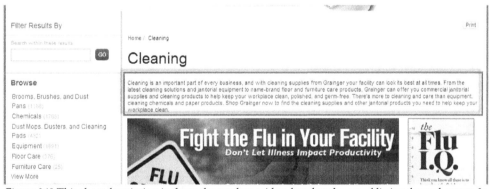

Figure 268 This short description is above the product grid and pushes the actual listing down the page. In this particular case, the description is not too long, but the marketing banners push the product grid even further down. Maybe an A/B test would clarify whether the banner should be there or not.

There's no question that more text content can help with SEO. But adding too much content above the products grid/listing can push the products below the fold, which can in turn confuse users and negatively affect conversion rates. On the other hand, putting the content below the product grid may not be as helpful—for SEO or for users—as having the content at the top of the page.

There are a few techniques to address this issue (e.g., collapse/expand more content at click or use JavaScript sliders). However, I find SEO-friendly **tabbed navigation** one of the most elegant solutions (for both the user and the search engine) to fit a lot of content at the top of the page—all within a limited amount of space and without being spammy.

Let's compare "before and after tabbed navigation" screenshots. This is how an older implementation looked on REI (without tabbed navigation):

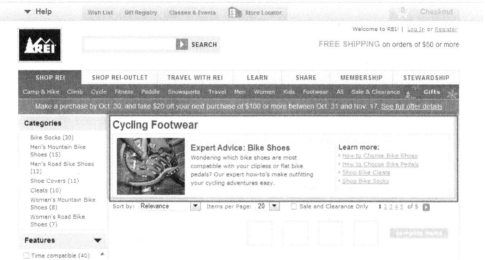

Figure 269 Notice how content at the top pushes the listing down the page?

And this is how the tabbed navigation version looks:

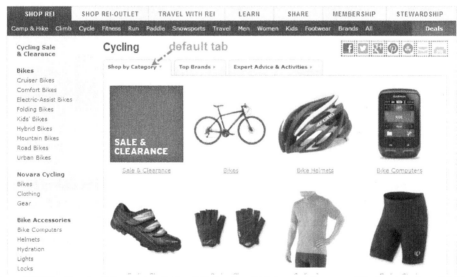

Figure 270 The *Shop by Category* view is the default tab, which is great for users. The last tab, *Expert Advice & Activities*, holds a whole lot of SEO value (see next image).

Figure 271 The above is not only well-written content, keeping users and conversion in mind (almost no SEO focus), but also "food" for search engines.

The content focuses on users rather than search engines (REI could probably easily add one or two contextual text links to thematically related subcategories or products to push some SEO equity to them). This type of content targets visitors at various buying stages and will move them further into the conversion funnel, which is great. It will also increase the category's chances of ranking better in SERPs.

The lesson here is that whatever content is placed in the tabbed navigation, it should be useful and not boilerplate text. As I mentioned before, ecommerce websites have to become content publishers (static and/or interactive) if they want to succeed in the long run.

In addition to the great content wrapped in this tab, REI added even more content at the bottom of the subcategories grid, outside the tabbed navigation:

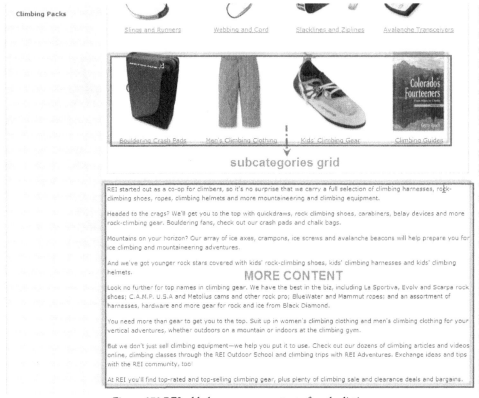

Figure 272 REI added even more content after the listing.

One great implementation of content at the bottom of the listing grid is on The Home Depot's website as depicted on the next page.

They placed buying guides, project guides and category-related community content, which is great (by this I mean really useful) for users. It would be interesting to test the effects on conversions if this type of content was moved up in the layout, to just above the product grid. This is a win-win tactic because:

- Users will get helpful content to assist with their needs and questions.

- Search engines will also love such content.

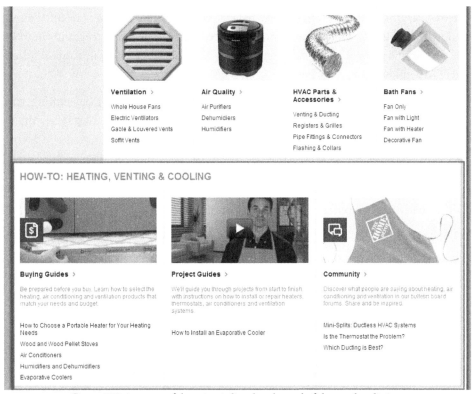

Figure 273 A very useful section is listed at the end of the product listing.

Another option for adding more content to category pages is to present a link/button to more content *above* the listing:

Figure 274 When users click on the *View Guide* button (top right), they are taken to another page. The guide is pretty long, but it doesn't add any content to the listing page itself.

However, instead of opening a new page at click, a better option is to open a modal window that contains an excerpt from the guide. Preload the text excerpt in the HTML code so that it's accessible to search engines. The modal window will contain a link to the HTML guide.

Creating content (especially interactive tools) is time and resource consuming, so you need to identify the top-performing or best-margin categories to start with, then gradually proceed to others.

4. Capitalize on UGC for categories

User generated content is a highly valuable SEO asset. Let's take a look at two types of UGC that you can implement on listing pages:

Product reviews

Adding relevant product reviews can influence conversion rates and search engine rankings:

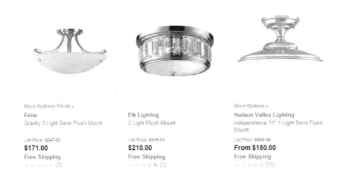

Figure 275 Ideally, the reviews are for the products in the listing.

If the listing is paginated, the reviews should be listed on the index page and should not be repeated on component (paginated) pages. If you have enough reviews to populate pages 2-N of the series, then do it. However, you may want to consider increasing the number of reviews you list on the index page (e.g., instead of listing three reviews, increase to five or 10).

You need to create rules to avoid duplicate content issues. For example, do not display more than two reviews for the same product on the same page, or display only five reviews on the same listing page and so on.

Forum posts

Community content such as forum posts can be handy not only in the Forum section of the website (if you have one) but on category pages as well:

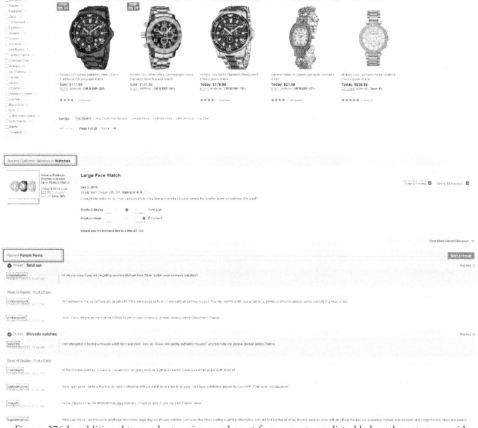

Figure 276 In additional to product reviews, relevant forum posts are listed below the category grid. Unfortunately, users need to scroll several thousand pixels to view this content, due to a very long vertical secondary navigation (not shown in the screenshot).

5. *Optimize for better SERP snippets*

Category pages get rich snippets in Google search result pages:

RUNNING Shoes @ ASICS

www.asics.com.au › Footwear ▾

40+ items	Our Footwear contains some of the most advanced technology ...

| Gel-Kayano 19. | Kayano 19 - As it approaches its 20th birthday, the ASICS ... |
| Gt-3000. | The GT-3000 continues on from its predecessor (the GEL ... |

Figure 277 Sometimes, Google displays only the number of items in the listing; other times, it displays a few item names as well.

Google's official recommendations don't go into much detail:[2]

"If a search result consists mostly of a structured list, like a table or series of bullets, we'll show a list of three relevant rows or items underneath the result in a bulleted format. The snippet will also show an approximate count of the total number of rows or items on the page (for example, "30+ items" in the screenshot below)."

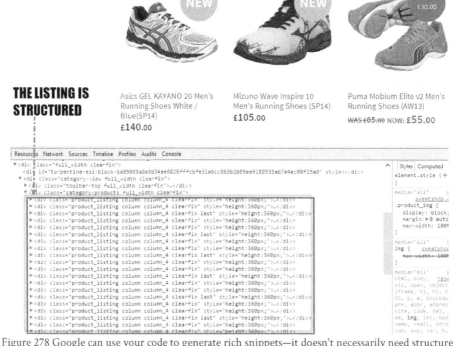

Figure 278 Google can use your code to generate rich snippets—it doesn't necessarily need structured markup such as Schema.org. That's why it's important to keep your code clean and well structured.

Keep in mind that if your category URLs show up in SERPs with rich snippets that contain item names, the meta description of the category page becomes shorter—to one line of text instead of two or three. You may want to check the impact on SERP CTR.

Here are some tips on how to get rich snippets for category listings:

Valid HTML code in the grid/list

If you open a *<li>* element but don't close it, or if you nest elements improperly, it will be more difficult for Google to understand the page structure.

Figure 279 Each product in the grid is wrapped in a *<li>* element that is properly closed. Also, notice the *DIV* and *UL* class names.

No breaks in HTML tables

The SERP rich snippet will display the number of items on the index page (e.g., "20+ items") if the product grid contains 20+ items in a table, but only as long as the table markup has no break. If something in between items 10 and 11 breaks the table, Google will instead display the message "10+ items" in the SERPs. If you list your products in multiple tables, Google will choose to display the count from only one of them.

6. Use suggestive HTML class names

It's been reported[3] that using the class name "item" in the item's DIV helps:

"Just to confirm, wrapped a few items in <div class=items> and the snippet has been updated. Took four days to appear in the SERPs..."

The above advice seems to be working, at least to some extent, as you can see on the next page.

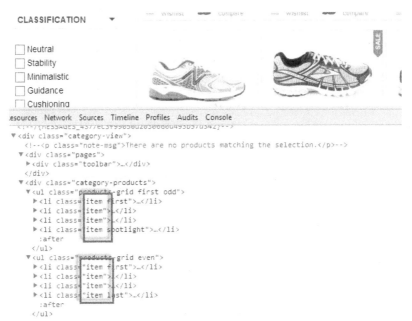

Figure 280 The *DIV* that wraps the product grid contains the word "products" (this seems to be common among websites that get rich snippets), and the *LI* contains the word "item".

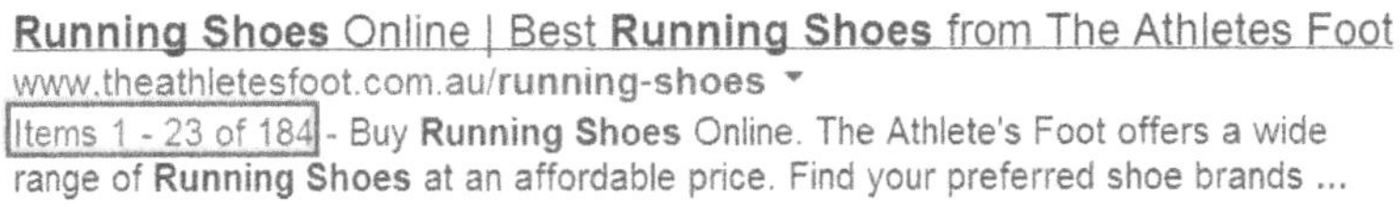

Running Shoes Online | Best **Running Shoes** from The Athletes Foot
www.theathletesfoot.com.au/running-shoes ▾
Items 1 - 23 of 184 - Buy **Running Shoes** Online. The Athlete's Foot offers a wide range of **Running Shoes** at an affordable price. Find your preferred shoe brands ...

Figure 281 The rich snippet for the shoes page.

A larger total of items in the list may attract more clicks (large selection is one of the things consumers look at when choosing where to click). This brings us to another optimization idea.

7. Reconsider the number of items in the listing

If the number of products within the currently viewed category is reasonably low and easily skimmable (e.g., 50 items in a grid of five rows by 10 columns), then load them all on one page. Depending on how many other links you have on the page and your overall domain's authority, you can sometimes pump up this number to 100 or even more.

If you think it's necessary from a user experience perspective, you can load 50/100/150 items in the source code in an SEO-friendly way, and use AJAX to display only 10/15/20 items, to avoid information overload. You can then use AJAX to update the page content based on users' requests (scroll, sort, display all, etc.).

If you have hundreds or thousands of products under the same category, consider breaking them into more manageable subcategories. You can list the subcategories instead of products after segmenting into smaller chunks.

8. Tag product reviews with structured markup

While product markup on category pages is not yet supported by search engines, it's easy to apply the markup to product listings as well if you already use a vocabulary like Schema.org to mark up product reviews on the product details page:

Figure 282 Product reviews are (or should be) displayed on listing pages.

To learn more about Schema.org product markup, visit this page.[4]

9. Add category related searches below the search field

Related searches sections have traditionally been used to link internally to other pages. Some websites still use them that way:

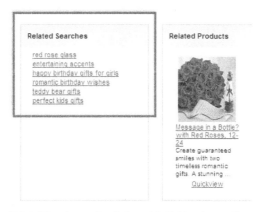

Figure 283 The *Related Searches* section helps with linking internally to other pages.

Related searches sections are there to help users find other items of interest to them. In this case, why not place them closer to where users will perform a search, such as the search field?

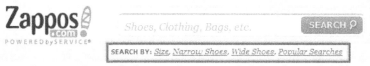
Figure 284 Zappos displays search options right below the search field.

The *Search by* links are placed prominently to push authority to the linked pages and to help users. However, the links are the same on every page, and they don't really make sense on the Bags section of the website:

Figure 285 *Size, Narrow Shoes* and *Wide Shoes* are not really useful for someone looking for bags.

Instead, you can change those links to something related to bags, maybe *Style* or *Lifestyle*.

If you don't want to use too much space to list 10 or more related popular searches, you can implement a modal window that opens at click on "Popular Searches". (Make sure its content is available to search engines.) You can list as many popular related keywords for each category as you like in this window:

Figure 286 The above is a possible implementation of popular searches with a modal window.

As mentioned in the previous chapter about home pages, you can use one of the following sources to identify searches helpful to users:

- Top searches performed on each category page.

- Products or subcategories most visited after viewing the category page.

- Whenever possible, top referring keywords (because Google and other commercial search engines hide search queries behind the "not provided" label, this is challenging).

10. Defer product/category thumbnail image loading

When you load tens of items in a listing, chances are that many of them will be *below the fold*.[5] Loading all thumbnail images at once is neither necessary nor recommended. Load only when the user scrolls down to view more products.

While image deferring has not been correlated with SEO rankings (as opposed to *Time To First Byte*, which shows a strong correlation with rankings[6]), it will help lower bandwidth and improve user experience.

Figure 287 Notice the scrollbar at the right. The products in the screenshot are several thousand pixels "below the fold".

A word of caution. The "fold" has a very clear meaning in print media (i.e., the physical fold of the newspaper is right at the middle), but with websites the meaning of "fold" is blurry. You will need to define and identify where the "fold" is for your websites, taking into account the browser resolution and the devices used by most of your users.

11. Remove or consolidate unnecessary links

Product grids often pose the issue of redundant links. For example, there's an image link on the product thumbnail image and another link on the product name, both pointing to the same URL.

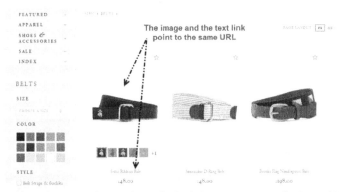

Figure 288 To address this issue, please refer to the *Link Position* section in the *Internal Linking* chapter.

Another issue very similar to the thumbnail-product name redundancy occurs when you place a link on the review stars and on the text link displaying the number of reviews for the same product:

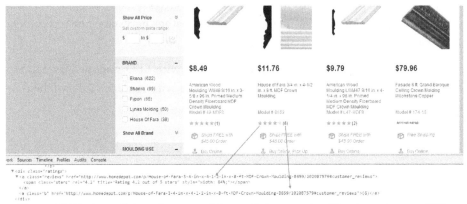

Figure 289 The image link on the stars and the text link on number "6" point to the same URL.

In this particular case—where both links can't provide strong relevance clues to search engines due to the lack of anchor text—you can keep only one link. I would keep the link on the star images, because you can add some more meaningful anchor text to the alt text, and because the link area on those star images is larger than the text numbers. The link on the number of reviews could eventually be JavaScripted.

Removing unnecessary links/elements can de-clutter the design, provide more white spacing between products and reduce the number of links that leak authority to the wrong pages:

Figure 290 It's unnecessary to display the *Special Offers* section for each product. JavaScript hovers can reveal the offer; small icons on thumbnail images are better alternatives.

Another element frequently listed in product grids is the "add to cart" button. Mind that I am not saying you should remove it without a proper analysis (and then follow up with an A/B test to see how it influenced conversion rate).

What I am suggesting is to track "add to cart" events and analyze whether users really add to cart directly from product listings. If they do, go a step further and see what type of users do that (e.g., returning customers, first timers, etc.). In many cases, those who add directly from product listings are return customers who are very familiar with your brand and with how your website works, and know exactly what they want. If you decide to remove the "add to cart" buttons, these users will know they can also add products to their cart from product details pages.

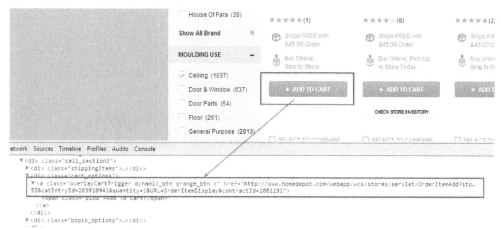

Figure 291 The usefulness of the "add to cart" buttons on product listings has to be tested. Test replacing them with other CTAs, adding more product details or removing the buttons altogether.

12. Make the listing view the default view

Usually, the list view allows more room for product-related content, which is useful for users and search engines.

Figure 292 This is the grid view. There's room to feature the name and price only.

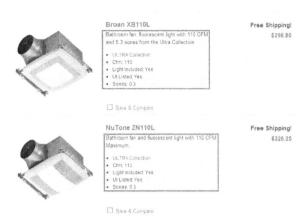

Figure 293 This is the list view. Products have more text details.

In this example, the list view is the default view for users and search engines. Users have the option to switch to *grid view* in the interface.

At the beginning of the chapter, we mentioned that there are two types of listings. Until now, we've discussed product listings. Let's talk about the second type.

Subcategory listings

Subcategory listing means that instead of listing products, you list subcategories. Generally, subcategory listings are implemented for the first two levels of categorization for categories containing a large number of items.

Let's look at how Home Depot implemented the subcategories grid in a user-friendly and search engine-friendly manner:

Figure 294 The first level in the ecommerce hierarchy, *Appliances*, lists several subcategory thumbnails (*Refrigerators, Ranges, Washers*, etc.), as well as subcategory links (e.g., for *Refrigerators* they list *French Door Refrigerators, Top Freezer Refrigerators, Side By Side Refrigerators*, etc.).

When you click on *Refrigerators*, another subcategory listing is displayed:

Figure 295 This is the third level in the hierarchy (*Appliances > Refrigeration > Refrigerators*), and it still lists subcategories instead of products. This encourages users to take a more deliberate selection path before the page displays tens or hundreds of products.

Implementing the first or the first two levels of the ecommerce hierarchy as subcategory listings has the advantages of:

- Sending more PageRank to subcategory pages. This is better than sending more PageRank to just a few products, because your link development efforts should point to category and subcategory pages (it is not economically feasible to target product pages with link building, unless you have either a large budget or only a few products in the catalog). This builds equity into category and subcategory pages, which then flows to item pages.

- Making a better user experience. Usability tests have shown[7] that users can be encouraged to navigate deeper into the hierarchy and make better scope selections.

The choice between product and subcategory listing on the first one to two levels of the hierarchy is particular to the conditions of each website, but usually subcategory listings are a better choice (especially for websites with large inventories). Deciding which subcategories to feature at which level of the hierarchy should be based on business rules (e.g., top five subcategories with highest margins, or top five bestsellers).

Here are several recommendations on how to build better subcategory listing pages:

1. To send some SEO love directly to products, add a list of featured/top items at the bottom of the listing:

Figure 296 Don't list too many products; five to 10 should be enough.

2. Keep the left sidebar navigation available to users (that is the spot we've been trained to look to for secondary navigation; this navigation pattern influences conversions[8]).

3. Display professional subcategory thumbnails, as exemplified on the next page.

Figure 297 Secondary navigation links are easier to scan and choose from. The secondary navigation won't contain filters until a user reaches the point where you list products instead of subcategories.

4. Add a brief description of the category whenever possible, and eventually link to buying guides or interactive product-finder tools that may help users decide which product is right for them. This is especially important if your target market is not familiar with the items you sell.

Figure 298 A brief description of each category may help first-time buyers understand your terminology and can provide more context for search engines.

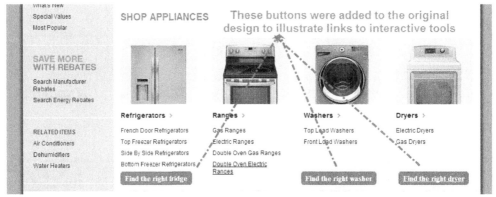

Figure 299 The original design doesn't include the CTA buttons along the bottom, but such links can be of great value to users.

5. Use an SEO-friendly *Quick View* functionality to add more details about each category.

Just as this functionality works on product grids, a similar approach can be implemented for subcategory listings to provide more information about each subcategory:

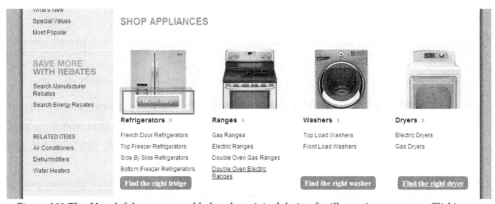

Figure 300 The *More Info* button was added to the original design for illustration purposes. Clicking on *More Info* opens a modal window.

In the modal windows, you can include details such as a brief explanation of the category (which can eventually be an excerpt from the subcategory description), what users can expect to find under this category, links to more subsequent subcategories in the hierarchy, and even FAQs.

Breadcrumbs

Breadcrumbs are navigational elements usually displayed between the header and the main body of content:

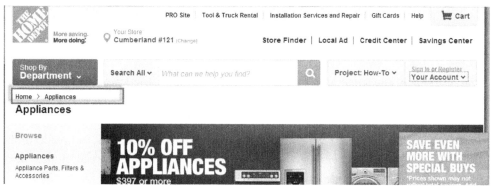

Figure 301 Breadcrumbs provide a sense of "location" for users.

For example, a breadcrumb on a website selling home hardware might read *Home > Appliances > Cooking. Home, Appliances* and *Cooking* are called *elements*, and ">" is called a *separator.*

Breadcrumbs are frequently neglected as an SEO factor, but here are few good reasons for you to pay more attention to them:

- Breadcrumb links are a very important navigational element that communicates the location of a page in the website hierarchy to users, and helps them easily navigate around the website.[9, 10]

- SEO breadcrumbs are one of the best ways to create silos, by allowing search engine bots to crawl vertically upwards and downwards in the taxonomy.

- Breadcrumb navigation makes it easier for search engines to analyze your website architecture.

- Breadcrumbs are one of the best places to use exact anchor text keywords with the lowest risk.

In spite of breadcrumbs' great usability and SEO benefits, a lot of ecommerce websites fail to implement them correctly, for users and/or search engines.

Figure 302 Which page is this? *Edition? Gifts? Designer Sale? Shop by Designer?* None of these, actually. It's the *Shoes & Handbags* category listing page. A breadcrumb would make it easier for users to understand where they are on the website.

If usability alone has not yet convinced you to pay more attention to breadcrumbs, then maybe it's time to remind you that properly implemented breadcrumbs show directly in Bing[11] and Google search results:[12]

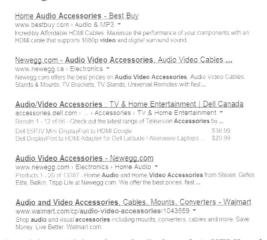

Figure 303 Walmart doesn't have rich breadcrumbs. Perhaps their HTML code for breadcrumbs is not properly tagged.

On the subject of featuring breadcrumb-rich snippets in SERPs (which can lead to better CTR), Google's patent[13] discusses the taxonomy of the website, internal linking, primary and secondary navigation and structured URLs, among other things. To increase the chances of breadcrumbs showing up in search engines, implement them consistently across the website and/or follow Google's official guidelines by using the *Breadcrumbs* structured markup, with microdata or RDFA.[14]

Breadcrumb-rich search result listings also allow users to click not only on the SERP title (usually blue and underline text), but on the breadcrumbs in the listing as well. This provides additional benefits:

- It promotes usability for both Google and your website.

- It provides more links in SERPs for users to click to get to your site.

If a product belongs to multiple categories, it's ok to list multiple breadcrumbs on a page,[15] as long as the product is not categorized in too many different spots. However, the first breadcrumb on the page has to be the canonical path to that product, because Google picks the first breadcrumb it finds on the page.

Depth-triggered breadcrumbs

Some ecommerce websites implement breadcrumbs only at a certain depth in the website architecture, but that's not optimal for users and search engines:

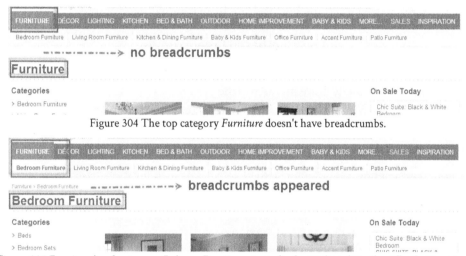

Figure 304 The top category *Furniture* doesn't have breadcrumbs.

Figure 305 Furniture's subcategory, *Bedroom Furniture*, starts displaying breadcrumbs. All subcategories of *Bedroom Furniture* thereafter have breadcrumbs.

Depth-triggered breadcrumbs may work fine for users (or search robots) who start navigating from the home page, but nowadays, every page on your website could serve as an entry point. This is why it's important to feature breadcrumbs from the first level of the website taxonomy, right below the home page. Additionally, featuring breadcrumbs only on some pages and not on others confuses users.

Figure 306 It's ok to repeat the category name in the breadcrumb and the heading.

Depending on how they are implemented, there are three types of breadcrumbs:[16] *path-based*, *location-based* and *attribute-based*.

Path-based breadcrumbs

This breadcrumb trail shows the path users have taken within the website to get to the current page (the *this is how you got here* clue for users). The breadcrumbs will dynamically update to reflect the user's *historical* navigation path. Page view history is achieved with either URL tagging or session-based cookies.

It is not a good idea to implement this type of breadcrumb anywhere except search result pages. Users landing from search engines can reach deep sections inside a website without ever needing to navigate through the website. In this case, a path-based breadcrumb becomes meaningless for users. The same applies for search engine bots, which can reach deep pages on your website from external referral sources.

Location-based breadcrumbs

This is the most popular type of breadcrumb, and it indicates the position of the current page within the website hierarchy (the *you are here* clue for users). It keeps users on a fixed navigation path based on the website's taxonomy, no matter which previous pages they saw during navigation. This is the type of breadcrumb recommended by taxonomists[17] and usability experts.[18]

You may generate a lot of almost-duplicate pages with location-based breadcrumbs, because an item can be categorized and accessible in multiple locations (URLs) for usability reasons. But as far as search engines are concerned, you need to point all multiple URLs to a single, canonical version of the item.

On top-level category pages, the breadcrumb will be just one link to the home page, and the category name will be plain text, not hyperlinked:

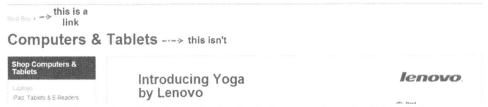

Figure 307 The breadcrumb for the first level under the home page has only a link to the home page.

The first element in the breadcrumb should be a link to your home page, but it doesn't necessarily have to use the anchor text "home page". You can use the company's name instead, or use a small house icon, with your company name in the alt text.

Figure 308 There are instances when using the main keyword in the anchor text, instead of "home page" anchor text, may make sense (e.g., your business name is *The Furniture Store*). But even then, use it with caution.

The subsequent levels in the breadcrumbs are the category and subcategory names used in your taxonomy.

Do not make the current page a link, because that will confuse users (clicking and not being taken to another page) and search engines (self-referencing leads to unnecessary crawling).

Attribute-based breadcrumbs

Attribute-based breadcrumbs, as the name suggests, use product attributes (e.g., style, color, brand, etc.) to create navigation that is presented in a breadcrumb-like fashion (the *this is how you filtered our items* clue for users):

Figure 309 A click on the *Comforter Sets* subcategory in the primary navigation opens the above page, which presents the breadcrumbs as filters.

Technically speaking, these are not breadcrumbs but, rather, faceted navigation. However, the above implementation mimics the traditional breadcrumbs usage, and users will expect the filters to be clickable, just as they expect the breadcrumbs to be displayed horizontally and not vertically.

I don't usually recommend replacing categories with filters for the top-level categories and the first subcategory levels. The choice between a category and a filter comes down to when it doesn't make sense to create separate categories for specific product attributes (e.g., having separate categories for shoe sizes does not make sense).

Separator

You need to clearly separate each element in the breadcrumb trail by using separators. The most common separator between elements is the "greater than" sign (>), while other good options may include right-pointing double-angle quotation marks (»), slashes (/) or arrows (→). Remember to mark them up with correct HTML entities.[19]

Pagination

SEO for category pages starts to get complicated when the listings need pagination. Pagination occurs on ecommerce websites because of the large number of items that have to be segmented across multiple *component pages* (aka *paginated pages*). It usually occurs on product listing pages and in internal site search results.

Figure 310 4,373 items spread across 113 pages is too much for users and search engines.

If pagination occurs on pages that list other subcategories instead of products, it's time you revise making subcategories available to users without pagination (e.g., increase the number of subcategories you list on a page, or break the subcategories into sub-subcategories).

Pagination is one of the oldest issues found on websites with large sets of items, and to address it is to aim at a moving target. Currently, the most recommended approach is with *rel="prev"* and *rel="next"*, but there were a couple of strategies to address pagination even before Google introduced these relationships at the end of 2011, such as noindexing all pages except the first, or using a *view-all* page.

Strangely enough, Google says that one of the options for handling pagination is to "leave as-is",[20] suggesting that they are capable of identifying a canonical page and handling pagination well enough.

However, anything you can do to help search engines better understand your website and crawl it more efficiently is advantageous. The question is not *whether* you need to deal with pagination but *how* to deal with it.

From an SEO perspective, a "simple" functionality such as pagination can cause serious issues with search engines' ability to crawl and index your site's content. Let's take a look at several relevant concerns.

Crawling issues

A listing with thousands of items will need pagination, since a huge listing like that won't help either users or search engines. But pagination can screw up a flat website architecture like nothing else.

For instance, in the screenshot below it may take search engines about 15 "clicks" to reach page 50. If the only way to reach the products listed on page 50 is by going through this pagination page by page, those products will have a very low chance of being discovered. Probably those pages will be crawled less frequently, which is not ideal.

Figure 311 Page 7 lists an additional three pages of pagination (8, 9 and 10) compared to page 1.

The odds that Googlebot will "click" through paginated content to crawl the final pages decreases with each page in the series, and more significantly at page 5.

Total number of Googlebot visits on all listing pages by their number

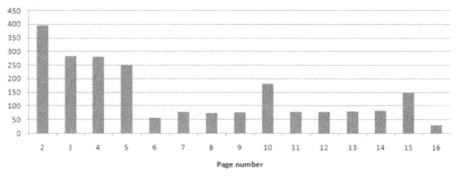

Figure 312 Google crawls component pages 6-N far less frequently.[21]

The experiment concluded that:

"The higher the page number is, the less probability that the page will be indexed.... On average, the chance that the robot will crawl to the next page of search results decreases by 1.2 to 1.3% per page."

If you have a large number of component pages, as in the above example, find a way to add links to intermediary pages in the series. Instead of linking to pages 1, 2, 3 and 4 and then jumping to the last page, 113, add links to multiple intermediary pages. In our example, we can break the series into four parts by linking to every 28th page in the series (113/4).

The pagination may look like this:

Previous   1 ... 4 5 6 7 8 9 10 28 .. 56 .. 86 ... 112   Next

Figure 313 Make sure the navigation on each page in the series makes sense for users.

Tip: If you use URL parameters to generate component pages, you can check the index saturation for each level of the pagination with Google Webmaster Tool's Internal Linking report. Once you've made changes to pagination, you can assess the impact after a week or two. Additionally, you can use your server logs to determine Googlebot's behavior before and after you've made updates to pagination.

Duplicate content

While the products listed on pages 2 to N are different, very often each component page has the same page title, heading and meta description (and sometimes even the same copy) across the series, maybe due to CMS configuration. Consider the following to avoid or improve upon this:

- Create a custom, unique title and description for page 1.

- Write unique title and description boilerplates for each of pages 2 to 5.

- Use boilerplate page titles for pages 5 to N. For instance, you can use the title of page 1 with some boilerplate appended at the end, "{Title Page One} - Page X/Y".

- You're ok with no meta descriptions on pages 5 to N.

While the effect on ranking for pages 2 to N will be minimal, doing the above helps Google differentiate between them, and component pages *might* send better internal quality signals.

Another duplicate content issue particular to pagination can occur between the category's index page and the first page in the series. The index page and the first page in the series are usually the same:

mysite.com/category/

mysite.com/category?page=1

Figure 314 Clicking on the page 1 link from pages 2 to N should not add a pagination parameter to the URL. Instead, the link on page 1 should point to the category index URL, *mysite.com/category/*.

Ranking signals dispersion

Sometimes, because component pages in the pagination series get linked internally or from external sites, they may end up in the SERPs. In such cases, rankings signals are dispersed to multiple destination URLs instead of to a single, consolidated page.

If we look at how PageRank flows, according to the first paper on this subject, published in 1998[22] (which notes that PageRank flows equally throughout each link and has a decay factor of 10 to 15%), then component pages seem to be PageRank black holes—especially those not linked from the first pages in the series.

Let's see how PageRank flows on a *view-all* page and on several paginated series. For our purposes, we'll split the PageRank between only the component pages (this assumes that all the other links are exactly the same on all pages):

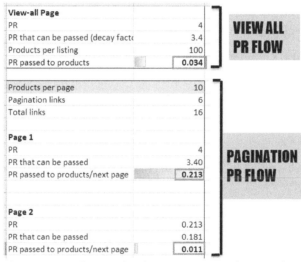

View-all Page	
PR	4
PR that can be passed (decay facto	3.4
Products per listing	100
PR passed to products	0.034

VIEW ALL PR FLOW

Products per page	10
Pagination links	6
Total links	16

Page 1	
PR	4
PR that can be passed	3.40
PR passed to products/next page	0.213

PAGINATION PR FLOW

Page 2	
PR	0.213
PR that can be passed	0.181
PR passed to products/next page	0.011

Figure 315 In the above scenario, the items listed on page 2 receive **three times less** PageRank than the items listed on a *view-all* page.

The above scenario is for a listing with 100 items on a PageRank 4 page. Due to the decaying factor, the page will send only 3.4 (4 x (1-0.15)) PageRank points to other pages. Each of the 100 items listed on the *view-all* page will receive **0.034** PageRank points.

We'll split the same listing into 10 pages in a paginated series (listing 10 items per page) and link to component pages *1, 2, 3, 4, 5...10*.

For the first page, we'll have the following metrics:

- The PageRank is the same as the *view-all* page (4), and the amount that can flow further is 3.4.

- The total number of links is 16 (10 links for items plus six links for pagination URLs).

Each item/pagination URL receives *0.213*.

The 10 items on the first page of pagination receive about *six times more* PageRank than items on the *view-all* page.

The second page has these metrics:

- The PageRank is 0.213 (from page 1), and the amount that can flow further is 0.181.

- The total number of links is 16 (10 links for items plus six links for pagination URLs).

Each item/pagination URL receives *0.011*.

The 10 items on the second page receive *three times less* PageRank than the items listed on the *view-all* page.

If a component URL is not present on the first page in the series (e.g., the page 6 URL shows up only when users click on page 2 of the series), the amount of PageRank that flows to items on page 6 is incredibly low.

- The PageRank is 0.011 (from page 2), and the amount that can flow further is 0.0096.

- The total number of links is 16 (10 links for items plus six links for pagination URLs).

- Each item/pagination URL receives 0.0006.

This means that the items on such pages will receive about *56 times less* PageRank than the items listed on the *view-all* page.

How the PageRank changes when you change the number of items on each component page (20 or 25 items per page) is depicted on the next page.

View-all Page	
PR	4
PR that can be passed (decay fact⌐	3.4
Products per listing	100
PR passed to products	0.034

Products per page	10		Products per page	20		Products per page	25
Pagination links	6		Pagination links	5		Pagination links	4
Total links	16		Total links	25		Total links	29
Page 1			**Page 1**			**Page 1**	
PR	4		PR	4		PR	4
PR that can be passed	3.40		PR that can be passed	3.40		PR that can be passed	3.40
PR passed to products/next page	0.213		PR passed to products/next page	0.136		PR passed to products/next page	0.1172
Page 2			**Page 2-5**			**Page 2-4**	
PR	0.213		PR	0.136		PR	0.117
PR that can be passed	0.181		PR that can be passed	0.116		PR that can be passed	0.100
PR passed to products/next page	0.011		PR passed to products/next page	0.0046		PR passed to products/next page	0.0034
Page 6							
PR	0.011						
PR that can be passed	0.0096						
PR passed to products/next page	0.0006						

Figure 316 Those interested in playing with this model can download a sample file from
http://www.ecommercemarketingbooks.com/companion-files.

This analysis suggests that:

- The items listed on the first page in a pagination series receive significantly more PageRank than those listed on component pages.

- The fewer links you have on the first page, the more important they are (and the more PageRank they receive)—no surprise here.

- If the link to a paginated page is not listed on the series' index page, it receives significantly less PageRank.

- Items listed on pages 2 to N receive less PageRank than if they were listed on a *view-all* page (except when they receive a lot of internal or external links).

In practice, however, PageRank is a metric that flows in more complex ways (e.g., it flows back and forth between the same two pages; more PageRank is passed for contextual links than for pagination links, etc.), and the amount of PageRank that gets into pagination pages is impossible for anyone except Google to compute.

But this oversimplified modeling shows that you can either pass a lot of PageRank to a few items on the first page of pagination (and significantly less to items on component pages), or you can pass a medium amount of PageRank to all items via a *view-all* page.

If you decide to use pagination, it is essential to put your most important products at the top of the list on the first page.

Thin content

Listing pages usually have little to no unique content—not much that search engines would consider worthy of indexing, except for product names and some basic item information. In fact, Panda filtered a lot of listing pages from their index.

Questionable usefulness

Do your users really make use of pagination? Look at your analytics data to find out. Do component pages serve as entry points, either from search engines or from other referrals? If not, the SEO and user benefits of a *view-all* might be much greater than having pagination.

Pagination may still be a necessary evil if the site architecture has already been implemented and it's too difficult to make updates, or if a large number of items cannot be divided and grouped into multiple subcategories.

If you want to minimize pagination issues, it's probably best to start with the website's architecture. You can avoid some challenging user-experience, IT and SEO issues by doing this. You should consider the following:

Replace product listings with subcategory listings

For example, on the *Men's Clothing* category page below, instead of listing 2,037 products, you can list subcategories such as *Athletic Wear, Belts & Suspenders, Casual Shirts* and so on. You will only have product listings deeper in the website hierarchy.

Figure 317 A typical category listing page.

The *Men's Clothing* category page above lists products, but instead it could list subcategories, as in the image below:

Figure 318 This is a mockup to demonstrate the replacement of product listings with subcategory listings.

Break into smaller subcategories

If you have a category with hundreds or thousands of items, maybe it's possible to break it down into smaller segments. This in turn will decrease, or even eliminate, the number of pages in the series.

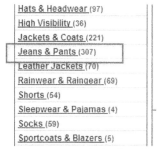

Figure 319 The *Jeans & Pants* subcategory can be broken down into two subcategories.

Segmenting into multiple subcategories may completely remove the need for pagination if you list a reasonable number of items. However, don't become overly granular; you want to avoid ending up with too many subcategories.

Implementing custom categories instead of listings will also assist users in making better scope selections.[23]

Increase the number of items in the listing

The idea behind this approach is simple: the more products you display on a listing page, the fewer component pages you have in the series. For example, if you list 50 items using a 5x10 grid on two pages and have 295 items to list, you will have six pages in the pagination series. If you increase the number of items per page to 100, you will need only three pages to list them all.

How many items you list on each page depends on how many other links are on the page, your web server's ability to load pages quickly, and the types of items in the list (e.g., funny greeting card listings may be scanned more slowly than fasteners), but generally, 100 to 150 items is a good choice.

Link to more pagination URLs

Instead of skipping pages in the pagination link series, link to as many pagination links as possible.

Show 18 per page   1 of 7 ⟶

Figure 320 The above pagination requires search engines and people to click *Next* (the right arrow) seven times to reach the last page. That's bad for SEO and for users.

Instead, the pagination should look like:

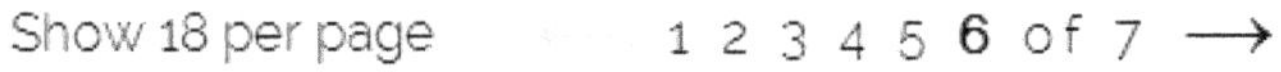

Show 18 per page   1 2 3 4 5 **6** of 7 ⟶

Figure 321 Adding links to a manageable number of pagination URLs will ensure crawlers get to those pages in as few hops as possible.

If you can, interlink all the paginated pages from each component page. For example, if the listing results in fewer than 10 component links, you can list all the links instead of just 1, 2, 3...10. If the listing generates an unmanageable number of component URLs, list as many as possible without creating a bad user experience.

While the above ideas can reduce the impact of pagination on SEO, in many cases pagination will still be necessary—and you will have to handle it.

The way you approach pagination is situational, which means it depends on factors such as the current implementation, the index saturation (the number of your pages indexed by search engines), the average number of products in categories or subcategories, and other factors. There's no one-size-fits-all approach.

Apart from the "do nothing" approach, there are various SEO methods for addressing pagination:

- The "noindex, follow" method.
- The *view-all* method.

- The pagination attributes (aka rel="prev", rel="next") method.

- The AJAX links method.

Note: Another (incorrect) approach to pagination is to use rel="canonical" to point all component pages in a series to the first page. Google states that:

"setting the canonical to the first page of a parameter-less sequence is considered improper usage."[24]

The "noindex, follow" method

This method requires adding *<meta name="robots" content="noindex, follow">* in the *<head>* of pages 2 to N of the series, while the first page will be indexable. Additionally, pages 2 to N can contain a self-referencing *rel="canonical"*.

Of the three methods, this is the least complicated to implement, but it effectively removes pages 2 to N from search engines' indices. Note that this method does not transfer any indexing signals from component pages to the primary, canonical page.

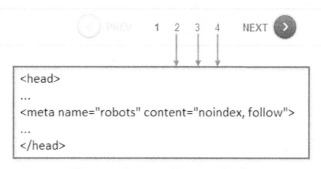

Figure 322 Pages 2 to N are *noindex*ed.

If your goal is to keep pages out of the index (e.g., because you have been hit by a thin content filter), this is the best approach. A good application of the noindex method can be on internal site search results pagination, since Google doesn't like "search in search".[25]

Blocking crawlers' access to component pages can also be done with *robots.txt* and within your webmaster accounts (these won't exclude pages from search engines' indices; they will only prevent further crawling). And while you can use Google Webmaster Tool to exclude component pages from crawling, it is better to block them in one place only (e.g., either with *robots.txt* or with GWT). Be careful—don't forget where you blocked content when you audit crawling and indexation issues.

The view-all page

This method seems to be Google's preferred choice for handling pagination, "because users generally prefer the *view-all* option in search results" and Google "will make more of an effort to properly detect and serve this version to searchers."[26] This seems to be backed up by testing performed by usability professionals such as Jakob Nielsen, who found that

> "the View-all option [was] helpful to some users. More important, the View-all option didn't bother users who didn't use it; when it wasn't offered, however, some users complained."[27]

The *view-all* method involves:

- Creating a *view-all* page that lists all the items in the specific category:

Showing 1 - 48 of 88 total   Items per page [48 ▼]   [View all 88 Items]   1 2 | Next

Figure 323 The *view-all* link list all the items.

- Making the *view-all* page the canonical URL of the paginated series by adding *rel="canonical"* to each component page pointing to the *view-all*:

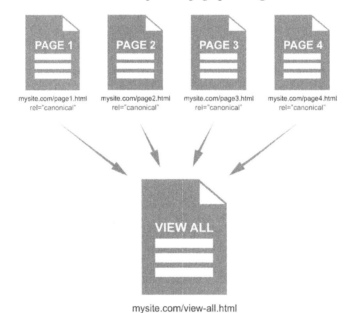

Figure 324 *The rel="canonical"* consolidates all link signals into the *view-all* page. However, all component pages lose their ability to rank in SERPs.

While the *view-all* page can be different from the default listing page, making the *view-all* the default listing page is also possible.

This method comes with advantages, such as better usability, indexing signal consolidation and relative ease of implementation, but there are several challenges to consider before creating a *view-all* page:

- Consolidating hundreds or thousands of products on one page can dramatically increase page load times, especially if you list product thumbnails (with or without deferring image loading). A fast loading time is considered under four seconds. Use progressive loading to make this happen.

- A *view-all* page means having hundreds or thousands of links on a single page (it has to list all the items listed in the component pages). While the compensation may be the consolidation of indexing signals from component pages to the *view-all* page, we don't have any official clues on how search engines will interpret such a large number of links on the *view-all* page.

- Sometimes, you don't really want to remove all other component pages and push the *view-all* to be listed in SERPs. If you'd like to surface individual pages from the pagination series, you should use the rel="next" and rel="prev" method.

- Implementation is a bit more complex than for the "noindex" method (but not as complex as the pagination attributes).

If you implement the *view-all* page solely for user experience purposes and you don't want search engines to list it in SERPs, make sure that the component pages in the series don't have a rel="canonical" pointing to the *view-all* page, and mark the *view-all* page with "noindex". Additionally, you may want to make the link to the *view-all* page available to humans only (AJAX, cookie-based, etc.).

If you're concerned with page load times, there are ways to deliver the *view-all* listing to non-JavaScript browsers (search engines) and present the results to JavaScript browsers (real visitors) on demand, without increasing load times. These implementations have to take into consideration progressive enhancement[28] and mobile user experience.

While depagination can work for websites that have a reasonably low number of items in their listings, for websites with larger inventories it may be easier to stay with user-friendly pagination that limits the number of items. From a usability standpoint,

"typically, this upper limit should be around 100 items, though it can be more or less depending on how easy it is for users to scan items and how much a long page impacts the response time."[29]

Pagination attributes (aka rel="prev" and rel="next" method)

This method, also known as the pagination attributes method, is probably the approach that best suits most of today's ecommerce websites, as it seems to generate good results without completely removing component pages' ability to rank in search results.

Each component page in the series is tagged with either the *rel="prev"* or *rel="next"* attribute in the *<head>* section of the page, to define a "chain" of paginated components. The *prev* and *next* relationship attributes have been HTML standards for a long time,[30] but they only got attention after Google pushed them as a hint (not a directive) to suggest pagination.

Let's say you have product listings paginated into the following URLs:

http://www.website.com/duvet-covers/

http://www.website.com/duvet-covers?page=2

http://www.website.com/duvet-covers?page=3

http://www.website.com/duvet-covers?page=4

On the first page (the category's index page), you'd include in the *<head>* section:

<link rel="next" href="http://www.website.com/duvet-covers?page=2" />

The first page only contains rel="next" and no rel="prev" markup. Typically, this is the page in the series that becomes the hub and gets listed in SERPs, but there are scenarios when users are sent to another page in the series.

On the second page, *http://www.website.com/duvet-covers?page=2*:

<link rel="prev" href="http://www.website.com/duvet-covers/" />

<link rel="next" href="http://www.website.com/duvet-covers?page=3" />

Pages 2 to the second-to-last page should have both rel="next" and rel="prev" markup.

Note that page 2 points back to the first page in the pagination as */duvet-covers/* instead of */duvet-covers?page=1*. This is actually the correct way to reference the first page in the series, and it doesn't break the chain, because

/duvet-covers/ will point to */duvet-covers?page=2* **and**

/duvet-covers?page=2 will point to */duvet-covers/*

On the third page, *http://www.website.com/duvet-covers?page=3*:

<link rel="prev" href="http://www.website.com/duvet-covers?page=2" />

<link rel="next" href="http://www.website.com/duvet-covers?page=4" />

On the last page, *http://www.website.com/duvet-covers?page=4*:

<link rel="prev" href="http://www.website.com/duvet-covers?page=3" />

The last page contains markup only for rel="prev", not for rel="next".

The pagination attributes method has a few advantages:

- The main one is that component pages retain and share equity with all other pages in the series.

- It addresses pagination without the need to "noindex" component pages (although in some cases, "noindex" can still make sense).

- It consolidates indexing properties (e.g., links signals such as anchor text and PageRank) between the component pages/URLs to the series as a whole, just as with a *view-all* implementation. This means that in most cases, it's the first page to show up in Google's SERPs.

- On-page SEO factors such as page titles, meta descriptions and URLs may be retained for individual component pages, as opposed to being consolidated into one *view-all* page.

- If the listing can be sorted in multiple ways using URL parameters (for example, by *most popular* or *bestsellers*), then these multiple "ordered by" views are eligible to be listed in SERPs. This is not possible with a *view-all* approach.

Note: It's not generally a good idea to mix pagination attributes with a *view-all* page. If you have a *view-all* page, point the rel="canonical" on all component pages to the *view-all* page, and don't use pagination attributes. You may also self-reference component pages to avoid duplicate content due to session IDs and tracking parameters.

Rel="canonical" with rel="prev" and rel="next"

Pagination attributes (rel="next" or rel="prev") and rel="canonical" are independent concepts, and both can be used on the same page to prevent some duplicate content issues.

For example, page 2 of a series could contain:

<link rel="canonical" href="http://www.website.com/duvet-covers?page=2" />

<link rel="prev" href="http://www.website.com/duvet-covers?sessionid=1235sfsd" />

<link rel="next" href="http://www.website.com/duvet-covers?page=3&sessionid=yeuy46"/>

The above tells Google that page 2 is part of a pagination series, and that the canonical version of page 2 is the URL with no parameters. Canonical should point to the current component page with no sorts, filters, views or other parameters, but rel="prev" and rel="next" should have the parameters.

Keep in mind that rel="canonical" should be used to deal with duplicate or near-duplicate content only. Use it on:

- URLs with session IDs, or URLs with internal or referral tracking parameters.

- Sorting that changes the display but not the content (e.g., sorting that happens on a page-by-page basis).

- Subsets of a canonical page (e.g., a *view-all* page).

Using rel="canonical" on content that spreads across multiple pages and is not part of a canonical page may not be feasible, since each component page may not be a subset of what you would like to point to as canonical.

Rel="prev", rel="next" and URL parameters

Although rel="prev" and rel="next" seems more advantageous than the *view-all* method, from an SEO standpoint (and also seems to be the preferred approach for ecommerce websites), it comes with implementation challenges.

Regarding URL parameters, the rule on paginated pages is that pagination attributes can only link together URLs with matching parameters (the exception being when you remove the pagination parameter for the first page in the series).

So to make pagination attributes work properly, you have to ensure that all pages within a paginated rel="prev" and rel="next" sequence are using the same parameters.

Pagination and tracking parameters

The following URLs aren't considered part of the same series, since the URL for page 3 has different parameters, and that **would break the chain**:

http://www.website.com/duvet-covers?page=2

http://www.website.com/duvet-covers?page=3&referrer=twitter

http://www.website.com/duvet-covers?page=4

In this case, you should dynamically insert the pagination key-value pairs based on the fetched URL. In the above example, when Googlebot fetches the page as

http://www.website.com/duvet-covers?page=3&referrer=twitter

the pagination should be dynamically inserted as

<link rel="prev" href="http://www.website.com/duvet-covers?page=2&referrer=twitter">

<link rel="next" href="http://www.website.com/duvet-covers?page=4&referrer=twitter">

Pagination and viewing/sorting parameters

Another frequent scenario with pagination is the sorting and viewing of listings that span multiple pages. Because each view option generates unique URL parameters, you will have to create a pagination set for each view.

Let's say these are the URLs for "sort by newest", displaying 20 items per page:

http://www.website.com/duvet-covers?sort=newest&view=20

http://www.website.com/duvet-covers?sort=newest&view=20&page=2

http://www.website.com/duvet-covers?sort=newest&view=20&page=3

On page 1, you will have the following pagination attributes:

<link   rel="next"   href="http://www.website.com/duvet-covers?sort=newest&view=20&page=2'>

On page 2:

<link rel="prev" href="http://www.website.com/duvet-covers?sort=newest&view=20'>

<link   rel="next"   href="http://www.website.com/duvet-covers?sort=newest&view=20&page=3'>

On page 3:

<link   rel="prev"   href="http://www.website.com/duvet-covers?sort=newest&view=20&page=2'>

This will be one pagination series. However, if users can also display 100 items per page, that's a new view option (*sort by newest, display 100 items per page*), and it will create a new pagination series:

http://www.website.com/duvet-covers?sort=newest&view=100

http://www.website.com/duvet-covers?sort=newest&view=100&page=2

http://www.website.com/duvet-covers?sort=newest&view=100&page=3

On page 1, you will have the following pagination attributes:

<link   rel="next"   href="http://www.website.com/duvet-covers?sort=newest&view=100&page=2">

On page 2:

<link rel="prev" href="http://www.website.com/duvet-covers?sort=newest&view=100">

<link   rel="next"   href="http://www.website.com/duvet-covers?sort=newest&view=100&page=3">

On page 3:

<link   rel="prev"   href="http://www.website.com/duvet-covers?sort=newest&view=100&page=2">

Additionally, you may want to prevent search engines from indexing bi-directional sorting options (sort by newest = sort by oldest, only in a different order). Keep one default way of sorting accessible—e.g., "newest"—and block the other, "oldest".

Adding a logic to the URL parameters not only can prevent duplicate content issues, it also can

"help the searcher experience by keeping a consistent parameter order based on searcher-valuable parameters listed first (as the URL may be visible in search results) and searcher-irrelevant parameters last (e.g. session ID). Avoid example.com/category.php?session-id=123&tracking-id=456&category=gummy-candies&taste=sour"[31]

Make sure that parameters don't change page content, such as session IDs, and are implemented as standard key=value pairs, not directories. This is necessary for search engines to understand which parameters are useless.

Here are a couple of other best practices for pagination attributes:

- Use absolute URLs (technically, you can use relative URLs as well), in case URLs are accidentally duplicated across directories or subdomains.

- Don't break the chain (page N should point to N-1 as the previous page and to N+1 as the next page—except for the first page, which won't have a prev attribute, and the last page, which won't have a next attribute).

- A page can't contain multiple rel="next" or rel="prev" attributes.[32]

- Multiple pages can't have the same rel="next" or rel="prev" attributes.

Probably the biggest downside of rel="prev" and rel="next" is that it gets tricky to implement, especially on URLs with multiple parameters. Also keep in mind that Bing doesn't treat the previous and next link relationships the same way as Google does. While Bing uses the markup to understand your website structure, it won't consolidate indexing signals to a single page. If pagination is a problem in Bing, consider blocking excessive pages with a Bingbot-specific robots.txt directive or noindex meta tag.

The AJAX/JavaScript links

With this method, you create pagination links that can't be crawled by search engines (AJAX, JavaScript or cookie-based links) but are available to users in the browser. The tradeoff is that users without JavaScript won't have access to component pages, but they can access a *view-all* page.

Figure 325 Users have access to sorting, viewing and pagination in the interface (1), but the source code (2) reveals a JavaScript implementation for the pagination. Google doesn't have access to those pagination URLs (3).

This approach has the potential to avoid a lot of duplicate content complications associated with pagination, sorting and viewing. However, it can introduce URL discoverability problems. If you prefer this approach, ***make sure that search engines have at least one other way to access each product in each listing***—for example:

- More detailed subcategorization that doesn't require more than 100 to 150 items in each list.

- Smart internal linking that links ***all*** products in an SEO-friendly way from other pages.

- Well-structured HTML site maps, along with XML Sitemaps.

- Other sorts of internal links.

Infinite scrolling

A frequent user interface design alternative for pagination is *infinite scrolling*.[33] Also known as *continuous scrolling*, it lets users view content as they scroll down towards the page bottom, without the need to click on pagination links. Visually, this alternative appears very similar to displaying all the items on the page. However, the difference between infinite scrolling and a *view-all* page is that with infinite scrolling, the content is loaded on demand (e.g., by clicking on a "load more items" button or scrolling down the page), while for a *view-all* page the content is loaded all at once.

Mobile websites use infinite scrolling more and more, since on small screens it's easier to swipe than to click. However, infinite scrolling relies on progressive loading with AJAX,[34] which means that you will still need to give search engines or users without JavaScript active links to component URLs. You will achieve this using a *progressive enhancement* approach.

In terms of SEO, infinite scrolling doesn't solve pagination issues for large inventories, and this is one of the reasons Google suggests paginating infinite scrolls.[35] Google's advice is ok, but I don't believe that infinite scrolling needs pagination when there aren't too many products in the listing; a *view-all* page with 200 items is preferable in many cases. However, pages that list more than 200 **and** use infinite scrolling should degrade to plain HTML pagination links for non JavaScript users (this includes search engine robots). Degrading to HTML links means that search engines may still get into pagination problems, though, so you will have to handle pagination with one of the methods described earlier in this chapter.

Figure 326 Above is the cached version of a subcategory page that uses infinite scrolling and degrades to HTML links for pagination when users don't have JavaScript on.

The above page displays the *Previous* and *Next* links for users without JavaScript active (or for search engines).

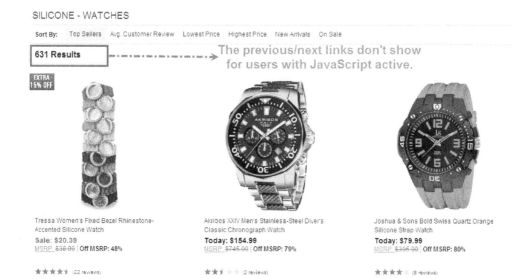

Figure 327 This is the same page in a web browser with JavaScript active. The *Previous* and *Next* links don't show up anymore. This was achieved by hiding the pagination section with CSS styling and JavaScript. Users can continuously scroll to see all watches.[36]

Continuous scrolling has many advantages (e.g., great user experience on touch devices, faster browsing due to elimination of page reloads, increased product discoverability, and external link consolidation). But there are disadvantages, too,[37] and it's worth knowing that infinite scrolling doesn't perform better on all websites.

For example, on Etsy (an ecommerce marketplace for handmade and vintage items), infinite scrolling didn't have the desired business outcomes, so they reverted to old-fashioned pagination.[38] Infinite scrolling led to fewer clicks from users, as they felt lost in a sea of items and had difficulty sorting between relevant and irrelevant. Consequently, users were less willing to click on items in the listing. But on other websites, it may work well.[39]

As with most ideas for your website, an A/B test will tell you whether it's a good or a bad one, and this is surely worth the effort.

If you plan on testing infinite scrolling, here are few things to consider.

Display visual clues that more content is loading

Not everyone's connection is fast enough to load content on demand in the blink of an eye. If your server can't handle fast user scrolling, let the users know that more content is on its way.

Figure 328 Loader icons are a good way to indicate that content is loading.

Consider a hybrid solution

A hybrid approach of infinite scrolling and pagination would display at the end of a preloaded list a "show more results" button (make it big, to combat fat-finger syndrome[40]), which loads another batch of items only when clicked:

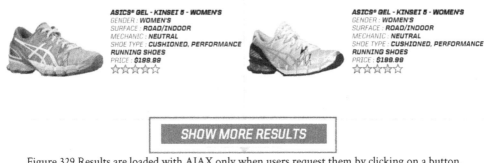

Figure 329 Results are loaded with AJAX only when users request them by clicking on a button.

Add landmarks when scrolling

Amazon uses "virtual pagination" in the horizontal scrolling, to give users a sense of how many pages are in the carousel and where they are at any moment:

Figure 330 The "virtual pagination" is in the top right corner.

In the case of vertical scrolling, adding landmarks such as virtual page numbers can help give users a feel for how much they have scrolled, and can create a mental point of reference (e.g., "I saw a product I liked somewhere around page 6.").

Figure 331 This screenshot was modified to exemplify a navigational landmark (the horizontal rule and the text "Page 2").

Update the URL while users scroll down

This is an interesting concept worth investigating. You can automatically append a pagination parameter to the URL when the user scrolls down past a certain number of rows.

This concept is best explained with a video, so I made a brief screen capture to illustrate it, just in case the original page[41] becomes unavailable. The file can be found at *http://www.ecommercemarketingbooks.com/companion-files/*.

But if you regularly have 200 or fewer items in a listing, it is better to load all the items at once to feed everything to search engines as one big *view-all* page. That's actually Google's preferred implementation to avoid pagination.

Of course, users will see 10 or 20 items at a time, and you will then progressively load the results in the interface, but from an already loaded HTML code. This has the potential to save a lot of pagination headaches. Depending on your website authority, you could go with even more than 200 items per listing.

If the list is huge, you should probably paginate, but even in that case you may want to consider a *view-all* page.

Complement with filtered navigation

Large sets of pagination should be accompanied by filtered navigation to allow users to narrow the items in the listing based on attributes, and to reach deeper into the website hierarchy with subcategory navigation.

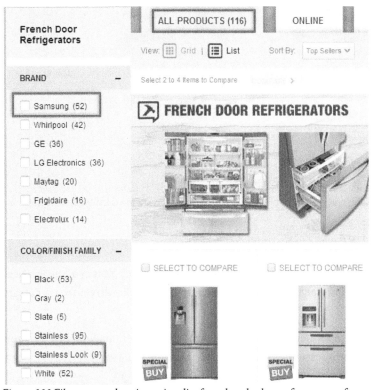

Figure 332 Filters can reduce items in a list from hundreds to a few tens or fewer.

If infinite scrolling produces better results for your users (and your bottom line, revenue), it's probably a good idea to keep it in place. But as mentioned, build it to work without JavaScript (keep the pagination in the code), and then use JavaScript to remove the pagination from the browser and implement infinite scrolling.

Secondary navigation

On listing pages, primary navigation is always complemented by some sort of ancillary secondary navigation. For the purpose of this book, we will refer to secondary navigation as navigation that provides access to categories, subcategories and items deeper in the taxonomy of an ecommerce website. It's usually displayed on the left sidebar on ecommerce websites.

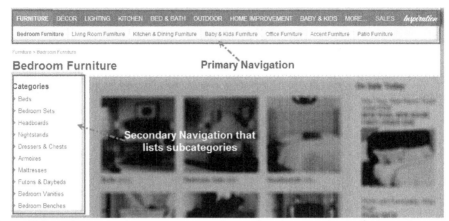

Figure 333 Secondary navigation can appear very close to the primary navigation (either at the top or on the left sidebar) and provides detailed information within a parent category.

In many cases, the secondary navigation on category and subcategory pages lists subcategories, facets, product attributes and product filters.

Figure 334 The entire left section is the secondary navigation; it includes filters, facets and subcategory facets.

Unlike in primary navigation, the labels in secondary navigation can change from one page to another to help users navigate even deeper into the website taxonomy. This change of links in the navigation menu is probably the most important difference between primary and secondary navigation.

From an SEO point of view, it's important to create category-related navigation. By doing so you offer users more relevant information, provide siloed crawl paths and give search engines better taxonomy clues.

Figure 335 Take Amazon, for example. When you are in the *Books* department of the website, the entire navigation is only about books.

Faceted navigation (aka filtered navigation)

Ecommerce sites are often cluttered, displaying too much information to process and too many items to choose from. This leads to information overload and induces *choice paralysis*.[42] It's therefore essential to offer users an easier way to navigate through large catalogs. This is where faceted/filtered navigation (what Google calls *additive filters*) comes into play.

Whether your visitors are looking for something very specific or just browsing, filters can be highly useful, helping them locate products without using the internal site search or the primary navigation (which in most cases shows a limited number of options).

Faceted navigation makes it easier for searchers to find what they're looking for by narrowing product listings based on predefined filters in the form of clickable links. Usability experts refer to faceted navigation as "arguably the most significant search innovation of the past decade".[43]

One retailer saw a

"76.1% increase in revenue, a 26% increase in conversions and 19.76% increase in shopping cart visits in an A/B test after implementing filtering on its listing pages."[44]

Below is a common design for faceted navigation displayed in the left sidebar:

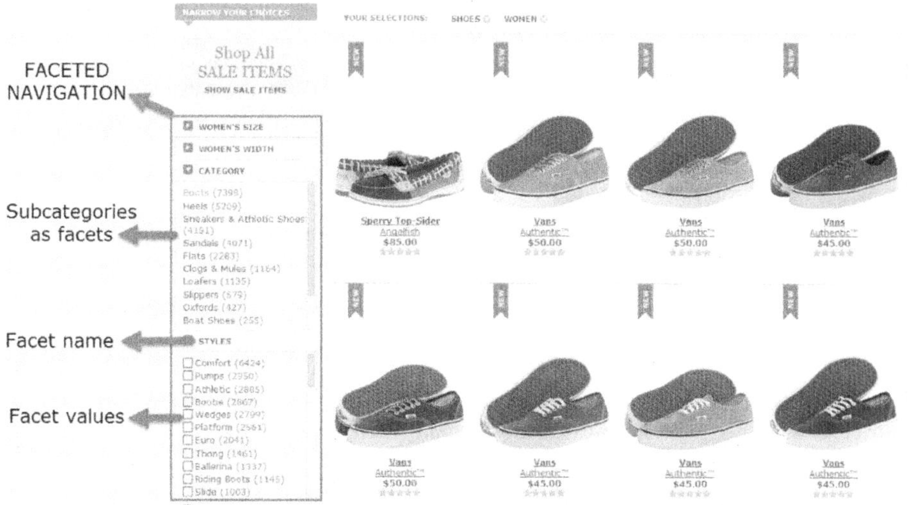

FACETED NAVIGATION

Subcategories as facets

Facet name

Facet values

Figure 336 It's common to present faceted navigation in the left sidebar, but it can also be displayed at the top of product listings. Subcategories can also be included in faceted navigation.

I will use the terms *filters* and *facets* interchangeably in this book, but it's important to know that they have slightly different meanings.

- **Facets** are dimensions/attributes shared by a group of items. In the image above, "Women's size", "Women's width", "Category" and "Styles" are the facets.

- **Filters** are the facet values. For the "Styles" facet, the filters will be "Comfort", "Pumps", "Athletic" and so on.

User can narrow based on 14 facets

Each of the 14 facets has a various # of filters

FACETS   FILTERS

Figure 337 Facets and filters.

Faceted navigation is a boon for users and conversion rates, but it can generate a serious maze for search engine crawlers. The major issues it generates are *duplicate or near-duplicate content, crawling traps* and *nonessential thin content.*

☆ **Googlebot found an extremely high number of URLs on your site:**

Googlebot encountered problems while crawling your site

Googlebot encountered extremely large numbers of links on your site. This may indicate a problem with your site's URL structure. Googlebot may unnecessarily be crawling a large number of distinct URLs that point to identical or similar content, or crawling parts of your site that are not intended to be crawled by Googlebot. As a result Googlebot may consume much more bandwidth than necessary, or may be unable to completely index all of the content on your site.

More information about this issue

Here's a list of sample URLs with potential problems. However, this list may not include all problematic URLs on your site.

Figure 338 Faceted navigation is one possible cause of the above message.

There's no better example of how filtering can create problems than the one offered by Google itself. The faceted navigation on googlestore.com (a site that sold 158 products), alongside other navigation types such as sorting and viewing options, generated 380,000 URLs.[45]

If you're curious to find out how many URLs faceted navigation could generate for a particular listing page, you can use the formula for counting possible permutations without allowed repetition, $P = n!/r!(n-r)!$, where n is the number of filters that can be applied and r is the number of facets. For instance, let's say you have the facets described below:

- Facet "Styles" with five filter options

- Facet "Materials" with nine filter options

In this case, n = 14 (5+9) and r = 2 (two facets), which could theoretically generate 91 URLs.[46] If you add another facet (e.g., "Color" with 15 options), you have n = 29 and r = 3, which will generate 3,654 unique URLs.

The above calculation assumes that you don't allow repetitive URLs. This means that if a user searches for (*style = comfort AND material = suede*), they get the same results as for (*material = blue AND style = comfort*) at the same URL. If you don't enforce an order for URL parameters, you will get 182 URLs for the example with two facets and a staggering 21,924 URLs for three facets.

Total indexed ⑦	Ever crawled ⑦	Blocked by robots ⑦
7,885	**3,746,406**	**0**

Figure 339 The huge difference between the total number of pages indexed and the number of pages ever crawled hints at a possible crawl trap issue.

price
5,272,167
Let Googlebot decide

Figure 340 The issue is confirmed by checking the URL parameters report in the webmaster account. The *price* facet generated 5.2 million URLs.

You can partially solve some duplicate content issues generated by faceted navigation by ***forcing a strict order for URL parameters*** (or directories) regardless of the order in which filters have been selected. For example, *Category* could be the first parameter and *Price* the second. Even if someone chooses *Price* first and then clicks on *Category*, you can make it so that the *Category* shows up first in the URL, followed by *Price*.

www.homedepot.com/b/Doors-Windows-Garage-Doors-Openers-Accessories-Garage-Doors/Double-Door/N-5yc1vZar38Z1z0ud51
www.homedepot.com/b/Doors-Windows-Garage-Doors-Openers-Accessories-Garage-Doors/Cherry/Double-Door/N-5yc1vZar38Z1z0ud51Z1z0vlmj

Figure 341 Although the *Cherry* filter was applied after *Double Door*, its position in the URL is based on a predefined order.

The same order is reflected in the breadcrumbs as well:

Home > Doors & Windows > Garage Doors, Openers & Accessories > Garage Doors > Double Door
Garage Doors
Home > Doors & Windows > Garage Doors, Openers & Accessories > Garage Doors > Cherry > Double Door
Garage Doors

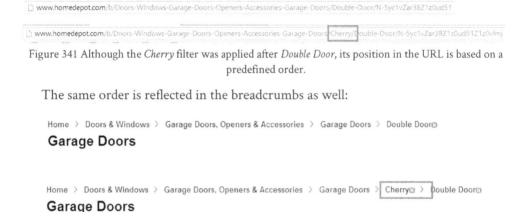

Figure 342 If you need a breadcrumb that reflects the order of user selection, you can store the order in a session cookie.

Another near-duplicate content issue generated by facets arises when one of the filtering options presents almost the same items as the unfiltered view. For example, the unfiltered view for *Ski & Snowboard Racks* has a total of 12 products, and you can narrow the results using two subcategory facets:

Shop By Category
Hitch Mount Ski Racks & Snowboard Racks
Rooftop Ski Racks & Snowboard Racks
Shop By Brand
INNO

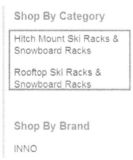

Figure 343 However, the *Hitch Mount Ski Racks & Snowboard Racks* subcategory includes 11 results from the unfiltered page. This means that with the exception of that one product, these two pages are near-duplicates.

Faceted navigation comes with a significant advantage over hierarchical navigation: the filter combinations will generate pages that could not exist in a tree-like hierarchy, because tree-like hierarchies are rigid and can't cover all possible combinations generated by faceted navigation. (The hierarchy is still good for high-level decisions, though.)

For instance, let's say that you sell diamonds and would like to rank for the term "square platinum pendants", but your website hierarchy only segregates into jewelry-type categories (pendants, bracelets, etc.), and then into material-based categories (platinum, gold, etc.). There's no shape-based category and therefore no page for "square platinum pendants". However, if you were to introduce the facet *Shape* on the *Platinum Pendants* product listing page, its filtering options would allow you to generate a *Square Platinum Pendants* filtered page that could be further optimized with custom content and visuals.

Necklaces & Pendants (830)   *Filter By:*   Designers & Collections   Materials   Gemstones   Price

Figure 344 An additional facet, *Shape*, would allow the targeting of more body and long-tail keywords.

If there's no *Shape* facet that could generate the "square platinum pendants" and there's no hierarchical navigation that could lead to such a page, you'll have to manually create a page that targets "square platinum pendants". Then you'll have to link to it internally or externally so search engines discover it. It's practically impossible to create hundreds of such pages manually.

Essential, important and overhead facets

Before discussing how to approach faceted navigation from an SEO perspective, it's important to break down the filters/facets into three types: *essential*, *important* and *overhead*.

Essential filters/facets

Applying these filters will generate landing pages that target competitive keywords with high search volumes, usually head terms. If your faceted navigation lists subcategories, those facets are essential (sometimes, these are called faceted subcategories).

Figure 345 "Bags", "Wallets" and the remaining subcategories are considered essential filters. You should always allow search engines to crawl and index such filters.

Essential facets could also be generated by a combination of filters under the *Brand* and *Category* facets—for example, using the filter "Nokia" for *Brand* and the filter "Cameras" for *Category*.

Note: In essence, *Category* or *Brand* can be considered facets, as they function like filters for larger sets of data.

You can handpick the top combinations of essential filters valuable for your users and your business, and turn those into standalone landing pages by adding content and optimizing them as you would a regular subcategory page. This is mostly a manual process, as it requires content creation, so it's doable for only a limited number of pages at once.

However, if you do this on a regular basis and you commit resources for content creation, it will give you an advantage over your competitors. Start with the most important 1% of facets and gradually move on. If you do a couple per day (you really need about 150 carefully crafted words for each), in a year you will have optimized hundreds of filtered pages. All essential facets should have unique titles (custom created, if possible) and descriptions (these can be boilerplate).

Note: Make sure that the search engines can find the links pointing to these essential filters/facets. In fact, these essential filters should be contextually linked internally from content-rich pages.

The URL structure for essential facets should be clean and, ideally, reflect (partially or exactly) the hierarchy of the website in a directory/subdirectory structure or other file-naming convention:

Figure 346 The URL for the subcategory facet *Bathroom Accessories* is parameter-free and reflects the website's hierarchy.

Important filters/facets

These filters/facets will lead users and search engines to landing pages that can eventually drive traffic for body and long-tail keywords.

If your analytics data proves that your target market searches for "red comfort shoes", this means that *red* (*Color* facet) and *comfort* (*Style* facet) are important filters. Search engines should be able to access important filters/facets, but you will have to define rules for what is and is not an important filter/facet, on a category or subcategory basis. For instance, the facet *Color* can be relevant and important for certain subcategories (e.g., for *Shoes*) but an overhead facet for others (e.g., for *Fragrances*).

A particular facet you need to pay attention to is *Sales* or *Clearance*. In the example below, the retailer lists *all the facets* for *all products* on sale.

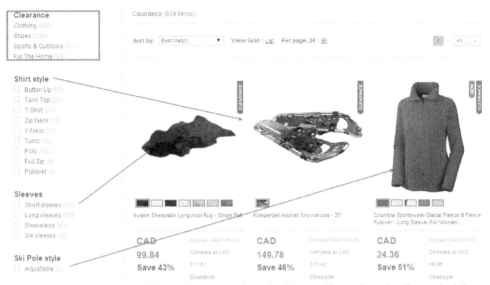

Figure 347 However, rugs don't have *Sleeves*, snowshoes don't have a *Shirt* style, and pullovers don't have a *Ski Pole* style.

This retailer should list the subcategories, not the products, at the top left. This will make it more likely that users will handle the ambiguous nature of the *Clearance* category by choosing a subcategory that interests them.

It's advisable to prevent search engines from discovering pages generated when more than one facet has been applied (after a faceted subcategory has been selected). This works best with multiple filter selections **on the same facet** (e.g., brand=Acorn AND/OR brand=Aerosoles) because users are less likely to search for patterns like "{brand1} {brand2} {category}" (e.g., "Acorn Aerosoles shoes"). Multiple selection facets are useful for users who might select "red and blue shirts", but they are not so useful for search engines.

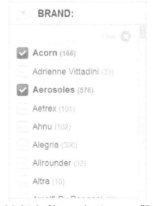

Figure 348 Multiple filters selection on a "Brand" facet.

However, blocking filtered URLs by default when multiple filters are applied will prevent bots from discovering pages created based on single filter selections **on different facets** (e.g., Color=red AND Style=comfort AND Category=shoes). You will miss traffic for a large number of filter combinations unless you manually create and optimize landing pages for all the important filters and facets, and allow the bots to crawl and index them.

Let your data decide which facets are important and which ones are overhead. Gather data from various sources, then programmatically replace the keywords with their facet name when appropriate (similar to the Labeling and Categorization technique I describe in the *Website Architecture* chapter). Identify patterns and see which facets/filters visitors use most. In your ecommerce platform, mark the ones that are important and therefore have to be indexed for each category or subcategory.

The URL structure for important facets has to be as clean as possible. It's ok to keep the important facets in a directory or in the file path structure, but it's also ok to keep them in URL parameters (two or three parameters are fine).

☐ www.homedepot.com/b/Bath-Bathroom-Accessories-Hardware-Bathroom-Accessories/KOHLER/N-5yc1vZbz99Z1qh

Figure 349 When an important filter is applied (under the "Brand" facet), its value is appended to the URL in a directory.

Tip: Avoid using non-standard URL encoding—like commas or brackets—for parameters.[47]

Often, search engines treat pages created by important filters like subsets of an unfiltered page. However, you need to create unique titles, descriptions, breadcrumbs, headings and, eventually, custom content on these filtered pages. Boilerplate title and description may be fine, but don't just repeat the title of the unfiltered view. Additionally, the breadcrumbs have to update to reflect the user selection; so do the headings. This may sound obvious, but it's amazing how many ecommerce websites don't do it.

One technique that can be useful for increasing the relevance of each filtered page and decreasing near-duplicate content problems is to write product descriptions that include the filters used to generate the filtered page. For instance, if you sell diamonds, when a user clicks on the *Material* facet, the product description snippet should include the value of the filter.

Let's take a look at the following example:

Figure 350 All the "quick view" product descriptions for the items in the listing generated when applying the filter Material = "White Gold" include the words "white gold".

These "quick view" snippets are actually different from the product description on the product details page:

Figure 351 Section 1 is the quick view snippet, section 2 the full product description.

Section 1 shows the quick view product description snippet in the product listing. As you can see, the snippet was carefully created to include all facet values. Section 2 depicts the product description in the product details page. These two product descriptions are different.

Writing custom quick view snippets for listing pages is a very effective SEO tactic even when you feature only 20 to 25 words for each product. However, it's difficult to write custom listing snippets for thousands of products. A workaround is to write the product descriptions to include as many product attributes (facet values) as possible at the beginning or end of the product description, and automatically extract the first/last sentence to the quick view snippet.

Another method is to dynamically add the facets and filters to the product listings as the new facet views are generated, but this can transform into spam if you're not careful. If you do this, make sure that you have rules in place to avoid keyword stuffing.

Overhead filters/facets

These facets/filters generate pages that have minimal search engine volume potential and that waste crawl budget on irrelevant pages. A classic example of an overhead facet is *Price*; in many instances, so is *Size*. But keep in mind that a facet can be considered overhead for one business but important or even essential for others.

You should prevent search engines from crawling pages generated based on these filters. Mark them as overheads on a category basis in your ecommerce platform. Whenever a combination of filters including an overhead value is selected, add a "noindex, follow" meta tag to the generated page and append the *crawler=no* parameter to its URL (more on this later in the chapter); then block the *crawler* parameter with *robots.txt.*

The directive in *robots.txt* will prevent wasting crawl budget, while the noindex meta tag will prevent empty results in the SERPs. If you have pages in the index that you need to remove, be careful about the combination of *robots.txt* and noindex meta tag, as *robots.txt* won't allow robots access to a page-level directive (noindex is a page-level directive). If your website doesn't have indexing-bloat or no-crawl issues, you may consider implementing rel="canonical" instead of *robots.txt.*

If progressive enhancement is not required, you can use AJAX to create the filtered pages for overhead filters. This way the URLs won't change, so search engine crawlers won't crawl useless content. If you need to degrade the code for users without JavaScript, you can use URL parameters, which can be placed either after a hash mark (#) or in a key that is excluded with *robots.txt.*

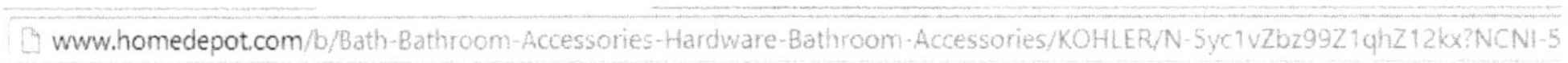

www.homedepot.com/b/Bath-Bathroom-Accessories-Hardware-Bathroom-Accessories/KOHLER/N-5yc1vZbz99Z1qhZ12kx?NCNI-5

Figure 352 When the pricing filter is applied, the NCNI-5 key is added to the URL.

URLs containing the NCNI-5 key are blocked with *robots.txt.*

*Disallow: /*NCNI-5**

To summarize, this is how Home Depot defines the filtered URLs for all three types of facets:

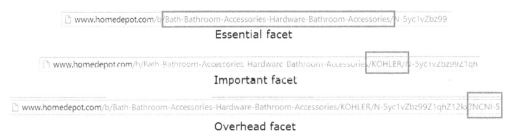

www.homedepot.com/b/Bath-Bathroom-Accessories-Hardware-Bathroom-Accessories/N-5yc1vZbz99
Essential facet
www.homedepot.com/b/Bath-Bathroom-Accessories-Hardware-Bathroom-Accessories/KOHLER/N-5yc1vZbz99Z1qh
Important facet
www.homedepot.com/b/Bath-Bathroom-Accessories-Hardware-Bathroom-Accessories/KOHLER/N-5yc1vZbz99Z1qhZ12kx?NCNI-5
Overhead facet

Figure 353 Each type of facet is handled differently.

Note: It is generally a bad idea to rewrite URLs to make overhead filters look like static URLs:

http://www.homedepot.com/b/Bath-Bathroom-Accessories-Hardware-Bathroom-Accessories/KOHLER/N-5yc1vZbz99Z1qh/Price/50-10

The above URL doesn't exist on Home Depot's website; I added the */Price/50-100* part to create the example. But remember that generating search engine-friendly URLs doesn't change the fact that there will be thousands of irrelevant pages.

In terms of URL discoverability, search engines don't need to find the links pointing to overhead filters/facets. If you absolutely have to allow search engines to crawl overhead facets, keep the filters in parameters with standard encoding and key=value pairs, not in directories or file paths. This helps search engines differentiate between useful and useless values.

A faceted navigation case study

When you search on Google for "Canon digital cameras", Overstock shows on the first page, OfficeMax on the fifth and Target on the seventh.

Overstock's approach to filtered navigation

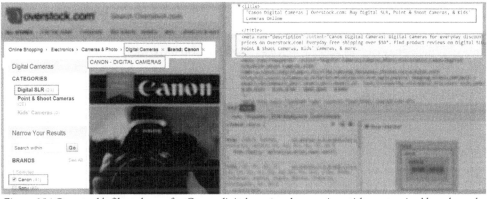

Figure 354 Overstock's filtered page for Canon digital cameras has a unique title, customized breadcrumbs and a relevant H1 heading. They also deploy a boilerplate description.

All these elements send quality signals to search engines. When users filter by another brand (e.g., Sony), the page elements update. If they didn't, the "Canon Digital Cameras" page would have the same H1, title, description, breadcrumbs, etc. as the "Digital Camera" page, which is not desirable.

Additionally, Overstock allows the crawl of essential and important filters, and it doesn't create links for "gray-end filters" (filters that generate zero results):

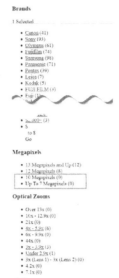

Figure 355 The "10 Megapixels" option generates zero results, so it's not linked.

Overstock's implementation of faceted navigation is SEO friendly, as it allows crawlers to access various filtered pages and it updates page elements based on users/crawlers.

Tip: Pay attention to gray-end filters. Whatever you choose to do in the interface (not show these filters at all, show them at the bottom, hide by default, or offer "show more" links), *gray ends should not be hyperlinked*. If you have to hyperlink them for some reason, the zero results pages should have 404 response code.

OfficeMax's approach to filtered navigation

Figure 356 The title, description and breadcrumbs don't update when the user selects a filter under the *Brand* facet.

On the OfficeMax site, there is no updating of title, description or breadcrumbs when the user selects a filter. This means that thousands of filtered pages will have very similar on-page SEO elements to, for example, the unfiltered page "Digital Cameras". Although the products on each filtered page will change, search engines will find a lot of near-duplicate content signals.

As a matter of fact, Google has not indexed the page resulting from filtering for *Canon*. The page that ranks for "Canon digital cameras" is their *Digital Cameras*, but that doesn't match too well with the user intent as stated in his query.

On Google's cached *Digital Camera* page, we notice that the faceted navigation is nowhere to be found:

No alternative can compete with the vast offerings of digital cameras. With point-and-click technology, digital cameras give yo

No alternative can compete with the vast offerings of digital cameras. With point-and-click technology, digital cameras give yo perfect travel companion. Since it fits neatly in your bag or pocket, you can quickly pull your camera out in time to catch a spl the nose bleed section that makes it look like you sat in the front row at your favorite concern or sporting event. With HD vide Hide

THE FACETED NAVIGATON IS MISSING COMPLETELY

Items Per Page: 15 View All
PAGE:
1 2 3 | Next >
Compare Selected Products
VIEW AS: Tile view Tile List view List
Reg: $109.99
Save 9% : $10.00
Your Price: $99.99
Instant Savings

Canon PowerShot A2500 16MP 5X Optical Zoom Silver Digital Camera

Figure 357 The faceted navigation is not accessible to search engines.

Maybe OfficeMax tried to fix some over-indexation issues or a possible Panda filter on thin content pages, but the current faceted navigation implementation is not optimal, as it completely ***blocks access to all filtered pages***. Unless OfficeMax creates manual landing pages for all essential and important filtered pages, they have closed the doors to search engines and the traffic those pages could bring in.

Target's approach to filtered navigation

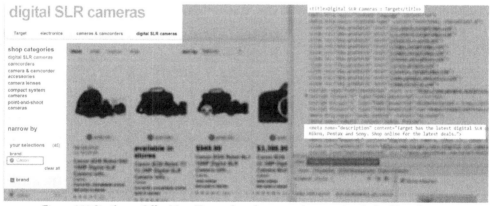

Figure 358 Similar to OfficeMax, Target doesn't create relevance signals for filtered pages.

At the Target site, the page title, breadcrumb, heading and description on the "Canon Digital Cameras" page are the same as on the unfiltered page "Digital Cameras", and they will be the same on hundreds or thousands of other possible filtered pages.

Moreover, since the page has a canonical pointing to the unfiltered page, its ability to rank is, theoretically, zero. But perhaps they have a "Canon Digital Cameras" page that can be reached from the navigation or from other pages. If they have one, Google was not able to identify it.

Figure 359 Google can't find a category or a filtered page relevant to "Canon Digital Cameras" on Target's site.

Google's cached version of the page shows that the faceted navigation doesn't create links:

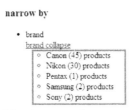

Figure 360 These are essential or important facet categories and need to be indexed.

Categories in faceted navigation

Hierarchical, category-based navigation is useful as long as it's easy for users to choose between categories. For instance, it could be more helpful for users if easy-to-decide-upon subcategories are listed in the main content area as opposed to being displayed as facet categories in the sidebar. Subcategory listing pages should be used

"whenever further navigation or scope definition is needed before it makes sense to display a list of products to the user. Generally, sub-category pages make the most sense in the one or two top layers of the hierarchy where the scope is often too broad to produce a meaningful product list."[48]

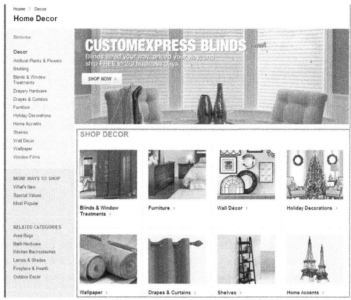

Figure 361 The subcategories are listed in the main content area. Faceted navigation is not yet introduced at this level of the hierarchy, and not even on the next one.

In this example, the category-based navigation ends on the third level in the hierarchy, and only then does the faceted navigation show up:

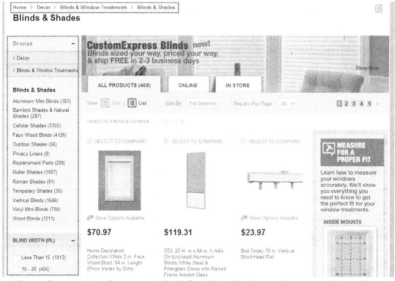

Figure 362 Faceted navigation shows up in the left sidebar for better decision making. The subcategory listing is replaced with a products listing.

It's important to keep hierarchies relatively shallow so users don't have to click through more than three to five layers of faceted navigation to find a product. Search engines will have the same challenges and may deem products buried so deep in the hierarchy as not important.

So what options do we have for controlling faceted navigation?

Option rel="canonical"

Because faceted navigation is a granular inventory segmentation feature, it generates a lot of superfluous content in most implementations. But it can also generate duplicate content—for instance, if you don't enforce a strict order for parameter filters in URLs. Although rel="canonical" is supposed to be used for identical or near-identical content, it may be worth experimenting with it to optimize facet URLs.

Vanessa Fox has suggested this approach for some cases:

> "If the filtered view is a subset of a single non-filtered page (perhaps the view=100 option), you can use the canonical attribute to point the filtered page to the non-filtered one. However, if the filtered view results in paginated content, this may not be viable (as each page may not be a subset of what you would like to point to as canonical)."[49]

Rel="canonical" will consolidate indexing signals to the canonical page and address some of the duplicate content issues, but search engine crawlers may still get trapped into crawling irrelevant URLs.

This is a good option for new websites or for adding **new** filtering options to an existing website. However, it is not helpful if you're trying to remove existing filtered URLs from search engines' indices. If you don't have indexing and crawling issues, you can use rel="canonical", as Vanessa suggests.

Option robots.txt

Robots.txt is the crawl control sledgehammer. Keep in mind that if you use *robots.txt* to block URLs, you will tamper with the flow of PageRank to and from thousands of pages. That's because while URLs listed in *robots.txt* can *accrue* PageRank, they don't *pass* PageRank.[50] Also remember that *robots.txt* does not prevent pages from being indexed by search engines.

But in some cases this approach is necessary—e.g., when you have a new website with no authority and a very large inventory of items that need to be discovered, or when you have thin content or indexing issues.

For example, if you use parameters in the URL and would like to prevent the crawling of all values of the *Price* facet, you would add something like this in your *robots.txt* file:

Disallow:*price*

Or, for URLs with unnecessary parameters, include a */filtered/* directory that will be *robots.txt* disallowed.

Robots.txt blocked URL parameter/directory

This method requires you to selectively add a URL parameter to control which filtered pages are crawlable and which are not. I have described this in the *Crawl Optimization* chapter, but I will repeat it here.

Let's say you don't want search engines to crawl the URLs generated when:

- More than one filter from the same facet is applied (multiple selections under the same facet); in this case, you will add the *crawler=no* parameter to all URLs generated when a second filter is added for the same facet.

OR

- More than two filters from any facets are applied; in this case, you will add the *crawler=no* parameter to all URLs generated when a third filter is applied, no matter which filtering options were chosen.

Here's the scenario for the second option:

1. The crawler is on the *Accessories > Battery Chargers* subcategory page, whose URL is:

    mysite.com/accessories/motorcycle-battery-chargers/

2. The crawler "checks" one of the *Brands* facet values: *Accessories > Battery Chargers > Brand*

    This is the first filter applied, so you will let the crawler fetch the page. The URL for this facet doesn't contain the exclusion parameter:

    mysite.com/accessories/motorcycle-battery-chargers/?brand=noco

3. The crawler now checks one of the *Style* facet filters: *Accessories > Battery Chargers > Brand > Style*

    Since this is the second filter applied, you will still let the crawler access the URL, which is still free of exclusion parameters:

    mysite.com/accessories/motorcycle-battery chargers/?brand=noco&style=cables

4. The crawler checks one of the "Pricing" options: *Accessories > Battery Chargers > Brand > Style > Price*

Since this is the third filter, you will append the *crawler=no* parameter to the URL. The URL becomes: *mysite.com/accessories/motorcycle-battery-chargers/?brand=noco&style=cables&pricing=1&crawler=no*

To block the above URL, the *robots.txt* will contain:

User-agent: *

*Disallow: /*crawler=no*

Note that blocking filtered pages based *solely* on how many filters have been applied poses some risks. For instance, if *Pricing* is applied first, the generated pages will still be indexed, since only one filter has been applied. You should have more solid rules—e.g., if an overhead filter has been applied, you should block the generated page anyway, whether one or N filters are applied.

Tip: It is also a good idea to limit the number of selections a search engine robot can discover (see the JavaScript/AJAX option). Important filters/facets will be plain HTML links, while you can present overhead as simple text to search engines but as functional text for users.

The blocked directory approach requires putting the unwanted URLs under a directory, then blocking that directory in the *robots.txt*.

In our previous example, when the crawler checks one of the *Pricing* options (*Accessories > Battery Chargers > Brand > Style > Price*), place the filtering ULR under the */filtered/* directory. The URL becomes:

mysite.com/filtered/accessories/motorcycle-battery-chargers/?brand=noco&style=cables&pricing

To block the URL, the *robots.txt* will contain:

User-agent: *

Disallow: /filtered/

Option nofollow

Some websites prefer to *nofollow* all unnecessary filters/facets. Surprisingly, this is one of Google's official recommendations for handling faceted navigation.[51] However, *nofollow* doesn't guarantee that search engines won't crawl the unnecessary URLs or that those pages won't be indexed. Additionally, *nofollowed* internal links might send search engines "don't trust these links" signals. Hence, *nofollow* doesn't solve current indexing issues. It works best with new websites.

It may be a good idea to either "back up" the *nofollow* option with another method that prevents URLs from being indexed (e.g., blocking URLs with *robots.txt* or using parameter/directory-based blocking) or nofollow the link and canonicalize it to a superset.

Option JavaScript/AJAX

We've established that ***essential and important facets/filters should always be accessible to search engines through plain HTML links*** (not JavaScript/AJAX links). Overhead filters, on the other hand, can safely be hidden from search engine bots.

Theoretically, you can hide the entire faceted navigation from search engines by loading it with search engine "unfriendly" JavaScript/AJAX. We've seen this deployed at OfficeMax. But excluding the entire faceted navigation is usually a bad idea and should be done only if there are alternative paths for search engines to reach pages created for *all essential and important facets*. In practice, this is neither feasible nor recommended.

One option is to allow search engines access to only the most important facet/filter links, while hiding the overhead links. For example, load only the important facets and filters as plain HTML links, and load the overhead filters/facets with AJAX. Users will be able to access both types of link, as they will be generated in the browser (e.g., using "see more options" links).

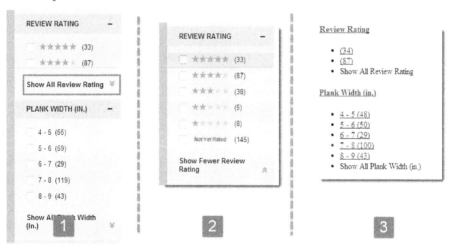

Figure 363 Some links are not accessible to search engines.

In the above example, users are presented just two filters for the *Review Rating* facets, with a link to *Show All Review Rating* (column 1). When they click on that link, they see all the filters (column 2). However, the *Show All Review Rating* is not a link for search engines. This will effectively limit the number of filters search engines discover. You can hide entire facets or just some filters.

For example, eBay initially presents users with only a limited number of filters and facets, then at click on "see all" or "More refinements" opens all of them in a modal window:

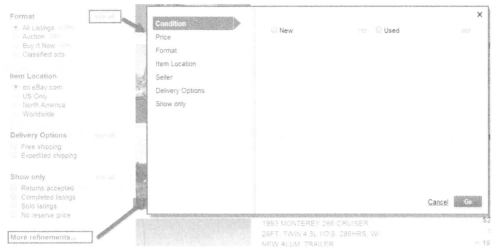

Figure 364 The modal window contains all the links users need.

The content modal of the modal window is not accessible to search engines, as you can see in the image below:

Figure 365 The *More refinements* link is not accessible to search engines.

One advantage of selectively loading filters and facets with AJAX is that it helps pass PageRank to important pages (PageRank sculpting). If you don't want useless pages in the index, why give Google access to them in the first place? Another advantage is that it will prevent unnecessary links from being crawled.

The hash mark

You can append the parameters after a hash mark (#) to avoid indexing of pages with filtering parameters. This means that you can let faceted navigation create URLs for every possible combination of filters. Currently, search engines ignore everything after the # sign (AJAX content is signaled with hashbang, #!), but this may change in the future.

For search engines, the page:

http://www.modcloth.com/shop/books#?price=28,70&sort=newest&page=1

has the same content as:

http://www.modcloth.com/shop/books

The hash mark could consolidate linking signals to *http://www.modcloth.com/shop/books*, but all the pages generated using with the hash mark won't be indexed; therefore, they can't rank.

However, you can selectively place just the overhead filters after the hash mark. Whenever an essential or important facet is selected, include it in a clean URL, before the hash mark. Multiple selection filters can also be added after #.

URL parameters handling tools

You can use Bing's and Google's parameter handling tools to hint to search engines about filtering (narrowing) parameters:

Figure 366 The above setup hints to Google that the *mid* parameter is used for narrowing the content. I prefer to hint to Google about the effect that each parameter has on the page content, but to *let Googlebot decide* which URLs to crawl.

The above setup is only a clue for search engines, so you still need to address crawling and duplicate content using another method (e.g., block overhead facets with selective *robots.txt* or hide them with AJAX), or with a combination of methods.

Option noindex, follow

Adding the *noindex, follow* meta tag to pages generated by overhead filters can help address "index bloat" issues, but it will not prevent spiders from getting caught in filtering traps.

Noindex, follow can be used in conjunction with *robots.txt* to prevent the crawling and indexing of new websites. However, if unwanted URLs have already been crawled and indexed, first you have to add *noindex, follow* to those pages and let search engine robots crawl them (which means you won't block the URLs with *robots.txt*). Once the URLs have been removed from the indices, you can block the unwanted URLs with *robots.txt*.

Sorting items

Users must be allowed to sort listings based on various options. The most popular sort options are *bestsellers* (or *best selling*), *new arrivals, most rated, price* (*high to low* and *low to high*), product names and even discount percentage.

Figure 367 Popular sorting options.

Sort order simply changes the order the content is presented in, not the content itself. This will create duplicate (or near-duplicate) content problems, especially when the sorting can be bidirectional (e.g., sort by price—*high to low* and *low to high*) or when the entire listing is on a single page (*view-all*). Google tells us that if the sort parameters never exist in the URLs by default, they don't even want to crawl those URLs:

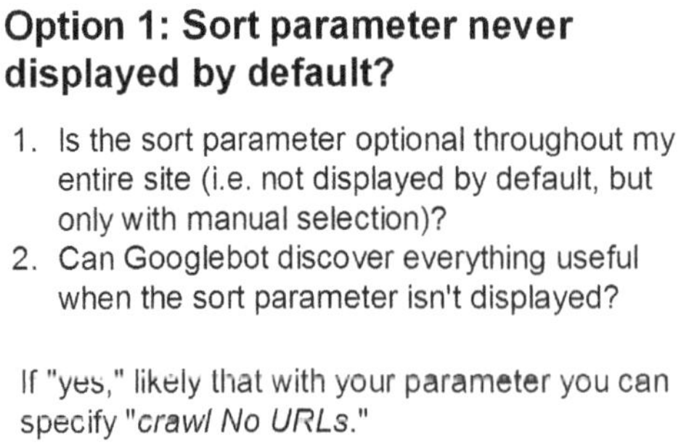

Option 1: Sort parameter never displayed by default?

1. Is the sort parameter optional throughout my entire site (i.e. not displayed by default, but only with manual selection)?
2. Can Googlebot discover everything useful when the sort parameter isn't displayed?

If "yes," likely that with your parameter you can specify "*crawl No URLs.*"

Figure 368 Screencap from *URL Parameters in Webmaster Tools* presentation.[52]

The best way to approach sorting is situational, depending on how your listings are set up. Here are several of the most-used approaches.

Use rel="canonical"

Many times, the sort parameters are kept in the URL. When users change the sort order, the sort parameters are appended to the URL and the page reloads with new content. In this case, you can use rel="canonical" on sorted pages to point to a default page (e.g., sorted by bestsellers).

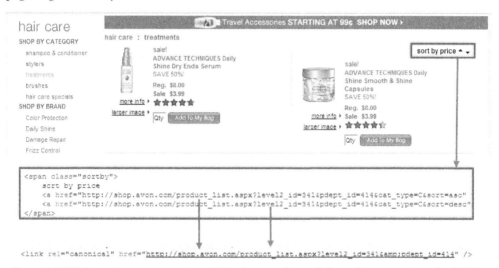

Figure 369 While sorting generates unique URLs for ascending and descending sort options, both URLs point to the same canonical URL.

The use of rel="canonical" is advisable when the sorting happens on a single page, because sorting the content will change only how it's displayed but not the content itself. This means that the content on each page, although sortable, will not be different, and that the generated page is a duplicate. For instance, when sorting reorders the content on a *view-all* page, you generate exact duplicates (given that the *view-all* page lists all items in the inventory). When the content is sorted on a page-by-page basis rather than using the entire paginated listing, you also create duplicate content.

Removing or blocking sort order URLs

This requires either adding rel="noindex, follow" to sorting URLs or blocking access to them altogether with *robots.txt* or within webmaster tools accounts.

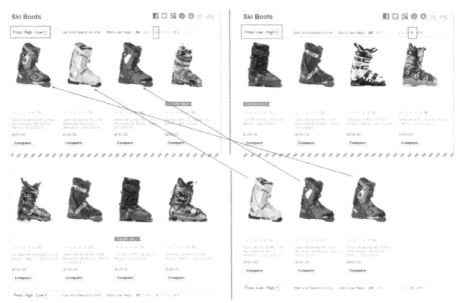

Figure 370 Items can be sorted in two directions (i.e., by *price high to low* and *price low to high*).

When items can be sorted in two directions, as in the above example, the first product on the first page sorted "High To Low" becomes the last product on the last page sorted "Low To High". The second product on the first page then becomes the second to last product on the last page, and so on.

One way to handle bidirectional sorting is to allow search engines to index in only one sorting direction and remove/block access to the other. For example, you allow the crawling and indexing of "High to Low" and block the "Low to High" view:

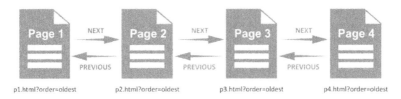

The order = newest key-value pair will be blocked

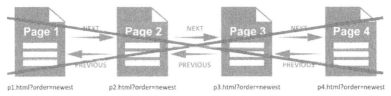

Figure 371 Removing or blocking sort-order URLs is the easiest method to implement and may help you address pagination issues quickly until you're ready to move ahead with a more complex solution.

Use AJAX to sort

With this approach, you sort the content using AJAX, and the URLs don't change when the user chooses a new sort option. All external links are naturally consolidated to a single URL, as there is only one URL to link to.

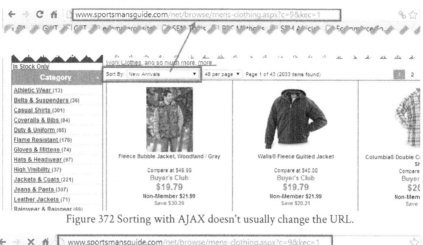

Figure 372 Sorting with AJAX doesn't usually change the URL.

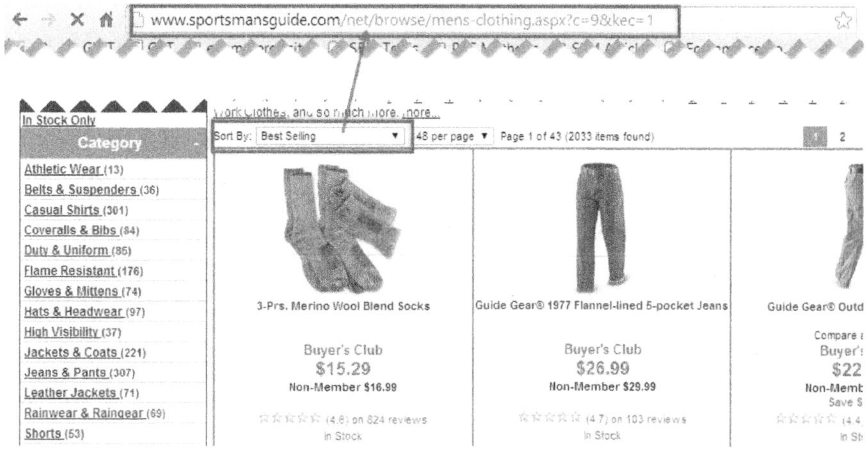

Figure 373 While the content changes when users select various sort options, the URL remains the same.

This method makes it impossible to link, share or bookmark a certain sorted view. But do people really link or share sorted or paginated listings? Even if they do, how relevant will a certain pagination or sorting page be a week or a month from the moment it was linked or shared? Products are added to and/or removed from listings on a regular basis, frequently changing the order of products in a particular listing. Chances are that the products listed on *page 2 sorted by price* today will be partially or totally different from the products listed on the same page the next week.

So, I don't think *shareability* and *linkability* should be concerns when you're deciding whether to implement AJAX. If it's better for users, do it.

Use hash marks in the URL

Using hash marks in the URL allows page reloading without the URL updating. It also allows sharing, bookmarking and linking to individual URLs. A rel="canonical" pointing to the default URL (without #) will consolidate eventual links to a single URL.

Figure 374 The default view sorts by *Most Relevant*. This will be the canonical page.

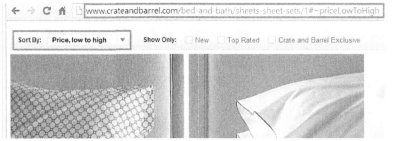

Figure 375 When sorted by *Price, low to high*, the URL contains the hash mark.

Currently, unless you use a hashbang (#!) to signal AJAX content, search engines typically ignore everything after the hash mark. This is because # is typically used by the browser, and using it in an URL doesn't cause additional information to be pulled from the web server.

The hash mark implementation is an elegant solution that addresses user concerns and possible duplicate issues.

View options

Just as various users prefer different sort options, some users want to change the default way of displaying listings. The most popular view options are *view N results per page* or *view as list/grid*. While good for users, view options can cause problems for search engines.

Figure 376 Users can choose to view the listing as a compact grid or as a detailed list; they can also choose the number of items per page.

Grid and list views

On most ecommerce websites, the list view and the grid view display the same item information:

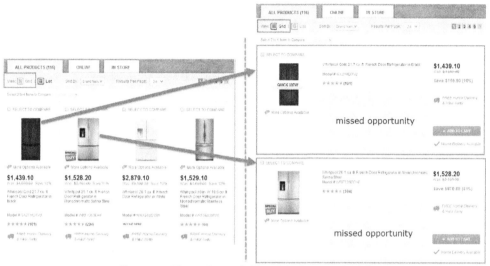

Figure 377 The grid view (left) and the list view (right).

Usually, both the grid and the list views present the same amount of product info, but the list view allows far more space, which could be filled with additional product information.

This space represents a big SEO opportunity, as it can be used not only to increase the amount of content on the listing page, but also to create relevant contextual internal links to products or parent categories.

The optimal approach for view options is to load the list-view content in the source code in a way that is accessible to search engines, then use AJAX/JavaScript and CSS to switch between views in the browser.

You don't really need to generate separate URLs for each view. But in case you do, those pages will contain duplicate content, and the way to handle them is with rel="canonical" to a default view.

For example, both URLs below point the rel="canonical" to */French-Door-Refrigerators/products* (which lists the items in a grid):

/French-Door-Refrigerators/products?style=List

/French-Door-Refrigerators/products?style=Grid

View N items

Many ecommerce websites have this feature, allowing users to select the number of items in the listing:

Figure 378 Typical dropdown for the *view N items per page* option.

If possible, your default product listing will be the *view-all* page. If *view-all* is not an option, you should display a default number in the list (about 20) and offer a *view-all* link or button.

MEN'S NIKEiD

Figure 379 Nike's *view-all* option is right in the menu.

If the *view-all* generates an unmanageable page, let users choose between two numbers, where the second number is substantially bigger than the default (e.g., 60 and 180). Remember to keep users' preferences in a session, or even a persistent cookie.[53]

464 Items | View 60 View 180 | 1 of 8 | ◀ 1 2 3 4 5 ▶

Figure 380 The second view option is substantially larger than the first one.

From an SEO perspective, *view N items per page* URLs are traditionally handled with rel="canonical" pointing to default listing pages—usually the index pages of the department, category or subcategory. For instance, on a listing with 464 items, the *view 180 items per page* parameter can be kept in the key-value pair *itemsPerPage=180* and the URL may look like:

www.mywebsite.com/seat-covers/10A522.aspx?itemsPerPage=180

This URL lists 180 items per page and will contain a rel="canonical" in the *<head>*, pointing to the category's default URL:

www.mywebsite.com/seat-covers/10A522.aspx

The URL above lists only 60 items by default, and that is what search engines will index.

This means that a larger subset (180) canonicalizes to a smaller subset (60). This approach can create some issues, because Google will index the content on the canonical page, while ignoring the content from the rest of the *view N items* pages. In this case, you need to make sure search engines can somehow access **each** of the items in the entire set (464)—for example, with paginated content that is handled with rel="prev" and rel="next" (so that Google consolidates all component pages into the canonical URL).

The use of rel="canonical" on a *view N items* page is appropriate if the canonical points either to a *view-all* page or to the largest subset of items. The former option is not desirable if you want another page to surface in search results (e.g., the first page in a paginated series with 20 items listed by default).

The approaches for *view N items* pages are similar to those for handling sorting: a *view-all* page combined with AJAX/JavaScript to change the display in the browser, uncrawlable AJAX/JavaScript links, hash-marked URLs or "noindex, follow" meta tags. I have listed these approaches in my preferred order, but keep in mind that while one approach might suit the particular conditions of one website, it may not work for another.

CHAPTER EIGHT

Product Detail Pages

Finally, we'll now discuss the bread and butter of ecommerce websites, the product detail pages (PDPs). Since that's where the *add to cart* micro-conversion happens, PDPs are almost unanimously considered the "money pages" and get the most SEO attention. After all, if you don't rank when someone searches for product names, you won't have the chance to make a sale.

While the focus of the product detail pages is to convince and convert, conversion has to be balanced with SEO. In this chapter, we'll break down the most important sections of product detail pages and look at ways to optimize for a better search experience.

URLs

It's a good idea to keep products on category-free URLs whenever possible, because products can move from one category to another or category names can change—although neither of these alterations is advisable, as re-categorization and/or renaming means that you will need to handle 301 redirects (possibly multiple 301s), which can quickly become a headache.

While a product can be accessed through multiple paths (due to multiple categorization), the final PDP URL should not contain categories or subcategories:

Use *www.mywebsite.com/product-name* instead of *www.mywebsite.com/category-1/product-name* and *www.mywebsite.com/category-2/product-name*

If you need to feature categories in the URLs (as in the above example), then point the rel="canonical" to the representative URL. Link to the canonical URL only in the navigation and on internal links.

If the product comes in multiple variations, the URL may contain some important attributes (e.g., manufacturer, brand name or even color, if this is an important attribute for your target market):

www.mywebsite.com/brand-product-name-important-attribute

Such URLs are ok since products usually belong to one brand only.

If you need to use categories or subcategories to generate PDP URLs:

- Set the category or subcategory name in stone.

- Use the product's canonical category and keep the product under this category or subcategory.

Do these to avoid 301 redirects and increased .htaccess files (which will slow your servers).

Images

Images are magnets for people's eyes. Users get product info from images, including details that aren't covered in the product descriptions (which are mainly skimmed, not thoroughly read). So it's no surprise that higher quality, multiple-angle and product-in-action images increase user satisfaction. But images also need to be optimized for search engines.

Savvy online retailers understand the importance of images, especially product images, when it comes to increasing conversion rates. A study[1] of online consumers found:

- 67% of consumers believe that an image is "very important" when selecting a product.

- More than 50% of consumers value the quality of a product's image more than product information, description, or rating and reviews.

From an SEO point of view, product images can drive organic traffic through *Google Image Search* and can also be used to improve document relevance and internal linking. For instance, search engines use the alternative text (the *alt* attribute of the *img* element) to gauge what the image is about.

We'll start with a very basic implementation of the *img* element, ending up with a highly optimized, SEO-friendly *img* tag. (Note: I'll use the terms *tag* and *element* interchangeably.)

<img src="0012adsds.gif" />

How do search engines analyze images?

Here are some signals that search engines use to understand, categorize and rank images:

- Colors, size and image resolution.

- Image type—does the image contain a face, photo, drawing or clip art?

- Weighting text by its distance from an image, and extracting context from text around an image.

- Overall theme of the website (e.g., adult websites will have all images labeled as "adult" and will be filtered).

- The *alt* attribute (directly used in document relevance analysis) and title attributes (not cached or ranked by search engines, but they can provide additional context).

- Image file names.

- Total number of thumbnail images located on the same webpage as the ranked image.

- Possibly OCR (optical character recognition).

As you can see, search engines take into consideration plenty of clues when analyzing images. A Microsoft patent application from 2008 provides an interesting description of how images are ranked for image search.[2]

Here are some image optimization best practices:

Take your own images

This will help you differentiate and can open doors for image licensing partnerships (which may come with some valuable backlinks). However, having familiar imagery is important when searchers look for a specific product they already know. If you do take your own product images, differentiate but don't be too unique.

Add an alt attribute to every significant image

Adding *alt* text to images is the best way to give search engines more information about them and about the page content. Without an *alt* text, the chances of the image being indexed in Google Images are low.

<img src="0012adsds.gif" alt="yellow t-shirt" />

The only attribute of the *img* element that gets cached by search engines is the content of the *alt* attribute.

Below is a typical product listing page:

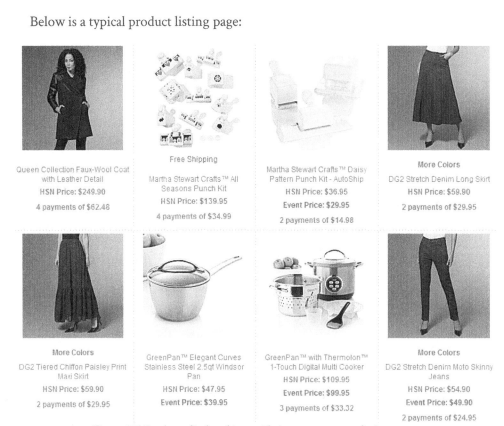

Figure 381 Products displayed in a grid view on a category listing page.

And below is the image data that will be cached by search engines, based on the content of the *alt* attributes:

Queen Collection Faux-Wool Coat with Leather Detail	Martha Stewart Crafts™ All Seasons Punch Kit	Martha Stewart Crafts™ Daisy Pattern Punch Kit - AutoShip	DG2 Stretch Denim Long Skirt
	Free Shipping		More Colors
Queen Collection Faux-Wool Coat with Leather Detail	Martha Stewart Crafts™ All Seasons Punch Kit	Martha Stewart Crafts™ Daisy Pattern Punch Kit - AutoShip	DG2 Stretch Denim Long Skirt
HSN Price: $249.90	HSN Price: $139.95	HSN Price: $36.95	HSN Price: $59.90
4 payments of $62.48	4 payments of $34.99	Event Price: $29.95	2 payments of $29.95
		2 payments of $14.98	

DG2 Tiered Chiffon Paisley Print Maxi Skirt	GreenPan™ Elegant Curves Stainless Steel 2.5qt Windsor Pan	GreenPan™ with Thermolon™ 1-Touch Digital Multi Cooker	DG2 Stretch Denim Moto Skinny Jeans
More Colors			More Colors
DG2 Tiered Chiffon Paisley Print Maxi Skirt	GreenPan™ Elegant Curves Stainless Steel 2.5qt Windsor Pan	GreenPan™ with Thermolon™ 1-Touch Digital Multi Cooker	DG2 Stretch Denim Moto Skinny Jeans
HSN Price: $59.90	HSN Price: $47.95	HSN Price: $109.95	HSN Price: $54.90
2 payments of $29.95	Event Price: $39.95	Event Price: $99.95	Event Price: $49.90
		3 payments of $33.32	2 payments of $24.95

DG2 Two-Tone Denim Trench Coat with Antique Buttons	Perlier Mini Shower Gel Assortment Gift Box	Perlier Mini Body Cream Assortment Gift Box	Perlier Mini Hand Cream Assortment Gift Box
More Colors	Perlier Mini Shower Gel Assortment Gift Box	Perlier Mini Body Cream Assortment Gift Box	Perlier Mini Hand Cream Assortment Gift Box
DG2 Two-Tone Denim Trench Coat with Antique Buttons	HSN Price: $19.95	HSN Price: $19.95	HSN Price: $19.95
HSN Price: $99.90			
3 payments of $33.30			

Figure 382 The *alt* texts are highlighted with a border.

The *alt* attributes should contain keywords but not be simply a list of keywords. When writing the alternative text for your product images, think of how you would describe the product to a blind person in a very succinct and relevant way (maybe fewer than 150 characters). That sentence will be your *alt* attribute.

Most of the time, the *alt* text of a product thumbnail image is the exact product name or, in the case of category listings, the category name. However, you can add a few more details on top of the product name. Instead of *alt="DG2 Stretch Denim Long Skirt"* you could use *alt="DG2 Stretch Denim Long Skirt in brown"*.

Spacer images, 1px gifs or other images used just for design purposes should still have an *alt* attribute, but it should be empty, *alt=""*. This is mostly for code validation and cross-browser compatibility. All other images that visually depict something important to visitors should have a descriptive text.

Microsoft recommends:

"Place relevant text near the beginning of the alt attribute to enable search engines to better correlate the keywords with the image. A copyright symbol or other copyright notice at the beginning of the alt attribute will indicate to the search engines that the most search-relevant aspect of the image is the copyright, rather than what the image actually depicts. If you require a copyright notice, consider moving it to the end of the alt attribute text." [3]

More of Microsoft's recommendations for the alt attribute can be found in their "Image Guidelines for SEO".[4]

Note: More and more websites have started using CSS sprites to reduce the number of HTTP requests made to the web server, thus improving page load times. While this is great, the implementation makes the use of standard *img* elements with *alt* attributes impossible, raising usability and SEO concerns. You can load icons, spacers and other small images with sprites, but product images should be loaded as single images.

Use the title attribute

The content of the title attributes for images is not cached by search engines. However, this doesn't mean that search engines don't use the title attribute to extract relevance signals, or that you shouldn't implement it. The title attribute displays as a tooltip on mouseover in many browsers and is used to give users additional information.

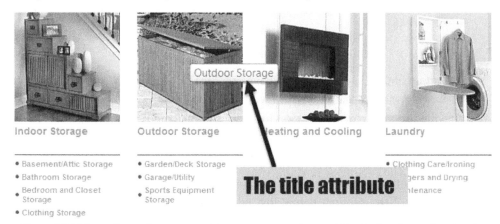

Figure 383 Title attributes show up as tooltips on mouseover images. The *Outdoor Storage* thumbnail contains the title attribute "Outdoor Storage".

If an image is representative, it requires an alternative text, and it can have a title attribute, too. The content of the title attribute shouldn't be an exact copy of the *alt* text but rather should complement it. Keep its title attribute short enough (below 255 characters) and don't just list keywords—create a meaningful sentence.

The initial sample *img* tag can now be improved to:

<img src="0012adsds.gif" alt="yellow t-shirt" **title="athletic women wearing a yellow tee shirt"** */>*

Don't underestimate the title attributes just because search engines don't cache their content. They can play a big role in providing context to users, and we don't really know how search engines use them to extract relevance.

Specify the width and height of the img tag

Let's improve the *img* tag further for better browser rendering and page load speed:

<img src="0012adsds.gif" alt="yellow t-shirt on a model" title="athletic women wearing a yellow tee shirt while running" **height="250" weight="100"** */>*

```
<div class="product-thumb">
<a href="http://www.williams-sonoma.com/products/beaba-multiportion-baby-food-freezer-tray/?pkey=ccooking-for-baby"
title="Beaba Multiportion Baby Food Freezer Tray">
<img alt="Beaba Multiportion Baby Food Freezer Tray" title="Beaba Multiportion Baby Food Freezer Tray"
src="http://www.williams-sonoma.com/wsimgs/ab/images/dp/wcm/201135/0029/img74t.jpg" height="165" width="165"
class="product-thumb"/>
```

Figure 384 The image has a *height* and *width* attribute for better, faster browser rendering.

Tip: For infinite scrolling or other image-heavy use, defer image loading until images are visible in the browser.

Use keyword-rich file names

You've probably noticed the unfriendly file name used in the initial example: *0012adsds.gif*. This type of file name doesn't help search engines understand what the image is about and should be avoided.

SRC	http://www.usautoparts.net/images/design/brake-discs.jpg
WIDTH	121
HEIGHT	89
ALT	Brake Discs

Figure 385 Good image file naming.

Your file names should include the product name, the category name, or whatever is depicted in the image. Having keywords in file names has long been recognized as an SEO factor, as stated by Matt Cutts in this video.[5]

A common challenge for large ecommerce websites that use hosted image solutions to manage, enhance and publish media content is that most of these solutions don't create SEO-friendly image names—for example:

http://s7d5.scene7.com/is/image/TerritoryAhead/116015_ZZZZ?$pdppreview_360$

Talk to your provider to find out whether there's a workaround to achieve a better file-naming convention.

Optimizing our example further, we now have:

*<img src="**yellow-t-shirt.gif**" alt="yellow t-shirt on a model" title="athletic women wearing a yellow tee shirt while running" height="250" weight="100"/>*

You should set and enforce image-naming rules, otherwise things can quickly get messy. For example, you could have a rule to add the image ID at the end of the file name, after two plus signs, i.e., *yellow-t-shirt++0012.gif.*

Provide context for your images by using captions and nearby text

Image captions or nearby text surrounding the image can provide context to search engines.

Switch between apps quickly.
The multitasking user interface allows you to quickly switch between apps. Just double-click the Home button to reveal your recently used apps. Scroll right to see more apps, then tap one to reopen it. No need to wait for the app to reload.

And pick up right where you left off.
Apps can remember where you left off. So when you return to the app, you can jump right back into playing your game, reading the news, finding a restaurant, or whatever you were doing.

Figure 386 The descriptions below the phone images provide context to search engines.

Apart from adding relevant image captions, you can provide better context for your images by placing plain text content nearby. Add a relevant sentence as close as possible to the image whenever possible, both visually and in the HTML code.

Here's how the *img* element can be improved even further by adding a caption:

*<li><img src="yellow-t-shirt.gif" alt="yellow t-shirt on a model" title="athletic women wearing a yellow tee shirt while running" height="250" weight="100" />**Adidas 2011 Summer Collection** </br> Yellow T-Shirt</li>*

In many cases, the caption will be the product or category name.

Create standalone landing pages for each image

If it makes sense (e.g., if you sell stock images), create dedicated landing pages for each image.

Figure 387 A clean, useful landing page dedicated to a single image on pixmac.com.

You can allow users to comment on, share or rate images on these pages and encourage them to generate content.

Create image XML Sitemaps

Create image XML Sitemaps and include information about your product and category images. Here are the official guidelines on how to do this.[6]

```
<?xml version="1.0" encoding="UTF-8"?>
 <urlset xmlns="http://www.sitemaps.org/schemas/sitemap/0.9"
  xmlns:image="http://www.google.com/schemas/sitemap-image/1.1">
 <url>
   <loc>http://example.com/sample.html</loc>
  <image:image>
    <image:loc>http://example.com/image.jpg</image:loc>
  </image:image>
  <image:image>
    <image:loc>http://example.com/photo.jpg</image:loc>
  </image:image>
 </url>
 </urlset>
```

Figure 388 XML Sitemap file with supplemental image information.

Submit the image Sitemap to Google. You will be able to specify information such as image caption, geo location, title attribute and license.

Add EXIF data to your images

At least one search engine (Google) has confirmed that it uses EXIF[7] data when analyzing images. More and more photo and mobile devices automatically add information—such as geo location, the owner of the picture or the camera orientation—to the EXIF data. If EXIF has the potential to give search engines additional info about a picture (and apparently it has), consider editing the EXIF data for your product and category images. Don't make this a top priority, though.

Adding image meta data such as *User Comments* can be a good way to reinforce your image's title or *alt* text. Other meta data that may be useful are *Artist, Copyright* or *Image Description*.

Metering Mode	Pattern
Flash	Flash did not fire, compulsory flash mode
Focal Length	10.6mm
Maker Note	1208 Byte
User Comment	Cypress Mountain covered with snow and a beatiful view of Pacific Ocean, just above Vancouver, Canada
Flashpix Version	Version 1.0

Figure 389 You can use EXIF editors to change images' meta data.

It may be worth testing how adding EXIF meta data affects traffic from Image Search. Also keep in mind that when you use image optimization software to reduce image size, you can accidentally remove existing EXIF data.

Group similar images into folders

If possible and appropriate, all images that can be logically grouped around a similar theme should be grouped into folders.

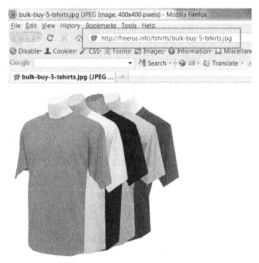

Figure 390 The t-shirt image is located under the */t-shirt/* directory that contains only t-shirt images.

The advantages of grouping into folders are that you will be able to (i) add keywords to the image URL and (ii) provide relevance clues to Google Image Search users. While they have limited influence on rankings, keywords in the directory structure are some of the signals search engines are looking for.

In our example, you can put the image under the */t-shirts/* directory. Now, the *img* tag becomes:

<li><img src="/t-shirts/yellow-t-shirt.gif" alt="yellow t-shirt on a model" title="athletic women wearing a yellow tee shirt while running" height="250" weight="100" />Adidas 2011 Summer Collection </br> Yellow T-Shirt</li>

Note: You should place your adult (or other sensitive) images into separate directories.

Use absolute image source paths

The way you reference the image source (*src*) doesn't directly influence rankings, but using absolute instead of relative paths can help to avoid problems with crawling, broken links, content scrappers and 404 errors.

If we update the *src* to reference an absolute path, our example becomes:

<li><img src="http://www.domain.com/t-shirts/yellow-t-shirt.gif" alt="yellow t-shirt on a model" title="athletic women wearing a yellow tee shirt while running" height="250" weight="100" />Adidas 2011 Summer Collection </br> Yellow T-Shirt</li>

Make the images accessible through plain HTML links

Don't use Flash or JavaScript to create slide shows, swatches, zooming or other similar features; these will make it impossible for search engines to find image URLs for important images. If you have to use JavaScript, provide alternative image URLs—otherwise search engines won't be able to crawl them easily, and the images might not get displayed in Image Search.

Search engines know that users like high-quality images, so always keep the high-resolution product image URLs accessible when JavaScript is disabled. Search engines can execute some basic JavaScript, but if the only way to reach a product image is with JavaScript enabled, crawlers may never discover that image.

Tip: Place your product images above the fold.

Implement plain text buttons

One technique for improving page load speed, and in some cases even the internal link relevance, is to create web buttons with CSS and HTML. Instead of using the classic web button made of an image, you mimic the appearance of a button by overlaying plain text on a CSS-styled background.

Here's what the implementation looks like:

More Popular Prescription Drugs

Buy Advair	Buy Celebrex	Buy Crestor	Buy Lipitor
Buy Nexium	Buy Norvasc	Buy Plavix	Buy Propecia
Buy Protonix	Buy Singulair	Buy Zocor	

Figure 391 The text "Buy Celebrex" is plain text that can be selected with the mouse.

Since search engines seem to assign a bit more weight to text links than to image alt text, this technique has the potential to increase the relevance of the linked-to page.

The opposite of this technique is to take "unwanted" text (e.g., site-wide boilerplate text) and embed it in images. For instance, if you have a global footer that includes a regulatory warning at the bottom of each page of the website, you could embed it into an image so that it's not diluting your overall site theme. This is a bit gray hat. Keep in mind that this technique is used mostly by spammers to pass email filters, and it can be flagged as spam on web pages, too. Use it at your own risk.

> These statements have not been evaluated by the FDA. This product is not intended to diagnose, treat, cure or prevent any disease.

> Information in this site is provided for informational purposes only. It is not mean to substitute for any medical advice provided by your physician or other medical professional. You should not use the information contained herein for diagnosing or treating a health problem or disease, or prescribing any medication. You should read carefully all product packaging and labels. If you have or suspect that you have a medical problem, promptly contact your physician or health care provider.

Figure 392 The above text is not plain text; it's actually embedded in an image.

Make images easy to share

Whenever appropriate, make it easy for users to share and embed your images. This way you can generate backlinks with the correct attribution. Take a look at how Flickr integrates social sharing and embeds codes:

Figure 393 It's pretty easy to share and embed Flickr images. Why not your product images, too?

So, we started with a very basic image source link:

<img src="0012adsds.gif" />

And we've ended up with this optimized version:

<li><img src="http://www.domain.com/t-shirts/yellow-t-shirt.gif" alt="yellow t-shirt on a model" title="athletic women wearing a yellow tee shirt while running" height="250" weight="100" />Adidas 2011 Summer Collection</br> Yellow T-Shirt</li>

Videos

A 2011 study[8] found that videos in search results have a 41% higher CTR than plain-text results. One online retailer found that visitors who view product videos are 85% more likely to buy than visitors who do not.[9] According to econsultancy Zappos, sales increase 6–30% on products with product videos.[10] There are multiple benefits to having videos on PDPs, so there's no doubt that you should do it if the budget permits.

Videos can be self-hosted (either on your own servers or using cloud solutions) or delivered by a third-party hosting provider (e.g., YouTube is free; Wistia is a paid secure hosting solution). If you go with a free third-party solution, you will miss the opportunity to gather links to your pages, but you will save money. However if the video goes viral, you will miss a lot of backlinks and social sharing.

For example, Dollar Shave Club launched their now viral video on YouTube[11] and gathered almost 20,000 backlinks. If they had self-hosted the video, people would have linked directly to their website, and the number of links could have been even larger.

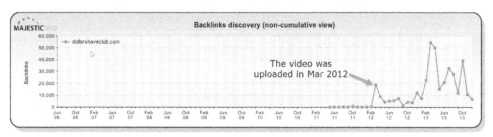

Figure 394 The number of backlinks for dollarshaveclub.com spiked after the video went viral.

Here are several tactics to get the most out of your product videos:

- Transcribe the video and make the text available to search engines, whenever doing so makes sense (e.g., when you have an expert video review of the product, or how-to videos).

- Add social sharing buttons and easy-to-use embed codes.

- Create video XML Sitemaps[12] and submit them using Google and Bing Webmaster accounts.

- Repurpose your videos to produce related content—e.g., presentations, user manual, instructographics,[13] podcasts, etc. (Note that conversely, you can also use other media types to create the videos.)

- Mark up the product video with schema.org vocabulary.[14]

- If possible, embed the video with HTML5 or Flash rather than iframes.

It's best to either self-host the videos or use a paid secure hosting solution (Wistia, Vimeo Pro or BrightCove), so you'll increase the chances of getting video-rich SERP snippets for your own domain name. YouTube provides rich snippets for the domains they are embedded on, but only sporadically.

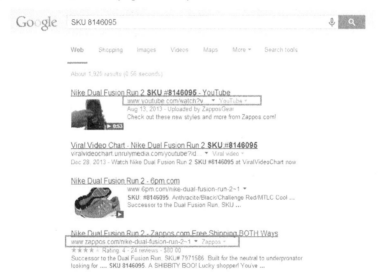

Figure 395 Google ranks a YouTube video first, while Zappos doesn't get a video rich snippet, although a video is included on their page.

Product descriptions

Product descriptions should be written so as to improve conversions by creating an emotional connection with the user (evoking any emotion is better than not evoking emotion at all) and enticing him to take action. While most people only skim the descriptions, if you carefully craft the first sentence to be engaging enough, you will increase the chances of making a sale.

The best product descriptions are written by copywriters with some basic SEO training and familiarity with the product, not by SEOs with basic copywriting skills.

| **PRODUCT INFO** | PRODUCT REVIEWS | FIND IN-STORE | SIZE CHART |

Whoa girl. You're blooming like nobody's business with our hot new floral print. Seen here in our 70s lowrider tie side bikini bottom, this style sits very low on your hips, with string loop side ties thrown in for fun. What's more, its full coverage makes it your best choice for surfing and swimming. Hand wash in cold water. 80% nylon/20% spandex. Imported.

Figure 396 Check out this swimsuit description. It doesn't read like the classic SEO style you're used to, does it?

It's a lot of work to write converting product descriptions, and therefore you may be tempted to skip it. However, the good news is that many of your competitors will not invest in product descriptions for the same reason. You can capitalize on their mindset and start differentiating your brand and gaining SEO advantage at the same time.

Prominently display a brief product copy crafted to sell the benefits of the product (aka the *benefits copy*) in an easy-to-spot place on the product page. You can complement it with a more detailed product copy that describes the product features (aka the *features copy*) on a less important area of the page. Try to incorporate the following into the copy:

- Product-related keywords (e.g., SKU, UPC, catalog number, IBAN, part number, etc.).

- The root of the product, variations, and synonyms (e.g., "seat", "seating", "chair").

- The product name (repeat it in the description at least once).

- Other names the product might be known by.

The above will be important not only for search engines, but for internal site search as well (given that the site search uses multiple data sources to score and rank items). So review your analytics data, incorporate frequently searched queries into your product descriptions, and use the same queries to feed your internal site search database.

Figure 397 Section 1 focuses on benefits, while section 2 lists the features.

In the above example, the layout of the PDP allows the *features copy* to follow immediately below the *benefits copy*, which is ideal but not always possible due to design constraints. In many cases, the page layout allows room for only one or two sentences, with a link to a section farther down the page for more detailed product info—for instance, in tabbed navigation:

Figure 398 Tabbed navigation allows space for longer product descriptions.

Tabbed navigation is a very common design element on PDPs, but there are some concerns about how search engines treat content that is not visible to users (e.g., in tabs or *read more* collapse/expand sections). Search engines will index this content, but we don't know whether they assign the same weight to content in tabs. Matt Cutts suggests that text hidden for design purposes is fine, as long as you don't hide too much content with too many links.[15]

You could put each tab on its own URL, but that would decrease the overall content on the product details page, which doesn't sound like the best idea either. And the user experience is better if the tab can be switched quickly, without reloading the page.

One solution is to display the entire product description without any expand/collapse or tabs. Search engines seem to prefer this, but design limitations introduce constraints.

Figure 399 This is a well-written product description, visible without any tabs. This is also a very good example of how a "boring" product can have a great description.

If you want to use tabs to make the user experience more pleasant, consider the following:

- Put the product description (or the other more important content) in the active/open tab. If search engines are able to understand which content is hidden and which is not, then putting the most important content in the open/active tab increases the chance of getting more out of it.

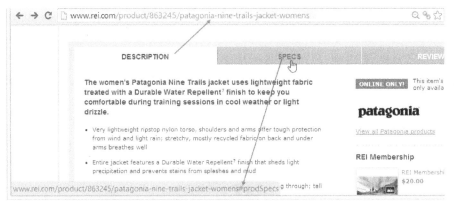

Figure 400 The product description is visible when the page is accessed. Additionally, the implementation uses hash marks to switch between tabs.

- Don't generate separate URLs for each tab unless the information provided is substantial enough to justify creating a new page.

- If you want the content inside the tabs to be indexed, make sure it's available with JavaScript disabled.

- If the tabs contain the same boilerplate text on all product detail pages (e.g., shipping information, legal, etc.), you can put the repetitive text in an iframe to avoid duplicate content issues.

- Consider placing user reviews outside the tabbed navigation.

Tip: Product descriptions are one of the best spots to feature internal contextual links. Ideally, you will link to parent categories in the same silo (think of the URLs in the breadcrumbs), but you can also link to other related pages. Because internal links may be taking users away from the product page, you should balance internal linking and conversion.

If you're not careful, however, product descriptions can generate duplicate content either on your own site (the same product description used across multiple product variations' URLs) or on external websites (when using generic manufacturer-supplied descriptions).

Manufacturer-supplied descriptions

The general SEO wisdom is that you should write your own unique product descriptions. That is indeed one of the best approaches to optimizing PDPs, if you can put it in practice. But keep in mind that this doesn't work with every product or within every industry. For example, it makes sense to write unique product descriptions for an expensive wristwatch, but not for a pencil. Also, this is often not economically feasible for websites with very large inventories.

And in some cases, Google ignores the product description and chooses to rank what's best for users based on their intent and location.[16] So while unique product descriptions may not always rank at the top, you still have to test the impact of writing 100- to 200-word product descriptions at scale, before deciding whether it will work to your advantage. Start with your top 10% most important items, write the descriptions for conversion and branding, then measure the impact on rankings and traffic. If 10% is too much based on your inventory size, then start with the top 100 to 150 products.

If the generic description provided by the manufacturer/supplier is just a small part of the content on a page, it should be fine, according to Matt Cutts.[17] If the manufacturer requires keeping their descriptions and that causes SEO problems, place each description in iframes with a noindex in the frame source. In this case, you'll need to add your own content to differentiate your website from others'.

Handling product variations

Even with your own unique product descriptions, you can run into crawling and duplicate content issues if products come in multiple variations. For example, the Nike Dual Fusion shoes come in red, green and black, and can generate unique URLs for each possible product variation. Product variations usually generate exact or near-duplicate content, and such cases are best handled with rel="canonical". But rel="canonical" is not the only solution.

Decide how to handle product variations once you understand how your target market searches online, and base the decision on your business goals. For instance, if your audience uses search queries that include product variation keywords, you may want to have unique URLs for each variation. Make those page URLs available to users and search engines, and don't use rel="canonical" to a representative URL. The challenge is to make these pages unique by adding unique product descriptions for each of them.

Let's look at a few approaches to handling product variations.

URL consolidation

You handle all different product options in the interface, with a design that makes sense for users. All product variations are listed on a single product details URL that doesn't change when an option is selected in the interface.

For instance, you can provide product options with dropdowns or swatches, as depicted on the next page.

Figure 401 Changing the color and size options with a dropdown selector doesn't change the URL.

Figure 402 These swatches change the product image and details, but on the same URL.

To increase the chances of the consolidated page surfacing in SERPs for variation queries such as "Nike Dual Fusion 2 Run Gray", include the variation as plain text copy in a search engine friendly way. For instance, the product description or the features/spec copy would include something like, "available in gray, red and blue".

If you already have unique URLs for each product variation and you want to consolidate them into one representative URL, you can either 301 redirect or use rel="canonical" to point to the authoritative URL.

Unique URLs for each product variation

This allows product variation pages to show up in SERPs for various product attributes queries, but since these pages are highly similar, they might compete against each other—or worse, be filtered completely from the results. These pages will have a self-referencing rel="canonical". Additionally, having individual URLs for each product variation dilutes indexing properties and links, because users may link to various URLs instead of one.

This approach should be implemented if your data shows your target market searches for various product attributes such as model numbers, colors, sizes, etc. (e.g., different tire sizes, like P195 / 65 R15 89H).

The challenge and key to success with this approach is to create unique enough content for each variation page, so that it doesn't get filtered by Panda or create duplicate content pages.

Unique URLs for each product variation, plus a canonical URL

A hybrid approach is to use the interface to allow users to change product options without changing the URL, but have separate URLs for each product variation *at the same time*. Each product variation URL can point to an authoritative product using rel="canonical". This is how Zappos handles product variations.

The canonical product page is *http://www.zappos.com/nike-dual-fusion-run-2~2*.

The following product variation URLs (different color models) point to the canonical URL above:

- *http://www.zappos.com/nike-dual-fusion-run-2-pure-platinum-dark-gray-gym-red-black*

- *http://www.zappos.com/nike-dual-fusion-run-2-black-pure-platinum-dark-gray-metallic-platinum*

- *http://www.zappos.com/nike-dual-fusion-run-2-pure-platinum-dark-gray-gym-red-black*

Because all color variation pages point to a canonical page, Zappos ranks in Google SERPs with the canonical URL even when someone searches for a color-specific product.

Figure 403 Zappos ranks with the canonical product (which is not red, as in the user's search query). Users will have to take additional steps to find the red color option, which is probably not the best search experience.

Some of the advantages of having separate URLs for product variations are that users can share each variation URL, and that you can get links to specific variations and list them on internal site search results, or even on category pages. For example, if an item is available in various colors, and someone visits the category page and selects "red" from the faceted navigation filters, you'll want to show items in red only. If you don't have separate URLs for "red", it's simply not possible for that user to share the red shoes page with someone else.

Additionally, if you run PPC ads for variation-specific keywords or product listing ads, you need to send users to the product variation landing page. Product attribute targeted landing pages tend to convert better than just one-size-fits-all pages that require users to find the product options.

I usually recommend creating separate URLs for the most important product variations—not just for SEO reasons but also to provide better landing pages for PPC and PLA campaigns. If you get into SEO issues (crawling, duplicate content or ranking cannibalization), you can always noindex or implement rel="canonical" to point to the primary URL.

"Google allows rel="canonical" from individual product variations to a general/default version (e.g., "Taccetti 53155 Pump in Beige" and "Taccetti 53166 Pump in Black" with rel="canonical" to "Taccetti 53155 Pump") as long as the general version mentions the product variations. By doing so, the general product page acts as a view-all page and only the general version may surface in search results (suppressing the individual variation pages)."[18]

Thin content

Even after creating unique descriptions for every single product in the database, you might find that pages have been filtered out of SERPs because they have been classified as "thin". This means that the amount of content on the PDPs is not "convincing" enough for Google to include the URLs in its results.

Figure 404 That's all the description for this product, and pretty much the entire text content on this page. Unless this page has a good authority, its chances of being included in the SERPs based solely on content are slim.

Ask your programmer or database administrator to provide a .csv file that contains the character/word count for each product URL (or, if the website is relatively small, run a crawl with Screaming Frog and sort the URLs by *WordCount*). Your data needs to include only non-boilerplate text that appears on each page (e.g., the character count for product description, user reviews, other forms of UGC and so on). List in Excel and sort by lowest count. Analyze those pages and add them to the copywriting queue based on their importance. If there are too many pages with thin content (I usually set that threshold at around 100 words of content unique to the site), you may even consider noindexing them until you are able to add more content.

Product names

Product names are one of the design elements that attract the user's eye within moments of him landing on a page. On most ecommerce websites, the design of the PDPs usually follows the same pattern: the product image is to the left, the product name is either above the image or to the right, and then some product info and *add to cart* are to the right of the product image.

This is probably why users scan PDPs using the well-known "F" pattern.

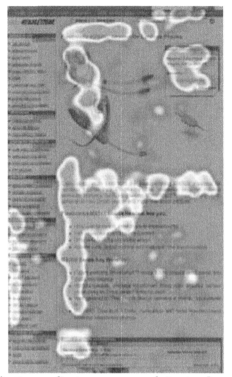

Figure 405 The "F" pattern applies to ecommerce websites, too. Image source: NNgroup

Although there seems to be little correlation between rankings and H1 headings,[19] Matt Cutts suggests[20] that Google assigns more weight to H1s. It's therefore still a good idea to wrap the product name in an HTML heading element, preferably the H1.

> *"Most product main pages have an opportunity to use one <h1> tag ... but they're currently only using other heading tags (<h3> in this case) or larger font styling. While styling your text so it appears larger might achieve the same visual presentation,* **it does not provide the same semantic meaning to the search engine that an <h1> tag does**. *The product's name and/or a few words about its features are great to have in an <h1> tag for the product main page."[21]*

But if the document structure requires it, an H2 will work, too. Note that the heading hierarchy on PDP templates can be different from the hierarchies on category and home pages. Visually, the product name should be the largest font size on the product page.

Don't be afraid to use long names (two-column layouts can easily accommodate this). Include the brand/manufacturer (especially if you carry multiple brands and the product is suited for searches—e.g., "Nike shoes"), model number or other important product attributes.

Figure 406 The product name includes brand, type and color.

Figure 407 This product name doesn't include the type (slippers). It may be obvious to users that they are looking at slippers, but not having "slippers" in the product name is not a good idea for search engines.

Admins who add new products to the catalogue should be trained to understand how the target market searches for those products, and should propose the long product names based on this data. This is not a complex process. If you want to make sure you don't mess up the product names, add just the shortest product names in the database and programmatically add other product attributes on the PDPs as researched and recommended by the people who add products to the database.

If you allow product names to be changed in the database, then give the update rights to one person only. Optimally, this person should know about the impact of changing names (e.g., new URLs for the same product, potential backlinks loss, internal linking updates, 301 redirects from old to new URLs, etc.). In most cases, it is a good idea to set product names in stone.

Use Schema.org *Product*[22] to mark up your code for product names, brands, manufacturers, images and a lot of other product properties. While many *Product* properties are not yet used by search engines, as long as you already have them in your database it won't be much of a hassle to mark up your HTML code subsequently. Google supports some of these properties[23] and will gradually support even more.

Reviews

No doubt about it—product reviews are good for users and for conversions. According to one study,[24] adding just the first review can increase conversion by 20%. Reviews enriched with additional info about the reviewer, or reviews that offer the ability to rate a particular product criterion (e.g., quality versus price) are even more useful for users.[25]

You can generate reviews by collecting them from people who purchase on your website, or you can integrate them from a reviews vendor. Since it can take a lot of purchases to get one review (it took Amazon 1,300 to generate one review[26] for *Harry Potter and the Deathly Hallows*), it's a good idea to implement both in-house and third-party reviews, especially if you're just starting out.

If you go with a vendor (e.g., Bazaar Voice, Reevo, Gigy, Pluck, etc.), you need to know whether their solution makes the reviews accessible to search engines. Usually, third-party reviews are placed inside a hidden div or a noscript tag that pulls data with a JavaScript code. Talk to your vendor to find out more about the add-ons they offer to make reviews more SEO-friendly.

The reviews can end up on multiple URLs, depending on the solution you chose and how you customized their out-of-the-box implementation, including URLs *on your own website, on the vendor's website* and/or *on other websites*. This is likely to create duplicate content issues, so you'll need to pay attention.

You need to decide which type of content you want to surface in SERPs for reviews: *PDPs* or *product review pages.*

If you want PDPs to show up in SERPs for "reviews" related keywords

In this scenario, the reviews should be placed on the PDPs and should be openly available to search engine robots. This means that the reviews will not be inserted in the code with JavaScript, AJAX or other technology that loads content on demand. The reviews should be available in the HTML source code when a bot fetches the PDPs. All other pages/sections/subdomains that contain the reviews should be blocked with *robots.txt.*

To check whether your reviews implementation is SEO friendly, look for content from your reviews in the cached pages of your products.

For instance, Amazon allows the reviews for *Kent Super 20 Boys Bike (20-Inch Wheels), Red/Black/White* to be indexed.

BROWSER   GOOGLE CACHE

Figure 408 The customer review at the left is included on the PDP and is cached by Google (right).

If you want product review pages, instead of PDPs, to show up in SERPs

Some vendors require a subdomain/directory to publish their reviews, e.g., *reviews.mysite.com* or *mysite.com/reviews/product*. This is not necessarily a bad thing, and it's a valid approach for merchants who plan to attract searchers in the research stage of the buying cycle. The *"reviews"* modifier (e.g., "under armour stormfront Jacket reviews") suggests that users are closer to a buying decision and that these keywords are pretty valuable. To increase the chances of product review pages ranking for "review"-related keywords, consider linking internally and externally with "reviews" in the anchor text.

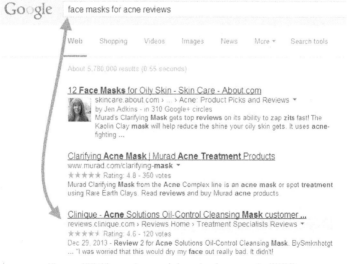

Figure 409 The reviews subdomain shows up in SERPs.

If you want product review pages, instead of PDPs, to show up in SERPs, be careful with same-site duplicate content issues. In many cases, you'll list some product reviews on both the PDP and the product reviews page. In these instances, you'll have to prevent crawlers from finding the reviews on the PDP. When you have the same reviews on multiple URLs, search engines will have difficulty sorting the right page to surface in SERPs.

To check whether your reviews generate duplicate content, just copy a few sentences, one at a time, from various reviews and do a "site:" search on Google:

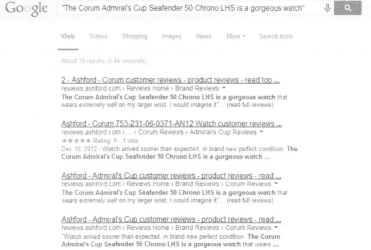

Figure 410 The same review shows on 15 URLs. This needs to be investigated.

However, if you list only a small fraction of the total number of reviews on the PDP (e.g., five out of 50), then you can let search engines access the reviews on the PDP as well as on the product reviews page. In this case, don't block the reviews subdomains/directory with *robots.txt*.

Figure 411 Amazon has a dedicated directory for product review pages.

The reviews for "Kent Super 20 Boys Bike (20-Inch Wheels), Red/Black/White (Sports)" are accessible to Googlebot and have been cached by Google. Amazon can afford this approach because the product reviews page lists three times more reviews than the PDP.

Figure 412 Amazon could improve the product reviews page by reducing it from three pages to one.

Amazon uses this strategy to rank multiple pages of reviews related to that bicycle:

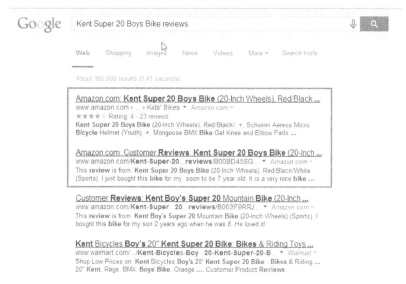

Figure 413 The first position is taken by the PDP, the second by the product review page.

Here are some SEO considerations you may want to keep in mind when implementing reviews.

Pay attention to duplicate reviews on other websites

If your provider also syndicates the same reviews in an SEO-friendly manner to other websites (accessible and indexable by search engines), that can cause duplicate problems.

In this case, you should allow crawlers access to duplicate reviews only if you add substantial unique content to the pages the reviews are listed on—for example, your own *Expert Reviews* and/or reviews you've collected, in addition to the reviews offered by your provider. If 90% of the reviews are syndicated somewhere else on the Internet, wrap them within an iframe, put on a *robots.txt*-blocked subdomain or AJAX them.

You also need to be careful if you syndicate your own reviews on comparison-shopping engines (CSEs).

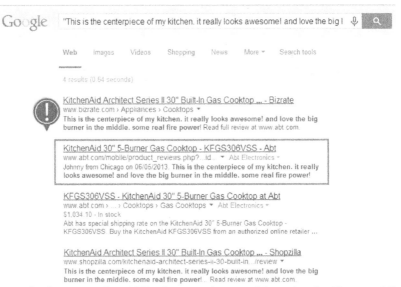

Figure 414 In the above screenshot, ABT is the original source of the review, but Bizrate and Shopzilla have the same content indexed.

If you plan to syndicate reviews on CSEs, select which reviews to keep for your website and which ones to syndicate.

Mark up reviews and ratings with structured data (microdata, microformats, RDF)

You can mark up the reviews and ratings with Schema.org markup to get rich snippets (stars, ratings, videos, etc.). The reviews/ratings have to be on the same page as the relevant product. Google explains their implementation in detail.[27]

This tool might come in handy: *http://schema-creator.org/product.php.*

Separate URLs for each review

If your current implementation generates separate URLs for each review, then using rel="canonical" to point to a *view-all* reviews URL is acceptable.[28]

Display reviews of related products

If a product doesn't have any reviews but there are other closely related items with reviews (e.g., the same Nike shoe in a different color), you can display the reviews for the related item. However, you have to ensure that the reviews make sense to users. You may want to place those reviews in a JavaScript or iframe for one of the product pages.

Tip: Reviews are one of the best ways to keep product detail pages "fresh". If you keep adding reviews to a product page on a regular basis, the page will be crawled more often and deemed more important. Other ways to freshen up are excerpts from relevant blog posts, or one to two sentences from research papers related to the product (if applicable).

Expired, out-of-stock and seasonal products

Product lifecycles and seasonality can rarely be avoided. Some products can expire for good, and others can go out of stock (some may come back in stock; others won't). Other products are available only during a certain season. Some products are evergreen and never change or run out of stock. The way you handle such products from an SEO perspective depends on factors such as future product availability or inventory availability.

There is no definite correct way to handle product lifecycles, but generally try to avoid:

- Removing the expired item's URL, which then returns a 404 response; if you absolutely need to return a 404 page, then at least create a custom one.

- Serving a soft 404, which is basically a 200 OK page that says "item no longer available".[29]

- 301 redirecting everything to the home page. Since the home page is unrelated to the product, 301 redirecting a PDP there may not always preserve indexing signals.

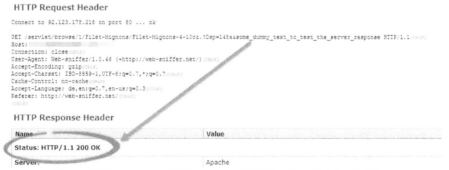

Figure 415 Every dummy URL returns a 200 OK code, which is a bad idea.

Discontinued products

These are products that have reached the end of their lifecycles.[30] For example, Canon stopped manufacturing the *Canon EOS-1Ds Mark III* model in 2012. Sometimes EOL (end-of-lifecycle) products are replaced with a newer model (*Canon EOS-1D X* replaced the older model), but other times they are discontinued for good.

If a product is replaced with a newer version, you can 301 the old page to the latest page. If possible, alert users with a message that the product they are seeking has been discontinued but replaced with a new one. The product name should not be close to the text "not available" in the source code, otherwise "not available" may show up in the

SERP snippet. You can even place the non-availability message in an iframe or JavaScript to avoid that.

Because the target market doesn't immediately stop searching for a product when the manufacturer discontinues it, you should redirect the users only after you notice a decline in the search demand for that product, or when all stocked items are sold out. Until that time, you can add a notice to the page announcing that the product has been discontinued, then eventually link to the newer version.

Some prefer leaving both pages alive indefinitely, with or without a notification message, depending on stock availability (after all, if you still have the discontinued item in stock, you want to sell it).

806124-102 Datacard YMCK Ribbon, 165 cards **This product has been discontinued, and replaced by the Datacard 806124-104**
by Datacard
Be the first to review this item

Price: $32.00 + $8.69 shipping

Only 3 left in stock.
Ships from and sold by ID ENHANCEMENTS, INC.

· Datacard 806124-102 YMCK Ribbon
· 165 cards

Figure 416 This page is still available (200 OK response code), although the product has been discontinued.

Upcoming products

Think of creating pages for *high-demand* products that have not yet been released but will be on the market in the near future (i.e., a few months down the road). Such pages have to be content rich and really useful so that they can gather links organically from trusted sources. The beauty of this tactic is that you can get those backlinks more easily, as the pages you are building are not yet commercial. A month before the launch, increase the amount of internal links to those pages (link even from the home page). Take pre-orders or capture contact info before the launch date. The moment the product becomes available, allow users to add to cart. If you plan well, you'll be positioned ahead of your competitors at the product release date.

Out-of-stock (OOS) products

If the product will never be restocked, you can 301 redirect to either:

- the most relevant product, which can be another variation of the product, or
- a similar product with a longer "web-life", or
- a parent category or subcategory.

You can leave the page alive as well (returning a 200 OK response code), with a clearly visible notice communicating the reason for unavailability and then guiding the users to new or more relevant pages. The "add to cart" button can be changed to "out of stock" and become inactive so that users can't add the item to cart. To minimize the effects on conversion rate, offer related items.

If the product goes temporarily out of stock

The page should return a 200 OK response to search engines and let customers know that the product is currently out of stock. It should also give them an estimated availability date. Eventually, you can offer an incentive to compensate for the inconvenience, and to collect their email address.

Irish Coffee Mug Temporarily Out of Stock

Email to a Friend
Be the first to review this product

Compare At: $17.00
$11.99
You Save: 29%

Add to Compare

High gloss finish ceramic
Dishwasher and microwave safe
Size: 5-1/2 by 3-1/2-inch, 13-ounce
Irish Coffee Recipe on back
Item # 130574

More Views   Temporarily Out of Stock

Figure 417 The *Temporarily Out of Stock* messaging is clear, but it should be separated from the product name.

If all products under a subcategory are unavailable and the page received qualified traffic in the past, 301 redirect to the parent category.

Keep in mind that shoppers may become frustrated if too much of your inventory is out of stock. In this case, mark the affected pages with noindex and remove them from navigation until your inventory improves.

These are subtleties that need to be tested, since users will react differently on each website, and even from product to product, depending on your messaging.

Seasonal products

If the product is seasonal, handle it in a similar way to out-of-stock items. If it will return the next season, leave the page in place, notify the users, and remove the ability to place orders. If it won't return, then 301 redirect to the most appropriate product or parent category.

Seasonal products require some attention for URL naming and maintenance. For example, if you put the year (or another time indicator that changes from time to time) in the URL, it's like starting over again when you update the URL the next year. You can do a 301 redirect from the previous year's URL to the current one, but generally try to avoid using URLs that designate a year or other time indicator. Instead, use a generic URL that can accommodate new dates or models in existing URLs.

For example, Ford uses *http://www.ford.com/cars/focus/* for their newest Focus model, the 2014. Toyota uses *http://www.toyota.com/corolla/* for all Corolla models.

Figure 418 This URL naming approach consolidates links to a single page.

The same applies to special-event URLs that occur regularly. Instead of *www.mywebsite.com/valentines-day-2014*, use *www.site.com/valentines-day/*. This page can be promoted (e.g., linked to from the home page) when the time comes, but it should not be allowed to return 404. With this method, the page continuously accumulates authority year after year.

Title tags

While <title> is not technically a tag (it's an HTML element), it's often referred to as a tag in SEO contexts.

An internal analysis[31] that Google performed on their very own Google product pages found that ***over 90% of those pages could improve their SEO simply by optimizing the title tag***.

Since search engines emphasize the SERP titles with blue and underline (Google did away with the underlining as of March 2014), these are the first things searchers gaze at after performing a search query. SERP titles play a big role in determining whether searchers will click on a particular listing. Titles are also one of the most important on-page SEO factors, and when others link to your pages organically, they tend to use the page titles as anchor text.

It's important to mention that, just as with AdWords, the SERP title of a listing has the biggest influence on CTRs. Hence, it pays to balance SEO and CTR.

The SERP title myth

Many otherwise knowledgeable webmasters, and even a few SEOs, believe that the content of the title tag is the only source Google uses to generate and display the SERP title excerpts:

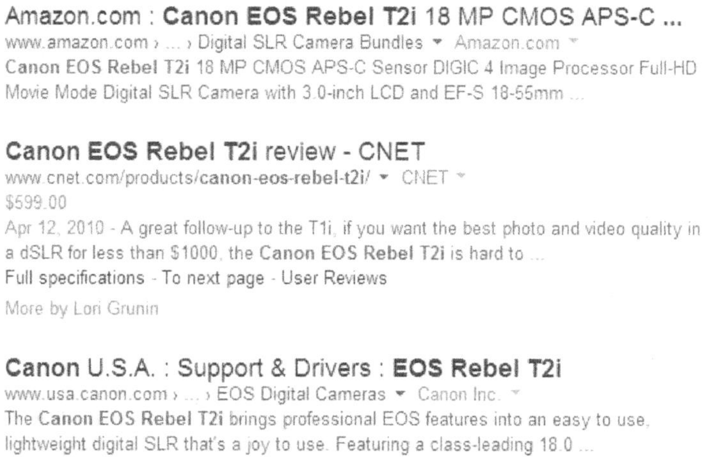

Amazon.com : **Canon EOS Rebel T2i** 18 MP CMOS APS-C ...
www.amazon.com › ... › Digital SLR Camera Bundles ▾ Amazon.com ▾
Canon EOS Rebel T2i 18 MP CMOS APS-C Sensor DIGIC 4 Image Processor Full-HD
Movie Mode Digital SLR Camera with 3.0-inch LCD and EF-S 18-55mm ...

Canon EOS Rebel T2i review - CNET
www.cnet.com/products/canon-eos-rebel-t2i/ ▾ CNET ▾
$599.00
Apr 12, 2010 - A great follow-up to the T1i, if you want the best photo and video quality in
a dSLR for less than $1000, the Canon EOS Rebel T2i is hard to ...
Full specifications - To next page - User Reviews
More by Lori Grunin

Canon U.S.A. : Support & Drivers : **EOS Rebel T2i**
www.usa.canon.com › ... › EOS Digital Cameras ▾ Canon Inc. ▾
The Canon EOS Rebel T2i brings professional EOS features into an easy to use,
lightweight digital SLR that's a joy to use. Featuring a class-leading 18.0 ...

Figure 419 Most of the time, the content of the title tag is displayed in SERPs, but not always.

However, the SERP title is not based solely on what is wrapped within the HTML title tag. Google's goal is to be *relevant*, so it's to be expected that they won't blindly use just the title tag to generate the most relevant snippets for users.

For example, let's say you forgot to add the product name in the title tag, and a user searches for that product. Google might classify the page as highly relevant for that search query due to great content—but the page title is not the best for users. In this case, Google may use other sections on the page to extract and display a title that is more useful to the searcher, meaning it will include the product name in the SERP title.

A very common question is: "Why is Google changing/rewriting/not indexing my title tag properly?" As mentioned, Google's goal is to provide the most relevant titles for searchers. They use various data sources and signals to accomplish this, analyzing the page content and looking for external relevance signals from other sources (e.g., DMOZ, Yahoo! directory or anchor text in backlinks) to match a user query with relevant content extracted from a page.

Below are some scenarios that may trigger search engines to alter the SERP titles:

- A malformed title tag.

- Titles that are too short or too long.

- A page blocked by *robots.txt*, but with backlinks related to the search query.

Getting a different title in the SERPs than the one in the HTML code doesn't mean that Google indexed your pages or titles incorrectly; it just means that the search query determines whether your HTML title tag is displayed.

SERP CTR and bounce rate

The *SERP CTR* (the click through rate on organic search results) and the *SERP bounce rate*[32] (searchers click on a SERP result and then go back to the initial results in a couple of seconds, or without interacting with other pages on the result they clicked on) are two "crowd-sourced" metrics used by search engines to self-evaluate the quality of their results.

For example, if a spam page managed to rank first for a competitive keyword but doesn't get clicks because users easily identify it as spam as soon as they see it in the listing—or if it gets clicks but searchers immediately bounce back to SERPs –that page may be deemed irrelevant in relationship to that keyword. Search engines may reduce its ranking because it's not useful for users.

In an older crowd-sourced test I ran in February 2011, the rankings of a URL went up a few positions (from #16 to #12) for a long-tail keyword after participants clicked on the targeted URL in SERPs and spent some time on the website. However, since this was not a large-scale experiment, it's possible that the fluctuation was just due to personalization or natural fluctuation.

It makes sense for search engines to test and analyze how users react to different results, and then lightly adjust results and algorithms based on SERP CTR and SERP bounce rate. Although it has not yet been officially confirmed, Matt Cutts suggests in a video that Google takes clicks into account when they test new algorithms on live results.[33]

Consider the following suggestions for improving the effectiveness of your titles.

Title tag and H1s matching

One way to reinforce the SEO relevance of a product page is to partially match the title tag with the H1 (both elements will contain the product name). This is generally a good idea because H1 and *<title>* should be conceptually related but not exactly the same.

The product name is usually wrapped in an H1 on PDPs and can have a pattern along the lines of the examples below:

- {Product_Name}
- {Brand} {Product_Name}
- {Brand} {Product_Name} {Variation/Attribute}

You can use the H1 product-naming convention in the title tag as well, but you need to change it a bit—for instance, by adding modifiers such as *Buy, Online, Free Shipping* or *{Business Name}*:

- {Product_Name} - {Business Name}

- {Brand} {Product_Name} - {Business Name}

- {Brand} {Product_Name} {Variation} - {Business Name}

Figure 420 Since the product name in H1 is very short, the title tag can easily be complemented with other useful product attributes.

Keep in mind that the keywords in the title tag should accurately reflect the page content and should also be present in the body content.

Category pages often list subcategories (e.g., in the faceted navigation or in the main content area). The titles of such pages can include some of the most important subcategories in the title tag as well.

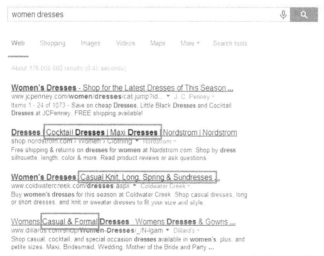

Figure 421 The title tag of the *Women's Dresses* category pages above includes several subcategories listed under "Women's Dresses".

Keyword significance consolidation

This tip works only for ecommerce websites that focus on a particular product line (e.g., only bar stools) or a specific niche (e.g., just furniture). It will help increase the main keyword's significance,[34] which in return will create more relevance around your website for that particular keyword:

- On the home page, place the main keyword at the very beginning of the title tag.

- Use the keyword towards the end of the title tag on every page of the website, even if the title will become longer than 65 characters (or 500 pixels).

- Mention the keyword within the body copy on each page of the website. If your pages are content rich, repeat the keyword at least once for each 100 words of non-boilerplate text.

- Consolidate the contextual anchor text from internal pages to point to the home page with the most important keyword that you placed at the beginning of the home page title tag. For example, if *speed boat parts* is your most important keyword, then each page on your website should contain the keyword *speed boat parts* in the body content (apart from navigation, menus or footer), and the first instance of *speed boat parts* should link to the home page.

Keywords

Below are the most common keywords Google found when crawling your site. These should reflect the subject matter of your site.

Keyword	Significance
1. shoprider (2 variants)	
2. scooters (2 variants)	
3. chairs (2 variants)	
4. dealer (2 variants)	

Figure 422 The website above sells just Shoprider scooters. Notice how Google deems those two words to be the most significant.

	Keyword	Occurrences	Variants encountered	
1				
2	shoprider		427 shoprider, shoprider's	
3	scooters		234 scooters, scooter	
4	chairs		193 chairs, chair	
5	dealer		170 dealer, dealers	
6	mobility		153 mobility	
7	eclipse		106 eclipse	
8	products		102 products, product	
9	lift		101 lift, lifts	
10	seat		81 seat, seating, seats	
11	accessories		75 accessories	

Figure 423 The website ranks in the top five for "Shoprider scooters" in Canada, close to Shoprider's official website.

Note: *Keyword significance* is not the same as *keyword density.* Keyword significance is measured at the domain level, while keyword density is measured at the document level.

Geo-targeting

Usually, ecommerce websites ship nationwide or even internationally. But there are cases when you can't ship outside a geographical region due to regulatory restrictions. For example, if you sell wine online in Canada, you are not allowed to ship inter-provincially.

If you sell only to a specific region/province/city, you can mention it in the title tag to increase the chances of showing up for a geo-personalized search query.

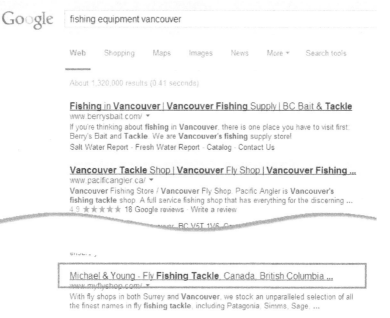

Figure 424 The URL ranked second contains the city name, while the URL at the bottom of page 1 doesn't.

If you are a retail chain, build separate landing pages for each store location. The store address (city and state/province, minimum) should be placed in the title tag, and the landing pages should reinforce the store locations with mention of surrounding landmarks or with geo-tagged images.

Holiday-specific titles

Searchers' behavior and the queries they use change around major holidays and events (e.g., Boxing Day, Mother's Day, Halloween, etc.). It is useful for searchers (and for SEO) if you can update the title tag to accommodate these changes. Around Valentine's Day, the title "***Valentine** Gifts for Her. All Items on Sale & FREE Shipping*" is more relevant to users *than "Gifts for Her. All Items on Sale & FREE Shipping"*.

Figure 425 Tiffany updated the page titles to match user behavior before Valentine's Day.

Character count and pixel length

Google doesn't index just 65 characters (which is about 500 pixels). Google *displays only* about 65 characters in the SERP title, but in fact *it indexes as many as 1,000 characters*. Knowing this opens the door to new experiments, such as thinking of your titles in blocks rather than 65-character units. For example, it may be worth testing titles made of two 65- to 70-character blocks:

- The first block of about 65 characters is where you craft your perfect title (category and subcategories, product names, branding, calls to action, etc.). Think of this as the title you would write if you were to enforce the character limit. Ideally, this will be the title seen by searchers on SERPs.

- The second block will contain second-tier keywords such as product attributes, model numbers, stock availability, plurals, synonyms and so on. You could eventually repeat the most important keyword for your website at the very end of the title on pages other than the home page.

If the title is a complete sentence and you want the entire sentence to show up in the SERP, it's best to keep that sentence under 65 characters.

Branded titles

The decision of whether to add your business name to the title tag depends on various factors, such as:

- The goal of your organic traffic campaign (branding versus rankings).

- How strong your brand is offline.

- The authority of your website (external links pointing to your site).

I usually recommend placing the brand at the end of the title tag. However, the final placement of the brand name should take the following into consideration:

- If you have a well-established brand and a more than decent website authority, you can place the brand at the beginning of the title tag.

- If you are trying to build a brand, place it at the beginning of the title.

- If your brand has only some recognition and the goal is to drive unbranded traffic, you should add the brand name at the end of the title tag.

- If your brand name is not known or if you don't care about branding, don't put your brand name in the title at all.

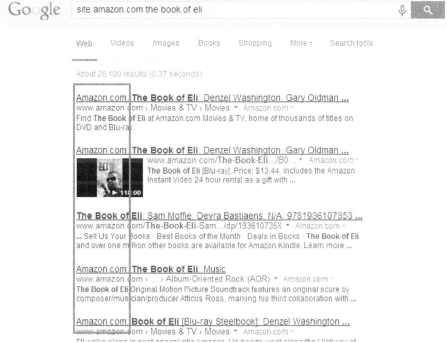

Figure 426 Big names like Amazon brand their page titles right at the beginning of the tag.

Keyword prominence

Prominence refers to the closeness of the keywords to the beginning of the title tag. For a category page, start the title with the category name; for a product details page, start with the product name (eventually, you can precede the product name with the manufacturer or brand).

Why is prominence important? First, search engines assign more weight to words at the beginning of the title. Second, western readers skim text from left to right, and it's important to reassure them that the page is relevant by placing the category/product name at the beginning. An exception to this is if you have an established brand (or are trying to build one)—then you can start the title with the brand name.

Keyword proximity

Proximity refers to how close two words are to each other. If your targeted keyword is the exact term *"women's dresses"*, you should not place other words between *women's* and *dresses*. The title "Women's Casual & Formal Dresses" is not ideal; instead, it should be "Women's Dresses: Casual, Formal, Going Out and more dress styles at {BrandName}".

Keyword (by relevance)		Avg. monthly searches ?	Competition ?
"women's dresses"	⬀	22,200	High
"womens dresses"	⬀	12,100	High
"women dresses"	⬀	8,100	High

Figure 427 "Women's dresses" has significantly more search volume than "womens dresses".

The importance of keyword prominence seem to have decreased after the Hummingbird update, as Google is not focusing on exact match keywords as much as it used to. However, it is still advisable not to break apart important words such as category or subcategory names.

User intent modifiers

User intent keyword modifiers are words that can be placed before or after the targeted keyword to target searchers at a specific buying stage.

Based on user intent, search queries can be categorized into three main categories: informational, transactional and navigational.

We discussed user intent in detail in the *Keyword Research* chapter. There, we saw that while the vast majority of search queries are not transactional, informational and navigational queries are valuable for later conversion assists. Hence, ecommerce websites should make efforts to capture consumers with relevant content at each buying stage.

One way of clarifying the purpose of a page to users is to include user intent keyword modifiers in the title tag:

- Transactional (e.g., words like *buy, sale, discount, cheap*) for category and product detail pages.

- Navigational (e.g., *Sears Store Vancouver, BC*) on store location pages, or adding the brand name on About Us and Contact Us pages.

- Educational (e.g., *learn, discover, read, find, guide)* for shopping guides.

Keywords order

In many cases, you will find that words have different search volumes, and even different meanings, if they are arranged in a different order. For example, "dog toys" has a different meaning than "toys dog" and a totally different search volume. When the order of words creates different meanings, you will have to create separate landing pages.

Singular versus plural

It's generally accepted that using the same keyword more than twice in the title tag may raise spam flags. But is the plural form of the keyword considered a repetition? When search engines analyze the content on a document, they use a process called *stemming*[35] to strip words to their root form (e.g., *dresses, dressed, dressing* are all variants of "*dress*"). If you view the matter from this angle, the plural will be considered a repetition.

However, there's more than just stemming when it comes to plural or singular—for example, there's user intent. Generally speaking, plural suggests that users are looking for a list of items rather than just one particular item. In some instances, the same word can have different meanings in singular versus plural—e.g., car cover (insurance cover) versus car covers (weather-proofing). So search engines have to consider more than just one factor when deciding which documents to rank in SERPs.

For ecommerce websites, I recommend using the plural on listing pages (category and subcategory) or on shopping guides, and the singular on PDPs:

Category Page – "Canon Digital SLR *Cameras*"

Product Details Page – "Canon EOS 60D 18 MP CMOS Digital SLR *Camera* with 3.0-Inch LCD (Body Only)"

Stop words

Words such as *and, or, the, in,* and *or* are called *stop words.*[36] Since these are usually deemed non-essential for relevance scoring, search engines will frequently filter them out when analyzing and classifying documents. Use as few stop words as possible; but don't get stuck on this, as it's not as important as one might think.

However, you should pay attention if you automatically remove stop words from titles and URLs, as some stop words are important for users. For instance, if you sell music online, if you automatically remove the word "that" from the band name "Take That", you will end up with a very suboptimal page title (e.g., *"Best Take Albums"* instead of *"Best Take **That** Albums"*.

Word separators

The word separator most used by SEOs is the pipe sign "|", but symbols such as hyphens and even commas are good choices, too. Google suggests you not use underscores,[37] and I would also recommend staying away from the following special characters: ' " < > { } [ ] ( ).

Some websites use catchy titles with a lot of non-alphabetic symbols—e.g., (~~~!FREE iPODS!~~~)—to grab searchers' attention and possibly higher CTRs. Keep in mind that the use of special symbols may get you a better CTR, but might also result in spam flags.

Character savers

If you need to squeeze in more text, you can replace certain words with their corresponding symbols—for example, "and" with "&", "or" with "/" or "copyright" with "©". Remember to implement special characters using HTML entities ("&" as & "©" as &copy).[38]

Other great space-saving options are abbreviations (e.g., instead of "extra-large" you could use XL) and shorter synonyms for a word (e.g., T-shirts instead of tee-shirts). The decision on which version of the keyword to use in the title has to be based on the search volume for those keywords, and also on the content targeted on the page.

Calls to action (CTAs)

A page ranked second but with a compelling CTA in the title could *theoretically* grab more clicks than the page ranked first but with a poor title. Remember that one of the most important elements tested in advertising and conversion rate optimization is the headline. On SERP listings, your title is the headline.

CTAs include action verbs, strong unique selling propositions (USPs) or promotional words. Sometimes, store/inventory-wide promotions can also affect CTR. An example of a promotional title is: "All Digital Cameras 60% OFF".

Competitive differentiators and free shipping

If you know your target market is sensitive to a particular feature or benefit that is part of your unique selling proposition (e.g., you offer a "lowest price guarantee") or a competitive edge (e.g., you are the exclusive retailer for a product/line of products), use this to attract more clicks on your listings and to differentiate yourself from competitors.

Khombu Boots, Shoes | Shipped FREE at Zappos
www.zappos.com/khombu ▾ Zappos ▾
FREE Shipping on Khombu boots & shoes for men, women, and kids! 365-day returns and 24/7 customer service with a smile at Zappos.

Lucky | Shipped Free at Zappos
www.zappos.com/lucky ▾ Zappos ▾
848 items - Free shipping BOTH ways on lucky, from our vast selection of styles. Fast delivery, and 24/7/365 real-person service with a smile. Click or call ...

Halter, Clothing | Shipped Free at Zappos
www.zappos.com/halter ▾ Zappos ▾
1053 items - Free shipping BOTH ways on Clothing, from our vast selection of styles Fast delivery, and 24/7/365 real-person service with a smile. Click or call ...

Figure 428 "Free shipping" works for conversion as well for better SERP CTR.

Test title patterns

SEO testing is theoretically possible[39] but very hard to statistically conclude, since search engines involve a lot of uncontrolled variables. However, title tag variations are one of the easiest SEO tests you can run. Here are some ideas for your tests:

- Place your brand at the beginning or end of the title.

- Add one or more important product attributes to the product name.

- Add the most important subcategory names before/after the parent category name.

- Test various USPs at the beginning or end of the title.

- Test various title patterns.

Conclusion

Now that you've made it to the end of the book, you've realized that on-page SEO for ecommerce websites is complex. I deliberately avoided subjects such as mobile or international SEO, since addressing them would have delayed the book's publication by two or three months. However, I plan to cover them in the future, so stay connected with me through my newsletter or blog to receive updates.

If you take the other important part of search engine rankings into consideration—link building—then you'll understand why lots of time and skilled resources are required to get to the top. But as long as you carefully optimize your website, add content and develop quality links, you'll make it.

See you at the top!

Notes

Chapter One: Introduction

[1] History of E-Commerce, http://www.spirecast.com/history-of-e-commerce/

[2] E-retail rolls in 2013, http://www.internetretailer.com/2014/02/18/e-retail-rolls-2013

Chapter Two: Website Architecture

[1] Information Architecture Institute, http://iainstitute.org/en/about/our_mission.php

[2] Rich snippets – Breadcrumbs, https://support.google.com/webmasters/answer/185417

[3] GoodRelations: The Professional Web Vocabulary for E-Commerce, http://www.heppnetz.de/projects/goodrelations/

[4] Three-click rule - Wikipedia, the free encyclopedia, http://en.wikipedia.org/wiki/Three-click_rule

[5] Testing the Three-Click Rule, http://www.uie.com/articles/three_click_rule/

[6] Opinion: Is SERP Bounce a Ranking Signal or a Quality Factor for SEO?, http://www.searchenginejournal.com/opinion-is-serp-bounce-a-ranking-signal-or-a-quality-factor-for-seo/35464/

[7] Solving the Pogo-Stick Problem - Whiteboard Friday, http://moz.com/blog/solving-the-pogo-stick-problem-whiteboard-friday

[8] Flat vs. Deep Website Hierarchies, http://www.nngroup.com/articles/flat-vs-deep-hierarchy/

[9] Highlights from Prioritizing Web Usability, http://cahdsu.wordpress.com/2010/01/03/highlights-from-prioritizing-web-usability/

[10] Supplemental Result, http://en.wikipedia.org/wiki/Supplemental_Result#Low_PageRank

[11] Visualizing Site Structure And Enabling Site Navigation For A Search Result Or Linked Page, http://appft.uspto.gov/netacgi/nph-Parser?Sect1=PTO1&Sect2=HITOFF&d=PG01&p=1&u=%2Fnetahtml%2FPTO%2Fsrchnum.html&r=1&f=G&l=50&s1=%2220110276562%22.PGNR.&OS=DN/20110276562&RS=DN/20110276562

[12] To slash or not to slash, http://googlewebmastercentral.blogspot.fr/2010/04/to-slash-or-not-to-slash.html

[13] Bot Herding: The Ultimate Tool for PageRank Flow, http://www.searchenginejournal.com/bot-herding-pagerank-sculpting/10352/

[14] PageRank sculpting, http://www.mattcutts.com/blog/pagerank-sculpting/

[15] Importance of link architecture, http://googlewebmastercentral.blogspot.fr/2008/10/importance-of-link-architecture.html

[16] Training set construction for taxonomic classification, http://patft.uspto.gov/netacgi/nph-Parser?Sect1=PTO2&Sect2=HITOFF&p=1&u=%2Fnetahtml%2FPTO%2Fsearch-adv.htm&r=1&f=G&l=50&d=PALL&S1=08484194&OS=PN/08484194&RS=PN/08484194

[17] Determining the User Intent of Web Search Engine Queries, http://www2007.org/posters/poster989.pdf

[18] Illustrating the Long Tail, http://moz.com/blog/illustrating-the-long-tail

[19] DIY Décor: Tree Stump Side Table, http://ext.homedepot.com/community/blog/diy-decor-tree-stump-side-table/

[20] A Backyard Makeover With A DIY Outdoor Game And A Place To Put Your Drink, http://ext.homedepot.com/community/blog/tag/diy-project/

[21] The Paradox of Choice, http://en.wikipedia.org/wiki/The_Paradox_of_Choice:_Why_More_Is_Less

[22] Cutting Down On Choice Is The Best Way To Make Better Decisions, http://www.businessinsider.com/too-many-choices-are-bad-for-business-2012-12?op=1

[23] Large-scale Item Categorization for e-Commerce, http://labs.ebay.com/wp-content/uploads/2012/10/Jean-David-Ruvini-Large-scale_Item.pdf

[24] Repeating full sentences (words) on multiple pages in one domain. (Is a disclaimer on every page not good seo?), https://productforums.google.com/forum/#!topic/webmasters/-B87jWN33j4

[25] Ten recent algorithm changes, http://insidesearch.blogspot.fr/2011/11/ten-recent-algorithm-changes.html

[26] Duplicate content, https://support.google.com/webmasters/answer/66359?hl=en

[27] ODP Data Dumps, http://rdf.dmoz.org/rdf/Changes.html

[28] Folksonomy, http://en.wikipedia.org/wiki/Folksonomy

Chapter Three: Keyword Research

[1] Keywords vs. Search Queries: What's the Difference?,
http://www.wordstream.com/blog/ws/2011/05/25/keywords-vs-search-queries

[2] Ecommerce conversion rates - Smart Insights Digital Marketing Advice,
http://www.smartinsights.com/ecommerce/ecommerce-analytics/ecommerce-conversion-rates/

[3] Into the Mind of the Searcher,
http://c.ymcdn.com/sites/www.sempo.org/resource/resmgr/Docs/searcher-mind.pdf

[4] Determining the User Intent of Web Search Engine Queries,
http://www2007.org/posters/poster989.pdf

[5] Determining the User Intent of Web Search Engine Queries,
http://www2007.org/posters/poster989.pdf

[6] Determining the User Intent of Web Search Engine Queries,
http://www2007.org/posters/poster989.pdf

[7] LEAKS: Best Buy's Internal Customer Profiling Document,
http://consumerist.com/2008/03/18/leaks-best-buys-internal-customer-profiling-document/

[8] A taxonomy of web search, http://www.cis.upenn.edu/~nenkova/Courses/cis430/p3-broder.pdf

[9] Search Quality Rating Guidelines,
http://www.google.com/insidesearch/howsearchworks/assets/searchqualityevaluatorguidelines.pdf

[10] Detecting Online Commercial Intention (OCI), http://research.microsoft.com/en-us/um/people/znie/WWW2006-oci.pdf

[11] Determining the informational, navigational, and transactional intent of Web queries -
http://faculty.ist.psu.edu/jjansen/academic/pubs/jansen_user_intent.pdf, page p1262 table 4

[12] The Changing Face of SERPs, Organic Click Through Rate -
https://web.archive.org/web/20130809032628/http://www.optify.net/wp-content/uploads/2011/04/Changing-Face-oof-SERPS-Organic-CTR.pdf

[13] Headsmacking Tip #4: Use Keyword Variations with Matching Intent Together, http://moz.com/blog/headsmacking-tip-4-use-keyword-variations-with-matching-intent-together

[14] IMPORTANT SHOPPING DATES 2013, http://cdn.shopify.com/static/images/other/ecommerce-calendar-2013.pdf

[15] Holiday 2010: Consumer Intentions, http://ssl.gstatic.com/think/docs/holiday-2010-consumer-intentions_research-studies.pdf

[16] Beat the Holiday Rush: Three Strategies for Getting Ahead, http://www.thinkwithgoogle.com/articles/3-strategies-to-prepare-for-the-holidays.html

[17] 2011 Post-Holiday Recap, http://ssl.gstatic.com/think/docs/post-holiday-learnings-for-2012_research-studies.pdf

[18] Consumer Trend Data, https://web.archive.org/web/20131103014217/http://www.nrf.com/modules.php?name=Pages&sp_id=449

[19] Many digital gift card buyers are last-minute holiday shoppers, http://www.internetretailer.com/2012/04/25/many-digital-gift-card-buyers-are-last-minute-holiday-shoppers

[20] INFOGRAPHIC: Americans Are Spending A Whopping $704.18 On Gifts This Year, http://www.businessinsider.com/what-americans-spend-on-christmas-2011-12

[21] How Much Do Americans Spend On Christmas, http://vizualarchive.com/2012/how-much-do-americans-spend-on-christmas-2012/

Chapter Four: Crawl Optimization

[1] Google Patent On Anchor Text And Different Crawling Rates, http://www.seobythesea.com/2007/12/google-patent-on-anchor-text-and-different-crawling-rates/

[2] Large-scale Incremental Processing Using Distributed Transactions and Notifications, http://research.google.com/pubs/pub36726.html

[3] Our new search index: Caffeine, http://googleblog.blogspot.ca/2010/06/our-new-search-index-caffeine.html

[4] Web crawler , http://en.wikipedia.org/wiki/Web_crawler#Politeness_policy

[5] To infinity and beyond? No!, http://googlewebmastercentral.blogspot.ca/2008/08/to-infinity-and-beyond-no.html

[6] Crawl Errors: The Next Generation, http://googlewebmastercentral.blogspot.ca/2012/03/crawl-errors-next-generation.html

[7] Make Data Useful, http://www.scribd.com/doc/4970486/Make-Data-Useful-by-Greg-Linden-Amazon-com

[8] Shopzilla's Site Redo - You Get What You Measure, http://www.scribd.com/doc/16877317/Shopzilla-s-Site-Redo-You-Get-What-You-Measure

[9] Expires Headers for SEO: Why You Should Think Twice Before Using Them, http://moz.com/ugc/expires-headers-for-seo-why-you-should-think-twice-before-using-them

[10] How Website Speed Actually Impacts Search Ranking, http://moz.com/blog/how-website-speed-actually-impacts-search-ranking

[11] Optimizing your very large site for search — Part 2, http://web.archive.org/web/20140527160343/http://www.bing.com/blogs/site_blogs/b/webmaster/archive/2009/01/27/optimizing-your-very-large-site-for-search-part-2.aspx

[12] Matt Cutts Interviewed by Eric Enge, http://www.stonetemple.com/articles/interview-matt-cutts-012510.shtml

[13] Save bandwidth costs: Dynamic pages can support If-Modified-Since too, http://sebastians-pamphlets.com/dynamic-pages-can-support-if-modified-since-too/

[14] Site Map Usability, http://www.nngroup.com/articles/site-map-usability/

[15] New Insights into Googlebot, http://moz.com/blog/googlebot-new-insights

[16] How Bing Uses CTR in Ranking, and more with Duane Forrester, http://www.stonetemple.com/search-algorithms-and-bing-webmaster-tools-with-duane-forrester/

[17] Multiple XML Sitemaps: Increased Indexation and Traffic, http://moz.com/blog/multiple-xml-sitemaps-increased-indexation-and-traffic

[18] How Bing Uses CTR in Ranking, and more with Duane Forrester, http://www.stonetemple.com/search-algorithms-and-bing-webmaster-tools-with-duane-forrester/

[19] How does Google treat +1 against robots.txt, meta noindex or redirected URL, https://productforums.google.com/forum/#!msg/webmasters/ck15w-1UHSk/0jpaBsaEG3EJ

[20] Robots meta tag and X-Robots-Tag HTTP header specifications, https://developers.google.com/webmasters/control-crawl-index/docs/robots_meta_tag

[21] Supporting rel="canonical" HTTP Headers, http://googlewebmastercentral.blogspot.ca/2011/06/supporting-relcanonical-http-headers.html

[22] Jaimie Sirovich, https://plus.google.com/100955965525617762614/about

[23] Configuring URL Parameters in Webmaster Tools,
https://www.youtube.com/watch?v=DiEYcBZ36po&feature=youtu.be&t=1m50s

[24] URL parameters, https://support.google.com/webmasters/answer/1235687?hl=en

Chapter Five: Internal Linking

[1] Browser-specific optimizations and cloaking,
https://productforums.google.com/forum/#!topic/webmasters/4sVFlldj7d8

[2] GET, POST, and safely surfacing more of the web,
http://googlewebmastercentral.blogspot.ca/2011/11/get-post-and-safely-surfacing-more-of.html

[3] Google Analytics event tracking (pageTracker._trackEvent) causing 404 crawl errors,
https://productforums.google.com/forum/#!topic/webmasters/4U6_JgeClJU

[4] Call of Duty: Ghosts - Xbox 360, http://www.amazon.com/Call-Duty-Ghosts-Xbox-360/dp/B002I098JE

[5] Free SEO Toolkit, http://www.microsoft.com/web/seo

[6] Getting Started with the SEO Toolkit, http://www.iis.net/learn/extensions/iis-search-engine-optimization-toolkit/getting-started-with-the-seo-toolkit

[7] One More Great Way to Use Fusion Tables for SEO, http://moz.com/ugc/one-more-great-way-to-use-fusion-tables-for-seo

[8] Visualize your Site's Link Graph with NodeXL, http://www.stateofdigital.com/visualize-your-sites-internal-linking-structure-with-nodexl/

[9] How To Visualize Open Site Explorer Data In Gephi, http://justinbriggs.org/how-visualize-open-site-explorer-data-in-gephi

[10] rel="nofollow" Microformats Wiki, http://microformats.org/wiki/rel-nofollow

[11] Interview with Google's Matt Cutts at Pubcon, http://www.stephanspencer.com/matt-cutts-interview/

[12] Use rel="nofollow" for specific links,
https://support.google.com/webmasters/answer/96569?hl=en

[13] PageRank sculpting, http://www.mattcutts.com/blog/pagerank-sculpting/

[14] Should internal links use rel="nofollow"?,
https://www.youtube.com/watch?feature=player_embedded&v=bVOOB_Q0MZY

[15] Damping factor, http://en.wikipedia.org/wiki/PageRank#Damping_factor

[16] Are links in footers treated differently than paragraph links?,
https://www.youtube.com/watch?v=D0fgh5RIHdE

[17] Is Navigation Useful?, http://www.nngroup.com/articles/is-navigation-useful/

[18] Ten recent algorithm changes, http://insidesearch.blogspot.ca/2011/11/ten-recent-algorithm-changes.html

[19] Link Value Factors, http://wiep.net/link-value-factors/

[20] Image Links Vs. Text Links, Questions About PR & Anchor Text Value,
http://moz.com/community/q/image-links-vs-text-links-questions-about-pr-anchor-text-value

[21] Are links in footers treated differently than paragraph links?,
https://www.youtube.com/watch?v=D0fgh5RIHdE&feature=youtu.be&t=40s

[22] VIPS: a Vision-based Page Segmentation Algorithm,
http://research.microsoft.com/apps/pubs/default.aspx?id=70027

[23] Block-Level Link Analysis, http://research.microsoft.com/apps/pubs/default.aspx?id=69111

[24] Document ranking based on semantic distance between terms in a document,
http://patft.uspto.gov/netacgi/nph-
Parser?Sect1=PTO2&Sect2=HITOFF&u=%2Fnetahtml%2FPTO%2Fsearch-
adv.htm&r=1&p=1&f=G&l=50&d=PTXT&S1=7,716,216.PN.&OS=pn/7,716,216&RS=PN/7,716,216

[25] Google's Reasonable Surfer: How The Value Of A Link May Differ Based Upon Link And Document
Features And User Data, http://www.seobythesea.com/2010/05/googles-reasonable-surfer-how-
the-value-of-a-link-may-differ-based-upon-link-and-document-features-and-user-data/

[26] Results of Google Experimentation - Only the First Anchor Text Counts,
http://moz.com/blog/results-of-google-experimentation-only-the-first-anchor-text-counts

[27] 3 Ways to Avoid the First Link Counts Rule, http://moz.com/ugc/3-ways-to-avoid-the-first-link-
counts-rule

[28] When Product Image Links Steal Thunder From Product Name Text Links,
http://www.goinflow.com/when-product-image-links-steal-thunder-from-product-name-text-links/

[29] Do multiple links from one page to another page count?,
https://www.youtube.com/watch?v=yYWlEItizjl

[30] Agave Denim, http://www.zappos.com/agave-denim

[31] How the Web Uses Anchor Text in Links [Study], http://searchenginewatch.com/article/2163780/How-the-Web-Uses-Anchor-Text-in-Links-Study

[32] Generic anchor text list, http://www.blackhatlinks.com/generic_kw_list.txt

[33] Will multiple internal links with the same anchor text hurt a site's ranking?, https://www.youtube.com/watch?v=6ybpXU0ckKQ

[34] Testing the Value of Anchor Text Optimized Internal Links, http://moz.com/blog/testing-the-value-of-anchor-text-optimized-internal-links

Chapter Six: The Home Page

[1] Does User Annoyance Matter? http://www.nngroup.com/articles/does-user-annoyance-matter/

[2] Mega Menus Work Well for Site Navigation, http://www.nngroup.com/articles/mega-menus-work-well/

[3] Findability, http://en.wikipedia.org/wiki/Findability

[4] The Paradox of Choice, http://en.wikipedia.org/wiki/The_Paradox_of_Choice:_Why_More_Is_Less

[5] 'How We Decide' And The Paralysis Of Analysis, http://www.npr.org/templates/story/story.php?storyId=122854276

[6] Avoid Category Names That Suck, http://www.nngroup.com/articles/category-names-suck/

[7] Interface Design >Navigation > Trunk Testing, http://jrivoire.com/ED722/trunktest.html

[8] Nine Techniques for CSS Image Replacement, http://css-tricks.com/css-image-replacement/

[9] Will I be penalized for hidden content if I have text in a "read more" dropdown?, https://www.youtube.com/watch?v=UpK1VGJN4XY

[10] Auto-Forwarding Carousels and Accordions Annoy Users and Reduce Visibility, http://www.nngroup.com/articles/auto-forwarding/

[11] Are carousels effective? http://ux.stackexchange.com/questions/10312/are-carousels-effective/10314#10314

[12] Are carousels effective? http://ux.stackexchange.com/questions/10312/are-carousels-effective/10314#10314

[13] WEB1009 - The <img> or <area> tag does not have an 'alt' attribute with text, http://msdn.microsoft.com/en-us/library/ff724032(Expression.40).aspx

[14] Using schema.org markup for organization logos, http://googlewebmastercentral.blogspot.fr/2013/05/using-schemaorg-markup-for-organization.html

[15] Thing > Property > logo, http://schema.org/logo

[16] Thing > Organization, http://schema.org/Organization

[17] The H1 debate, http://www.h1debate.com/

[18] Survey and Correlation Data, http://moz.com/search-ranking-factors

[19] Whiteboard Friday - The Biggest SEO Mistakes SEOmoz Has Ever Made, http://moz.com/blog/whiteboard-friday-the-biggest-seo-mistakes-seomoz-has-ever-made - Check #4 starting around 5:00

[20] Don't Make Me Think: A Common Sense Approach to Web Usability, 2nd Edition - http://www.amazon.com/Dont-Make-Me-Think-Usability/dp/0321344758/ref=la_B001KHCFUU_1_1?s=books&ie=UTF8&qid=1387533022&sr=1-1

[21] The Elements of User Experience: User-Centered Design for the Web and Beyond (2nd Edition) (Voices That Matter), http://www.amazon.com/Elements-User-Experience-User-Centered-Design/dp/0321683684/ref=sr_1_1?s=books&ie=UTF8&qid=1387533087&sr=1-1&keywords=jesse+james+garrett

[22] Persistent Shopping Carts vs. Perpetual Shopping Carts, http://www.getelastic.com/persistent-shopping-carts-vs-perpetual-shopping-carts/

[23] Should I use rel="nofollow" on internal links to a login page? https://www.youtube.com/watch?v=86GHCVRReJs

[24] PageRank: will links pointing to pages protected by robots.txt still count?, http://webmasters.stackexchange.com/questions/5534/pagerank-will-links-pointing-to-pages-protected-by-robots-txt-still-count/5548#5548

[25] Will a link to a page disallowed in robots txt transfer PageRank, https://www.youtube.com/watch?v=j6H3xBcvkZY

[26] PageRank sculpting, http://www.mattcutts.com/blog/pagerank-sculpting/

[27] Eric Enge Interviews Yahoo's Priyank Garg, http://www.stonetemple.com/articles/interview-priyank-garg.shtml

[28] SEO and Usability, http://www.nngroup.com/articles/seo-and-usability/

[29] Link schemes, https://support.google.com/webmasters/answer/66356?hl=en

[30] Smarter Internal Linking - Whiteboard Friday, http://moz.com/blog/smarter-internal-linking-whiteboard-friday

[31] Smarter Internal Linking - Whiteboard Friday, http://moz.com/blog/smarter-internal-linking-whiteboard-friday#comment-189218

[32] How to Build an Effective Footer, http://graywolfseo.com/seo/build-effective-footer/

Chapter Seven: Listing Pages (Department, Category and Subcategory Pages)

[1] Prioritize: Good Content Bubbles to the Top, http://www.nngroup.com/articles/prioritize-good-content-bubbles-to-the-top/

[2] New snippets for list pages, http://insidesearch.blogspot.fr/2011/08/new-snippets-for-list-pages.html

[3] More rich snippets on their way: G Testing Real Estate Rich Snippets, https://plus.google.com/+MarkNunney/posts/RqzNcKE9NSc

[4] Product - schema.org, http://schema.org/Product

[5] Below the fold, http://en.wikipedia.org/wiki/Above_the_fold#Below_the_fold

[6] Improving Search Rank by Optimizing Your Time to First Byte, http://moz.com/blog/improving-search-rank-by-optimizing-your-time-to-first-byte

[7] Implement the First 1-2 Levels of the E-Commerce Hierarchy as Custom Sub-Category Pages, http://baymard.com/blog/ecommerce-sub-category-pages

[8] Usability is not dead: how left navigation menu increased conversions by 34% for an eCommerce website, https://vwo.com/blog/usability-left-navigation-menu-bar-conversions-ecommerce-website/

[9] User Mental Models of Breadcrumbs, http://www.angelacolter.com/breadcrumbs/

[10] Breadcrumb Navigation Increasingly Useful, http://www.nngroup.com/articles/breadcrumb-navigation-useful/

[11] Breadcrumbs, http://www.bing.com/webmaster/help/markup-breadcrumbs-72419f3f

[12] New site hierarchies display in search results, http://googleblog.blogspot.fr/2009/11/new-site-hierarchies-display-in-search.html

[13] Visualizing Site Structure And Enabling Site Navigation For A Search Result Or Linked Page, http://appft.uspto.gov/netacgi/nph-Parser?Sect1=PTO1&Sect2=HITOFF&d=PG01&p=1&u=%2Fnetahtml%2FPTO%2Fsrchnum.html&r=1&f=G&l=50&s1=%2220110276562%22.PGNR.&OS=DN/20110276562&RS=DN/20110276562

[14] Rich snippets – Breadcrumbs, https://support.google.com/webmasters/answer/185417?hl=en

[15] Can I place multiple breadcrumbs on a page? https://www.youtube.com/watch?v=HXEYryd3eAY

[16] Location, Path & Attribute Breadcrumbs, http://instone.org/files/KEI-Breadcrumbs-IAS.pdf

[17] Taxonomies for E-Commerce, Best practices and design challenges -http://www.hedden-information.com/Taxonomies_for_E-Commerce.pdf

[18] Breadcrumb Navigation Increasingly Useful, http://www.nngroup.com/articles/breadcrumb-navigation-useful/

[19] HTML Entity List, http://www.freeformatter.com/html-entities.html

[20] Pagination and SEO, https://www.youtube.com/watch?v=njn8uXTWiGg&feature=youtu.be&t=11m

[21] Pagination and Googlebot Visit Efficiency, http://moz.com/ugc/pagination-and-googlebot-visit-efficiency

[22] The Anatomy of a Large-Scale Hypertextual, Web Search Engine, http://infolab.stanford.edu/pub/papers/google.pdf

[23] Implement the First 1-2 Levels of the E-Commerce Hierarchy as Custom Sub-Category Pages, http://baymard.com/blog/ecommerce-sub-category-pages

[24] Five common SEO mistakes (and six good ideas!), http://googlewebmastercentral.blogspot.ca/2012_03_01_archive.html

[25] Search results in search results, http://www.mattcutts.com/blog/search-results-in-search-results/

[26] View-all in search results, http://googlewebmastercentral.blogspot.ca/2011/09/view-all-in-search-results.html

[27] Users' Pagination Preferences and 'View-all', http://www.nngroup.com/articles/item-list-view-all/

[28] Progressive enhancement, http://en.wikipedia.org/wiki/Progressive_enhancement

[29] Users' Pagination Preferences and 'View-all', http://www.nngroup.com/articles/item-list-view-all/

[30] HTML <link> rel Attribute, http://www.w3schools.com/tags/att_link_rel.asp

[31] Faceted navigation best (and 5 of the worst) practices, http://googlewebmastercentral.blogspot.ca/2014/02/faceted-navigation-best-and-5-of-worst.html

[32] Implementing Markup For Paginated And Sequenced Content, https://web.archive.org/web/20140527145918/http://www.bing.com/blogs/site_blogs/b/webmaster/archive/2012/04/13/implementing-markup-for-paginated-and-sequenced-content.aspx

[33] Infinite Scrolling: Let's Get To The Bottom Of This, http://www.smashingmagazine.com/2013/05/03/infinite-scrolling-lets-get-to-the-bottom-of-this/

[34] Web application/Progressive loading, http://docforge.com/wiki/Web_application/Progressive_loading

[35] Infinite scroll search-friendly recommendations, http://googlewebmastercentral.blogspot.ca/2014/02/infinite-scroll-search-friendly.html

[36] Infinite Scrolling: Let's Get To The Bottom Of This, http://www.smashingmagazine.com/2013/05/03/infinite-scrolling-lets-get-to-the-bottom-of-this/

[37] Infinite Scroll On Ecommerce Websites: The Pros And Cons, http://www.lyonscg.com/insights/infinite-scroll-on-ecommerce-websites-the-pros-and-cons/

[38] Why did infinite scroll fail at Etsy?, http://danwin.com/2013/01/infinite-scroll-fail-etsy/

[39] Brazillian Virtual Mall MuccaShop Increases Revenue by 25% with Installment of Infinite Scroll Browsing Feature, https://web.archive.org/web/20131106172124/http://www.ereleases.com/pr/brazillian-virtual-mall-muccashop-increases-revenue-25-installment-infinite-scroll-browsing-feature-135237

[40] Typographical error, http://en.wikipedia.org/wiki/Typographical_error

[41] Better infinite scrolling, http://scrollsample.appspot.com/items

[42] The Paradox of Choice, http://en.wikipedia.org/wiki/The_Paradox_of_Choice:_Why_More_Is_Less

[43] Search Patterns: Design for Discovery, [page 95]

[44] Adding product filter on eCommerce website boosts revenues by 76%, https://vwo.com/blog/product-filter-ecommerce-ab-testing-revenue/

[45] Configuring URL Parameters in Webmaster Tools,
https://www.youtube.com/watch?v=DiEYcBZ36po&feature=youtu.be&t=1m37s

[46] Permutation, Combination – Calculator, http://easycalculation.com/statistics/permutation-combination.php

[47] Faceted navigation best (and 5 of the worst) practices,
http://googlewebmastercentral.blogspot.ca/2014/02/faceted-navigation-best-and-5-of-worst.html

[48] Implement the First 1-2 Levels of the E-Commerce Hierarchy as Custom Sub-Category Pages,
http://baymard.com/blog/ecommerce-sub-category-pages

[49] Implementing Pagination Attributes Correctly For Google,
http://searchengineland.com/implementing-pagination-attributes-correctly-for-google-114970

[50] Do URLs in robots.txt pass PageRank? https://productforums.google.com/forum/#!category-topic/webmasters/crawling-indexing--ranking/OTeGqIhJmjo

[51] Faceted navigation best (and 5 of the worst) practices,
http://googlewebmastercentral.blogspot.fr/2014/02/faceted-navigation-best-and-5-of-worst.html

[52] URL Parameters in Webmaster Tools,
https://docs.google.com/presentation/d/1xWy5TOkB4rwoUHXFPgwVMgl2Op9PayZOWa5wdW7ZB-o/present?pli=1&ueb=true#slide=id.g6205f11_0_28, page 18

[53] Persistent cookie, http://en.wikipedia.org/wiki/HTTP_cookie#Persistent_cookie

Chapter Eight: Product Detail Pages

[1] It's All About the Images [Infographic], http://www.mdgadvertising.com/blog/its-all-about-the-images-infographic/

[2] Ranking Images For Web Image Retrieval, http://appft1.uspto.gov/netacgi/nph-Parser?Sect1=PTO2&Sect2=HITOFF&u=%2Fnetahtml%2FPTO%2Fsearch-adv.html&r=1&p=1&f=G&l=50&d=PG01&S1=20080097981.PGNR.&OS=dn/20080097981&RS=DN/20080097981

[3] WEB1000 - The 'alt' attribute of the <img> or <area> tag begins with words or characters that provide no SEO value, http://msdn.microsoft.com/en-us/library/ff723935(v=expression.40).aspx

[4] Image guidelines for SEO, http://msdn.microsoft.com/en-us/library/ff724026(v=expression.40).aspx

[5] Is it better to have keywords in the URL path or filename?
https://www.youtube.com/watch?v=971qGsTPs8M

[6] Image Sitemaps, https://support.google.com/webmasters/answer/178636?hl=en

[7] Does Google use EXIF data from pictures as a ranking factor? https://www.youtube.com/watch?v=GMf6FmRus2M

[8] Video SEO White Paper, http://www.aimclearblog.com/2011/04/04/download-aimclear%C2%AE-video-seo-white-paper/

[9] Pop-ups, video buttons and color swatches can turn site search results into selling tools., http://www.internetretailer.com/2010/03/31/inside-search

[10] Six retailers that used product videos to improve conversion rates, https://econsultancy.com/blog/61817-six-retailers-that-used-product-videos-to-improve-conversion-rates#i.1k2dagwxune85p

[11] DollarShaveClub.com - Our Blades Are F***ing Great, https://www.youtube.com/watch?v=ZUG9qYTJMsI

[12] Creating a Video Sitemap, https://support.google.com/webmasters/answer/80472?hl=en

[13] Using Instructographics For Online Marketing, http://www.pitstopmedia.com/sem/using-instructographics-for-online-marketing

[14] schema.org markup for videos, https://support.google.com/webmasters/answer/2413309?hl=en&ref_topic=1088474

[15] Will I be penalized for hidden content if I have text in a "read more" dropdown? https://www.youtube.com/watch?v=UpK1VGJN4XY

[16] Webmaster Central 2013-09-27, https://www.youtube.com/watch?v=R5Jc2twXZlw&feature=share&t=20m49s [min 20:49]

[17] Will having the same ingredients list for a product as another site cause a duplicate content issue?, https://www.youtube.com/watch?v=LgbOibxkEQw

[18] SEO tips for e-commerce sites, http://maileohye.com/seo-tips-for-e-commerce-sites/

[19] Whiteboard Friday - The Biggest SEO Mistakes SEOmoz Has Ever Mad, http://moz.com/blog/whiteboard-friday-the-biggest-seo-mistakes-seomoz-has-ever-made

[20] How many H1 tags should be on each HTML page? https://www.youtube.com/watch?v=Hgy3Oc9zfOw&feature=youtu.be&t=42s [min 00:42]

[21] Google's SEO report card, http://static.googleusercontent.com/external_content/untrusted_dlcp/www.google.com/en/us/webmasters/docs/google-seo-report-card.pdf

[22] Thing > Product, http://schema.org/Product

[23] Non-visible text, https://support.google.com/webmasters/answer/146750?hl=en#product_page

[24] PowerReviews Spreads Consumer Reviews Between E-Commerce Sites, http://techcrunch.com/2011/07/26/powerreviews/

[25] Ecommerce UX: 3 Design Trends to Follow and 3 to Avoid, http://www.nngroup.com/articles/e-commerce-usability/

[26] The Magic Behind Amazon's 2.7 Billion Dollar Question, http://www.uie.com/articles/magicbehindamazon/

[27] Rich snippets – Reviews, https://support.google.com/webmasters/answer/146645?hl=en

[28] Can I specify the canonical of all of a product's review pages as a single URL?, https://www.youtube.com/watch?v=AXnbBsRbKDA

[29] Farewell to soft 404s, http://googlewebmastercentral.blogspot.ca/2008/08/farewell-to-soft-404s.html

[30] End-of-life (product), http://en.wikipedia.org/wiki/End-of-life_(product)

[31] Google's SEO report card, http://static.googleusercontent.com/media/www.google.com/en//webmasters/docs/google-seo-report-card.pdf

[32] Opinion: Is SERP Bounce a Ranking Signal or a Quality Factor for SEO? http://www.searchenginejournal.com/opinion-is-serp-bounce-a-ranking-signal-or-a-quality-factor-for-seo/35464/

[33] What's it like to fight webspam at Google? https://www.youtube.com/watch?v=rr-Cye_mFiQ&feature=youtu.be&t=2m50s&noredirect=1 [min 02:50]

[34] Content Keywords, https://support.google.com/webmasters/answer/35255?hl=en

[35] Stemming, http://en.wikipedia.org/wiki/Stemming

[36] Stop words, http://en.wikipedia.org/wiki/Stop_words

[37] Is comma a separator in a title tag?, https://www.youtube.com/watch?v=jHSqLYUPq8w

[38] HTML Character Sets, http://www.w3schools.com/charsets/default.asp

[39] SEO Tip: Titles matter, probably more than you think, http://www.thumbtack.com/engineering/seo-tip-titles-matter-probably-more-than-you-think/

Lightning Source UK Ltd.
Milton Keynes UK
UKOW07f1825170915

258830UK00005B/88/P